THE ANNOYING LIFE

KNOWLEDGE OF ALL BUT POWER OF NONE

AND LITTLE HEART AGNES

N. K. S. R. NANTU ROY (Ashim Kumar)

DME, DIM, B.Sc., PGDIM, PGDOM, MBA
Working Fields: Engineering, Science & Tech., Philosophy, Religion, Political Analysis, Social Sciences, Health general maintaining, Literature, Arts, Novels, Children Books, Women Empowerment, Painting and sculpture

M r. Salween Roy (Replica of Scientist)

First Published in May 2023

ISBN: 978-93-93385-29-1

BLUEROSE PUBLISHERS

www.BlueRoseONE.com

info@bluerosepublishers.com

+91 8882 898 898

Cover Design:

Aman Sharma

Typographic Design:

Namrata Saini

Distributed by: BlueRose, Amazon, Flipkart

Annoying Life and Little Heart Agness

Harry dreams of David and Abraham when two people come to his house. David is the younger brother and Abraham is the elder brother. Harry asked them how to be able to take responsibility for us at an older age? Abraham said, "I shall take your responsibility." Abraham entered Harry's house.

Later behind David enter to Harry's house

Harry gets up and goes to job and thinks about his life. Harry has one daughter named "Pearl" and thinks that next may have to be two sons.

After two years his dream became reality and his son was born and given the name" Abraham".

After three years his one daughter was born and was given the name" Ziva" but the next year a son was born. Harry becomes happy and thinks he has seen a real dream and son's name is David. But as a new born baby activity people started to call Tapon (Temperament Always personally operate normalization) whereas the actual name given **Tappan Ishim as nickname Nanai.**

Harry was in the village but came to the City as he has three brothers and one sister and depending on the elder brother becoming unhappy. In empty hand came to the city and at night school was getting education, thereafter getting a job. Harry has a poor family and leads a happy life.

Contents

Rebirth Again and Again

Nanai becomes ill and on a bed remaining silent. Mother crying and thinking about what happened. Nanai tells his mother you are trying to care and the man is mortal so do not think more. The mother remained silent to hear the answer from her child. Nanai has knowledge about arts, sculpture, poem writing and thought about creating an all-rounder vehicle and other defiance vehicles. He has creativity and far sightedness by birth. Devoted to Lord Vishnu as well as Jesus as Orthodox peoples. As liberal always believe Hindu, Islam and Christianity have no difference. His worship and meditation remain as a mixed community. Mother Sova is not restricted to him and gives freedom to believing as his own style. He offers foods to God by testing a little bit of fruits, or Prepared foods like hospice and others which he offers to God.

Life comes under danger four Physicians fail to diagnose what happened to him. Nanai, deeply thinking and meditation done to gods and goddess as lying on bed. Dreams come and see. It is his fifth rebirth and within the last five hundred he several times got birth and he should feel each life work is what he has done in the past.

David Meikles

When He Came first in India that was 1615 when British started Business in Vijayanagar Emperor executed and Madres formed a new Business spot. Actually in 1908 British flowed to the root of Portuguese and landed to Surat and later from Mughal Emperor Jahangir got permission to business in Surat but within some period that 1913 gave permission to business in Madres called Malappuram. As Legal Advisor "Edward Alva" came to India with a British company for business establishment and progress.

In 1600 Joint Stock company founder for establish business at Indian ocean region and Edward Alva started to works as legal adviser who law practice in Glaxo city of Scotland

The agents of the East Indian Company first visited the provinces of Bengal and Bihar for trade during the period of Ibrahim Khan (1617 to 1624), the Subhadra of Bengal at the time of Mughal Emperor Jahangir.

The influence of Renaissance in life inspires us to learn different fields. The Northern Renaissance that we regard as beginning in Italy and most of the 15th century and 16th century become the most versatile change in European nations. The English Renaissance and Scottish Renaissance are somewhat different but Arts, Sculpture and multiple activities have become part of European life. Multi-talented and intellectual personality are remaining as Lorenzo de Medici, Leonardo da Vinci, Michelangelo, Nicolaus Copernicus, Petrarch, Raphael, Galileo Galilei, Michel de Montaigne, Niccolò Machiavelli, William Shakespeare. All great personalities changed European thought and social change.

Martin Luther, a German priest, reforms society and gives new root Protestant that Catholic conservative mode changes and society gives new root flows that peoples entering to scientific mode.

Leonardo da Vinci, became the ideology of life as an all-rounder personality and hence wanted to be an all-rounder. Different arts, sculptures and scientific works started in life but life does not stand in single ways. Come to India with Father. Old Friendship ended and now friendship started and assimilated with the Mughal Family in India. Angela Agnes remains in Life as a best friend and thought she may be my life partner but change of life is a basic matter for everyone. Which you want that may or may not be getting in life. I visited Bengal and returned to Madras where Angela Agnes met with me but she became afraid and came to my house with her husband. Angela Agnes, my childhood friend who remained as a neighbor and came to my house at Glaxo. In our garden playing and picking flowers, running together and becoming closer friends.

Dance and Song love too much so new friends get me to their entertainment house called Bijee House where dance performances by young girls and drinking win. Sometime done more affairs with Bijee than body relationship affairs also. Bijee had no social status and actually Bijee remained a slave of rulers who enforced dans and entertainment forcefully. After meeting with Angela Agnes mind not remaining stable and health conditions disturbed due to lack of care.

Man is mortal and it is the right thing and when it comes people do not know. Suddenly I became ill and Tuberculosis attracted me. Proper medicine is not available so death should come. I become separated as it is a communicative disease and ultimately die.

Actually, it is my rebirth that participation in Renaissance that character remain in life style as remain Michelangelo

Michelangelo Di Lodovico

Michelangelo Di Lodovico Born 1475 in Italy. Learned from and was inspired by the Scholars and writers in Lorenzo's intellectual circle and works forever be informed what he learned about philosophy and politics in those years. He refined technique under the tutelage of Bertoldi and keeper of Lorenzo's collection of ancient Roman Sculptures and noted sculptor himself. He worked for the Florentine. He chose to depict the young David from the Bible as heroic, energetic, powerful and spiritual. The sculpture considered by scholars to be nearly technically perfect. Paintings at Sistine Chapel: In 1505 Pope Julius II commissioned to Sculpt a grand tomb with 40 life size statues and artist began works But the Pope's shifted away from the project as he become embroiled in military disputes and his founds become scarce and a displeased Michelangelo left Rome. In 1508 Julius called Michelangelo back to Rome for a less expensive, but still ambitious painting project on the ceiling of the Sistine Chapel, a most sacred part of the Vatican. He remained an architect and poet and worked from 1520 to 1527 on the interior of the Medici Chapel in Florence including wall designs, windows and cornices. After he left Florence permanently in Rome, he wrote many lyrical letters to his family members who remained there. He died of a short illness in 1564. He remained a member who participated in Italian Renaissance and as artist sculptor and poet work forever and apprenticed to printer Domenico Ghirlandaio, particularly known for his murals.

Leonardo da Vinci, became the ideology of life as an all-rounder personality and hence wanted to be an all-rounder. Different arts, sculptures and scientific works started in life but life does not stand in single ways. Come to India with Father. Old Friendship ended and now friendship started and assimilated with the Mughal Family in India. Angela Agnes remains in Life as my best friend and thought she may be my life partner but change of life is a basic matter for everyone. Which you want that may or may not be getting in life. I visited Bengal and returned to Madras where Angela Agnes met with me but she became married and came to my house with her husband. Angela Agnes, my childhood friend who remained as a neighbor and came to my house at Glaxo. In our garden playing and picking flowers, running together and becoming closer friends.

Dance and Song love too much so new friends get me to their entertainment house called Bijee House where dance performances by young girls and drinking win. Sometime done more affairs with Bijee than body relationship affairs also. Bijee had no social status and actually Bijee remained a slave of rulers who enforced dans and entertainment forcefully. After meeting with Angela Agnes mind not remaining stable and health conditions disturbed due to lack of care.

Man is mortal and it is the right thing and when it comes people do not know. Suddenly I became ill and Tuberculosis attracted me. Proper medicine is not available so death should come. I become separated as it is a communicative disease and ultimately die.

Near to Jesus payer the songs called Garland offer to God

Garland offer to God

Oh, Jesus you crucified life
Sinner torture to You
Your mind is the truth of life.
You sacrificed life for innocent who suffer
Depress by cruel king and misguide us
Oh, you are Lord in Social Life.
You remaining to mind and a life all time
Peoples remember to your story
Memorable days of social life.
Peoples believing You come again
You rebirth again to save society
Your Epithet remains all time.

Michelangelo Di Lodovico died but David Life of Genesis influenced him too much and social reformation remains an aim in life. Rebirth again but life remained in a changed mode and the social system changed all time. Michelangelo Di Lodovico rebirth and parent given name David. David Meikles thought about Angela Agnes and Love to his mind too. But his father left Great Britain and came to India and love was lost in Life. Indian people enjoy dancing in different ways than Young lady dancing who was captured by a land lord of Islamic or Hindu called Tayyab or Baiji. New Islamic friends meet and get to study of Islamic culture and feel it is also right. Moony Bai met several times that he danced the Baiji dance of Lucknow Gharana as it liked Uzbek dress and style. Whereas in Jaipur the same type of dance is famous in Hindu dress up only. Mughal culture attracts too much and after David Meikles

Die rebirth again at the Mughal family in the West part of India. The new parents are named Allam Khan.

Badshah Allam Khan

Badshah Allam Born in Sultanate family. Alarm when become 11 years old that time 1972 Mughal sultanate becoming under pressure of Marathi raj and Salwar of Nashik Region battle held and the family started to be called Salwar.

Sant Suman:

Devotees of Goddess Kale Born in Landlord family Central India and have one sister and one brother. The Central provinces have their own Temples of Lord Shiva and Goddess Kale. Dave Sakti worshiping is done from childhood as he visits temples with his mother Namrata. Father remaining Landlord Nagpal. As once upon a time Nagvanshi (Serpentine Community) ruled here and Kale remained Family goddess.

Landlord Ravi Kant:

Ravi Kant remained landlord of Dacca district area Khalapara Where He made a Farm house and Estate controlling as Get lice from British Government as small ruler of Several Villages. Ramie, when become younger than

Ravi Kant, was attracted to her as so beautiful. Even Ravi Kant is married but becomes a fan that keeps a dancer called Nachaniya in the Landlord house. Forcefully arrested Ramie and kept in the House of Dance called Nach Ghar. As Ravi Kant remains powerful, it becomes difficult to free Ramia from his hand to Ramie by her family. Several times Ramie's father and mother wanted it may be possible to give status to the wife of Ravi Kant but as Landlord Status it was not possible.

Nanai

Works as Artist, Sculptor and Multi field works. Poem writing is one activity but nowadays poems have become uninteresting to common peoples. British rule ended and the human mentality of India changed and it became the mentality of Indians to go back about hundred and thousands of years. Ramayana, Mahabharata mythology given more priority than scientific temperament. When the British started Western Education that time Scientist, Social Reformer became highly influential and the superstition system started to diminish but today Common peoples as well as Educated peoples remain believers of Mythology even reading Science and technology. Only it become tradition to get education for job and proudness but have not little bit of social development contribution and they degradation society by dark cloud by which peoples entering in conservative mentality.

Worldly Renaissance remain aim of Life and Social Globalization Liberalism remaining aim to neutralist racism and conflict around social groups

Neither feel Christian, nor feel Islam or Hindu, I am Human and give priority to Humanity

Flow of life in Struggle

Under That life is the name of Struggle and **Tappan Ishim** understands his life is wavy and hence left the house of Friends forever. Surjatapa should not remain in his life as his farsightedness sees her marriage should be held at Bardhaman City and mostly her husband be remaining at Clerical Job. So, it is better to leave her forever.

Educational field damage due to negligence and sickness in life that leads to negativity. A letter was sent to Sujatapa that my life was in darkness and I left the city for ever and went so far away. Sometime arts and making sculpture as love of nature and creativity of life. Songs and Music love too much but god for nothing that makes life too spoiled. A daughter in laws that wife of a relative brother Mousomi suggest that left Music, Arts and other activity and restart Student life again as a Brilliant student

The best love story about Raja Ram Mohan Roy, Ishar Sharma, Dirozio, as they have done renaissance in Bengal. Learning several languages, cultures and songs become hobbies in life. Arts and Sculpture making habit remaining in life Wooden craft, San Schuster, clay modeling, cemented and stone sculpture making done easily and casting leaning from friend.

Tayler, Hosiery, press owner, painter, Ornament Businessman, become friends

Business Concept

i. Edible Oil production Unite: Mustard oil. Groundnut Oil and Coconut Oil production are simple systems and can be produced in a single unit.

ii. Wholesaler of Vegetable and Grocery: Potato, Onion, Garlic, Ginger, are better to done business with Rice, Wheat, Pulse can business wholesaler system together

iii. Fishery and Polity farming: Fishing culture learned from a friend who has a business farming fish.

iv. Flour Mill where grains, Grams (Roasted and raw) powders, and Spice power production together

v. Pickles and Process food products: Learn from my mother and hence thick to establish business.

vi. Ladies and Gents Readymade Dress material production (Inner and General): tailoring works and garment making learn to establish clothing business.

vii. Heavy Vehicle Driving and own bus ownership: When nothing is done then learn driving and think of driving a heavy vehicle and doing business.

viii. Steel and wooden Furniture organization: Wooden works and fabrication works learn and make conception to establish business.

ix. Publication Press and Register Copy Manufacturing: As poet, author, as novelist and learn to make register and book binding and press works to establish publication.

x. Commercial, fine Arts and Crafts Sculpture Works: As artists and sculptors want to establish life.

xi. General Multiple Retail Store Business: When nothing is done then want to establish a retail business.

Good for nothing and life turns to other ways.

Philosophy of Life

Nanai (Neither Awarded Nor Achievement implement) and Santai (Simple Alive No Tension Always Inside)

1. What I get with me that I left. When life starts that has nothing and when gone that death will come then nothing remains. Each and every thing started and remained on earth and finished here.

2. Today, memories work but tomorrow I may not be able to work. Today I have knowledge, relatives and properties and tomorrow that may be lost.

3. Dress up, make up, Style, all are social needs and only natural needs are food, shelter and sex. Offspring produced by reproduction is the main aim to make the generation that replica should remain in our life who were born, brought up and die like everyone.

4. Properties of life remain static and flouting and those transfer from generation to generation but there are not any guarantees that future generations should be able to use.

5. Struggle is part of life by which we survive. We are like actors who come on stages and play drama and leave

forever as humans are also mortal like other living organisms.

6. God and Lord are actually our own old generation who guides us to survive life. Farming, work, and other activities to earn money are system development as the social system is manmade.
7. Humans are one type of animal, as it is cordate, mammalian, terrestrial, social and most intelligent animals.

Migratory Life

A job is essential in life. But how to lead life as a basic need required to fully feel to survive life. Shelter and cloth as social need and food, life partners naturally need that as a root of life.

Friends' relations build up and go on in life which is called the mobility of society. When I remained that child, I made friends to play and enjoy. We together played Family works where cooking, marketing and grocery and vegetable business making playing themes. Male and female friends playing together. Rumi, Soma, Jhuma, Sraboni, Shamol, Babu, Narayan all remaining child friends.

When becoming younger than life started to change and thought came, we were required to study and get a job. Several friends started small businesses and Soma, Rumi, Sraboni and Jhuma became parts of life. I don't understand what Spampa likes. But I like Rima too. Jhuma and Sraboni remain junior to me and like sweet babies like them and kiss them.

Tuition life becomes an irritating life. Students get something from each other. Friend introduces to getting Students but life becomes disturbing in the path of establishment. Sati, Shipra become friend

Today I understand that several like and love to me but I left them forever. At ancient age Multi marriage system

Eight sisters became friends when they came to Ratlam. Gunjan and Tina become closer and We visit Kale temples together for a fresh mind.

Transferred to Ujjain and joined as a Junior Engineer. Karishma Becomes Friend.

Nanai and Santai

Marriage Held on Suddenly Nanai returned to the house that wanted to meet with parent and left the house forever to participate in Church Missioner. Marriage Held on Suddenly

Death of Creativity and Innovation Mind

Understand that innovation is base of nation to development and economic independence

Social Reality Researching

The social system is manmade. The Spiritual system has come to remember an old generation that in society who remained into a highly influential personality. Hence, they offer food, cloth, and other daily essential commodities.

Most Popular Society and Royals Ruling in Godism:

Heaven:

Heaven is where the Norse Language originated and Norse Community rehabilitation is in the Baltic States. Jutland,

Denmark is heaven where the Norse God and Goddess ruled. Due to the Poly Ethnic system transformed to Christianity under St. Peter's Church to European continents Heaven assimilated to Jannat.

Jannah/ Jannat:

Ancient Yardon/Jordan and Israel are Jannah/ Jannat where the El generation and Yahweh generation ruled. Origin of Genesis was the generation of Ancient Godism which executed Germanic peoples who continued to be attracted to Egypt to execute the white race and ended Black Sub Saharan ruling. Jews, Christian, Islamic Communities are the next generation of White race of the Euro-Asia Region. Later the Mediterranean came under European rule. El garden/ Yahweh Garden/ Eden was at the Jordan River side where several waterfalls, Hot springs remained which are also described in the Hebrew Bibles.

Paradise/ Paradeisos:

Paradise/ Paradeisos are Greek Godism royal sites where Greek gods and goddesses ruled Mount Olympus which range from execution in present Greece. Ancient Persian Royal Enclosed Garden called Paradise as reformatted words of Paradeisos.

Sarga / Sarga:

The Indu rulings executed at the mountain range of Hindu Kush to Himachal range. Indu transformed to Hindu by Aryan who invaded later and mixed to form as Hindu.

Sargha/ Sarga and La Sarga or other related places situated at these mountain ranges. The explanation of Sarga in Hindu ancient Text has similarity to this region. Hence the actual Indu region called Sarga is the Mountain range of Himalayan to Hindu Kush range. But Lateral stages of Hindu Godism several Hill/ Mountains comparisons with Sargha like the same name of place, were found where such descriptions were done in different lateral texts.

Tianmen:

The mountain range of Tianmen is actually ruled by Godism in China. Tianmen Mountain of Hunan province of China, hence Tianmen was given status as Heaven as a Norse community by the Chinese/ Mongoloid peoples.

Nebesa:

It was ruled at Slavonia by Slavić Community groups. We got text of Slavic rules and for compression confuse and forget the social system is man-made.

Tian Shan:

It is the place where Slavic Germanic groups, Assyrian Turkey groups mixed with Mongoloid peoples and hence in old Turkey called Tengir – too ruled also.

Indo-Iranian Racism that Life feel Bitter Test

Job entered the Central Part of India. Hindi racism started after the British ruled and in 1968 a new act passed that reform the official language. Hindi becomes an official language by cheating as English and Hindi get the same voting in parliament but one vote given by the president which does not remain entitled. Hindi people use English as they are unable to walk in a professional field without English. Actual ancient Arabian culture executed by West, Central and North India that Jat, Marat, Tater, Nathan, Gujar Community migrated from Sinai and in Uttar Pradesh have Evidence that Sinaili excavation that assyrian peoples migrated and rehabilitated as Sin stand for Sinai peoples Ayli means Farming and in these area marathi, Marawary, Gujar, Panjabi, Kashmiri, Hariyani all are Indo-Iranian language.

Revolution and Rebellion thought

Hindiana became most Dangerous for Non-Hindi peoples that Hindi Force Racism started. When remaining in a Non-Hindi region that time you should not properly understand the policy of Hindi racism but when you enter the Hindi region in India then it is realized that there is discrimination, isolation and partiality among Hindi and Non-Hindi. When a Person become unable to describe any things in Hindi than officers and other also saying that why a Non-Hindi person remaining in India that Hindi peoples thought that Indi is only for their own land where as Hindi peoples are basically Indo-Iranian who invaded India at ancient age and we read Dava- Ashur conflicts in our old Text. Actually, North West India is majority of Indo-Iranian who called Ashur in ancient India. Deva were basically Dravidian whereas Ashur were Assyrian peoples of Sematic Samarian peoples who were also called as Indo-Iranian /Indo-Aryan.

United Liberal Bharat formation Dream

North Eastern, East Central and South Indian regions are Non-Indo-Iranian or Non-Aryan Regions which are required to form as Sovereign Independent Nation to protect Identity, languages, cultural and social system faith. It is historical background that

Visit with Angela Agnes

Tappan Ishim remains troublesome, hurtful and inpatient so remaining worry and thoughtful and life enter a negative root. A life story such as that which remained a depressing condition where the living side remained zero but making positive and guiding others as positive to lead life. An all-rounder personality but knowledge of all power of non-personality.

David Meikles life remained a struggle and after a long time he is thinking about his life, that many friends remained his life and so many loves too and left for ever from life. Sometimes remember the British ruled in India what system changed and how much we came forward. Rebirth again and again but friendship remained with Agnes as she remained in mind but not remained in life. Suddenly some problems came and separated forever but remained friends in life. David Meikles Remember the rebirth story and singe some song as-

Faster than fairy and faster witches,
From Far distance I am returning to house owe,
My little heart Agnes wants to meet with me.
I love her too much but left her for long time,
Life change and ever not return again time,

Love and hidden Agnes remained in life.
Life is struggle that sometime sweet sometime bitter,
What happen that not known by us,
Loves remain in life and lead something that changes forever.

From a remote Town Ratlam of Madhya Pradesh (At British Time Central Province) Tappan Ishim is traveling by a train and wants to reach Kolkata (At British India Calcutta). Tappan Ishim wants to meet with Surjatapa. It has a background in the rebirth story of David Meikles and Angela Agnes. It was the time that Life remained with joy and laughter and childhood passed Agnes and David remained childhood friends. Both played in their garden. The Glasgow City covered with Hill and mountains and in outside of city little house remained made by stone structure remained and in backside and front remained rose and another flower garden. The swimming pool remained at the back where David Meikles sometimes swam and Angela Agnes came to meet with him. Sing songs and enjoy games that remain in life. Take study in a remote school and return to home. I was waiting for Angela Agnes to wear a red dress. Snowfall in winter and we went inside the house. We played indoor games such as chess.

But time changed and Father deputed to India as Attorneys of British India and David Meikles came with Jam Adware Meikles. As a law Adviser remained in Madras Province. David Meikles a young that scientific mentality and creativity walk up life to done some things new and researches working started. He wanted to do a vehicle as an all-rounder which can be operated to every field as run to land or water and sky.

Some things are drawing and some things are drawing done but time is not staying for any one that changed. David Meikles shifted to Calcutta and some new friends came into his life. Some bodies' landlord and they were entertained at their Farmhouse where dance and drinking win as they enjoy life.

One day suddenly met David Meikles with her husband at Park Street when returning from a party with landlord groups. Angela Agnes was married to Pettier John. David Meikles left Scotland for a long time and was unable to meet with Angela Agnes. Life is not staying for anyone and that changes all time.

Angela Agnes' parents wanted David Meikles to be their son in laws as both remained inmate friends. But love should not turn to love as breaking is the mode of operation in life.

David Meikles Shocked and his life value came to an end and participated in Dancing programmed. Indian songs should not be understood but love as the theme of sweetness. David Meikles became ill as too much about Angela Agnes. Jam Adware Meikles took him to climate change at Darjeeling. Natural David Meikles likes remaining creative and writing poems as explaining the sorrow of his life and how he leads life without love.

Life trance to end that he wanted to see Angela Agnes but a sweet song was sung by a young girl at a tea garden hearing but last breath came.

David Meikles dies but rebirth again and again to meet with his love Angela Agnes all time.

Love is unable to end if you really like it too much. Life is the root of sorrow and joy and it flows through. Tappan Ishim traveling in a train with his wife Lupamudra and child Ashine. He remembers his entire girlfriend when he was in class ten. One group remained: Surjatapa, Shachaita, Manica, Rupa, Taporshi, Mala, Dolbaby and others. One Group remains Sunandita, Sukhla, and Suchandana. The group remained as close to me as Soma, Rima, Jhuma and their friends Dalya, Preethi, and Eti. At different times meet with them and other groups remain Dola, Moon, and Garland mala. Different times thought something and all came in life for a certain time and they all left. Tappan Ishim sings songs in mind forever. Soma, Rima, and Jhuma remind me of my childhood friend. Surjatapa, Shanchaita, Manica, Rupa, Taporshi, Mala, Dolbaby were Tuition coaching friends. Dola, Moon, and Garland mala remained college level friends. Dalya, Preethi, and Eti became friends as friends of Rima. Oh, that time each and every one came and remained friends of life. Someone love I and someone like which that time not understand as life turned to negative point. Poems written and those lost in life. Sunandita, Sukhla, and Suchandana remained friends in the Arts class.

Sunandita and Suchandana were my art teacher Ashoka's Daughter. Suchandana spent the maximum time playing badminton in the afternoon with me. Suchandana, the elder daughter of my art teacher, returned from college and she also played with me. Shukla remains a friend who talks when

Sunday meets with her at Art Schooling. Sukhla offered to meet me in the afternoon everyday but I refused her offer as I remained with Sunandita. Every enjoyment ends and I become sick which destroys my life forever.

Lost the Poems

I lost the poems I wrote in my life.
The value of sorrow is most important
I am happy as it remains the maximum time in my life.
The Happy remain inelastic in a life
Which should be remain less time for ever
Then sorrow came again and went later from life.
Sorrows elastic are more in life which more and more
How much a person thought again and again?
Which become endless at that time and
Sometimes I feel it should not end at any time in my life.
I thought about some things but got others in my life.
If a life is full of sorrow than stopped the cry
That becomes an integrated part of life.
I forget happiness in life when
Become saturated with sorrow of life.
I write the dream in a poem again but erase every time
Happy come like as full moon light but
Sorrow remain as noon sun light
Which heat up body, sweet up body and
Life is suffocating at all times.

Monica got married and I got news from Anupama, the sister of Manica. I became happy that her life started with a house. I also met with Anupama as she also became my friend.

Monica came to my house with Anupama and basically talked about my intelligence. For only Three months Attended coaching class at Matriculation but they remained friends. After three months I became sick and no one physician diagnosed what happened in my life. After all, a Medical Professor saved my life. Dr. Roy FRCS saved who said that it was a case to save about 5% patients only and I was within those lucky persons.

I remained sick but not cried for my life. My patient tried their best. I remained on my bed and thought about Surjatapa. I wanted to see her face one time that may have lost life forever. Surjatapa my little heart Agnes dreams in life as a real friend from one after another life.

Surjatapa was my best friend in life. Her mother and father feel my mother and father her system and brother as my brother and sister. I remained as a Son in this family. I had a dream that my last birth was held to a family at Decca (Presently called Dhaka the Capital of Bangladesh). A Land Lord family where I got birth named Ratan Devnath. One sister named Mona and brother Sourav remained. I was brought up and involved with landlord groups. We had a farm house where I went for entertainment and sometime visited the dancer house Kothi Nach Ghar.

In early Student life meet with Ellina Desuga, a rich merchant Anglo person daughter.

She visited me at my house as my father agreed for a coal mine and tea garden. WE remained happy. Ellina Desuga was my older friend Agnes who remained in my previous life when I was David Meikles. But life turned as my marriage settled with Rumki but I did not love her in my life. Ellina Desuga was Anglo so it remained impossible to marry her as she remained Christran but love remained hidden. Hence remained alone sometime and otherwise remained at Natch Ghar/ Dressing Room. Poor family girls came to River Padma to pour water as River water drunk at that time. Sweet and young Maliny travel in the muddy road. My mind started to think about her. One day I thought I wanted her in my arms. I kidnapped her and kept at our Farm House to make her a dancer. Horse riding and went to the farm house to meet with her but she could not tolerate me as I kept her forcefully under me for my enjoyment. Life turned and Ellina Desuga married a merchant and went to England forever. My Mother Anjali and Father Ramcharan became older and left for ever one after another. Sister Mona's marriage and Brother Sourav maintained business but I maintained the Estate.

Ellina Desuga was born as Surjatapa. My parents became her parents and my sister's brother became her. But in my mind, she remained and was always seen as her as Angela Agnes. After sickness I remained under tension that life may end at any time so one day left her house forever when her mother said you are only a friend of Surjatapa and should not make any intimacy with sister. My sister how I forget and how it should make another relation with her. My Friend Surjatapa marriage would hold to be in Burdhaman as her life remained separated all in by rebirth. I left her forever because I wanted to see her happy like a sweet little heart in my rebirth and re meet again in life.

I was remembering the face of a friend who married an Islamic boy. I feel sorrow about this news but remember her as a good friend and hear that she has three girl children now. Her name Monica as star of my life as I learned Indian dance.

A black sweet face and melody voice

I want to speak and I want to chat with her,
A black bright face with bright way comes at mind,
Her smile makes me happy; her words are like melodies.
I saw her long time ago but remember in mind,
I talk with her on mobile phone some time,
Her sound; I like too much to talk all time.
She may be like to talk some time with me,
She remains in my heart called affection,
A good friend remains that I tell all words in life.
Human is mortal and everyone should die,
She will die and I will die but who will die before,
God only knows the matter of our future.
Someone dies before another in our daily life,
Friendship end in our life and feel loneliness in life
Again, will meet in heaven when another dies in life.

-: Stop: -

Monica was my previous life friend when I was born at the Salar estate where Nuri Begum lived but real estate remained under our hands. Arts and sculpture love too much and the house is covered with arts and sculpture. Nuri Begum remains close to estate works. I remained bachelor in life. Everyone called me Badshah Khan Husain. Namaj done as a religious faith addicted as one time at last birth some Islamic sultan remained a friend where learn Islamic text at their house ever as a Christian as Anglo as ruler of British India as Attorney my father Jams. David Meikles came to India but after death rebirth again and again. After Surjatapa married, Monica came to my house as a friend. I completed Diploma Engineering but did not get a good job. As IVth class staff was working at Madras in Southern Railways where they remained unhappy. Monica worked at Sarojini Naidu College as a Computer Instructor but her friend wanted her as a life partner as she told me if any gay came to visit with her every one asked her how much money she got. Her colour is dark but remains sweet as black queen and I like her too. When I became fed up with my life, I thought I might accept her as my life partner. I visited with her but Taporshi met in a way and offered a partnership business in the computer field. I will explain about Taporshi. My mind might turn and Monica told me you should be married to Taporshi. I became unable to express my thoughts as I want her as a life partner.

I remain in struggle and God as my beloved superpower. I lead life and remember god's name and sing songs.

*God, the power of mind *

Wherever I went for peace,
I saw same sceneries and
People were weeping forever.
I was feeling that I had most
Sorrowful life around the world
And anything that I want to god,
That should not get in my life.
I went to temple of Hindu,
Meet with so many peoples
Where persons find that
They were weeping near to god,
Idols of god and goddess remain in the temple.
I went to temples of Jain,
Meet with so many peoples
Who was weeping near the idol?
Idol of Parasnath and Mahavir of Jain
I went to Christian church,
I meet with so many peoples
Whom were weeping hear to idol,
The idol of Jesus Chariest remains in church.
I went to Mosque the Islamic holy place,
The Islam is believer of no image of god
But there are seen weeping persons
Who remains like the other as sed.?
I am not only man that I am weeping
But we are all together who are sad.
When we expect some things but
Those should not full feeling as

Per expectation then we become sed.
When we should not expect but
Some things good happen than
We become maximum happy in life.
When we should not expect and
Bad things happen in life suddenly
Our mind full fill with sad and
Someone should not tolerate than kill him
Or she finds the path to the end of life forever.
Human life covers with happy, sorrow,
Filtration, tension expectation, unexpected
And many more, there have less person
Who may guide proper than?
We required confessing to some
Where do you relish your tension?
Where I confess than creeper required to us
Where we believed there has none or believes,
There have someone control to us
We explain god or goddess or prophet or guide.
We confess and cool our mind.

-: Stop: -

God has remained life as power and to lead life with sorrow as part of life. Each and everywhere seen peoples cried nearby god as sorrow remained to maximum peoples as integral part of life. I feel faithfulness required to god as if sorrow explains to someone who may get an undue advantage or to harm in life and it is better to remember the name of god that cool my mind. Sing again.

Our Faithfulness to God

I a little child nearby God;
A child play with his parent and
Believe in superpower nearby him.
He believes whatever he required
Those should be from parents.
I believe God is supreme power and
He should provide all required of my life;
I am a child of him remain as child
As innocent as I should not understand
Any things more and not afraid him
That he became angry at me.
He is my own power and myself
Power that I believe God, he might help me
I believe in the supreme power of life.
I am little child nearby God and
I am innocent of doing anything with him.
If I become afraid than I remember his name
And I get power to my mind than
I walk forward bravely to do my job.
Oh God! You are my power, my life anthem;
Nothing's I kept my mind to afraid to you;
You are the power of my life to do work.
-: Stop: -

Several people came in life as Uncle Monoranjan as a misguide to my father and lost my three years. After sickness 10+2 completed and the progress report came down. I was feeling depression and negativity of life full as darkness felt all over. I love nature. I wanted to remain at Darjeeling or nearest Jalpaiguri as a hill locality covered with Tea garden and mind fresh by which mental relaxation felt and arts and sculpture become more integral parts that took the path to forget the sorrow of my life. Again, a song remembered by me.

Oh God! You give punishment to enemy of me

Social enemies always push back society,
It is a real fact that they have little knowledge.
Social reformer realized the system of society
They reformed to build on truth and faith.
If we read life of greater man than seen same type,
Musa lead life simple and was face problem,
Isa Mossy crucified to killed, Gautama Buddha torched
And Hazarat Mohammad left from Makkah to Madinah.
They believed God is great and nature is beautiful,
God bless you and apologies sin of life;
Oh God! You punish the enemy of me.
The sinner is poor knowledgeable to changing;
You give purity to their mind as they do not know
That what they have done wrong;
They killed thousands of innocent people.
Oh God! You punish the enemy of society.
-: Stop: -

My life is full of sorrow and I only remain a friend as God in my life and always travel to temples or Church or mosque where I might get peace in mind. I was the only path to control life and thought Oh Jesus a great Lord Sacrifice life for truth, peace and love. I feel the best way to lead life is to remember the name of God.

We required remembering name of god

The Morning, moon and evening worship or
Meditation system created by human in their life,
Developed on the base of sun rise, and sun set,
General conception of life started to believe in god.
When started to believe Moon and stars are god
Then main priority given to moon, Venous and
Jupiter in different regional side and worship
Or meditation or both have done as started in life.
Little Knowledge danger for life, society and
World call as social truth that seen in social life
Who force to sped up their believed and?
Push back the social civilized system of life.
We required to liberalized our life
And believe go as you like to kept
Peacefulness and beatified the world human life.
The food habit, dressing and living style;
All are depending on climatic condition and availability
Of those places and changed from time to time.
Liberal faith creates birth peace and better life
We create harmony around the world and life.
-: Stop: -

I remember my rebirth and present life where Hindu, Christian and Islamic culture remained as mixed as my intimate one friend called me. My worshiping and meditation remained as something different. I remained liberal from the beginning in my life. It was hard for Islamic peoples to save my life in childhood and a Christian Sister given the first set of home tuition who loved me much as my activity remained good. Liberalism gives me a way of life.

Liberal faith creates peace and harmony

Someone believed guide is supreme Authority in life
To safe home, someone believe ancient concept sun,
Fire and moon are his god as believed primitive life
And goddess' someone believed river,
Tree, animal all have god in its sprite
And worship those by simple and common man.
Someone believe god is invisible
And single to create the world, Planet, living being,
Human and society and require to meditate
Only in his life; who is not take any offer,
All believe in human beings in life.
Animals should not create conception of god,
Tree has not any brain to create conception
To think to indicate chemical natural reaction
Chemicals give birth to living beings around the world as nature.
In the world but general peoples maintain body and
Mind by physical exercise and Physiological
Concentration recycles the mind of humans.
Someone offering food to idol and image of god

Who remains as lord or guide of society or done job?
Dressing, singing and dancing; decorated by flowers
And clothes and beatified the environment of the place
Who believed place as the purity of life and mind?
Someone called Mandir, someone call mosque and
Someone called pagoda and someone called temple
All palaces are believed to be the purity of life and mind.
Sun rise and sun sign than sun set every day,
That Earth revolves around Sun and rotating on its Axis
But then why fight against others for the belief of god?
It is your mater nothing anything you believe god
You lead life like as living human as sleep, walks,
We have done work all the time and got to rest.
It is believed four times or after interval of four hours

In my life irritation feels too much and I remember God to save my life. God remained as a friend as I talked in my mind and felt God tell me what will happen next time. God only helps me to make me happy. After left Surjatapa's house I staying at Rima's house and she remains intimate to much but relation breaks and called god make me happy.

* Oh God! Make Me Happy*

I am fed up with the Society who criticizes me.
You are superpower and you are all of my heart;
You help me to make me happy as I saw as little child
I am crossing a road as blind as unable to see.
I unable to walk without help of you, worship, homage
I meditated for you to lighten and brightness of mind.
Thank God! I believe you otherwise may be mad;
They want to see me that I remain like as them
To cry all the time if someone becomes happy.
If anyone does not want to talk than talking along;
If anyone does not want to walk with me a walk along;
If anyone does not play with me, I am playing along.
Oh God! You are my Friend; you are my all;
When I remember you, quickly I sleep on the bed.
You come on the dream and playing with me;
Guide me; tell me the path to release tension of mind.
You are my power, my heart and love to help all time
A fresh mind makes it cool to lead life forward.
Oh God! Make Me Happy and I am leading my life.

-: Stop: -

Four Sister in Life

Rima is my most loved as she remained most close to me. Sitting together and talking together. I told her that I want to marry her. Rima remained a great part of my life. Three Sisters were Soma, Rima and Jhuma.

Sraboni was their cousin. Sraboni came to my house and I kissed her on check and love too. But her mother left them when remain as a child and a love affair was done to their maternal uncle. I feel that was actually wrong with her and she remained with her brother Sanjeev. Her father thought what to do? Sraboni and her brother remain alone in the house. I sometimes went to their house and kissed sometimes. It was my teenage activity at that time and it was not prominent about love. Sraboni loves me and is waiting near the window of my room. One day her mother returned as her father thought that she must take care of the children. Her mother balm to her father that whenever she wanted to visit to some traveling place or wanted to gone at market then maximum time seen her mother with uncle of Sraboni. Actually, her father remained busy in his business but social life remained a factor and love and relation happened. Her uncle's marriage holds on and her mother returns back to the pavilion. Sraboni became young and some intensity created to mine to Joy. Joy, a local resident boy. Joy's father left his mother Arati as sister and become wife. Sraboni met with Joy when she went to school and returned from school. This news gets to me and I feel so sorrowful. I try to avoid her for some time. Her mother got this news and sought Joy. She came to my house to get tuition and three months continued and left for ever and left schooling at class nine. I love her but do not explain that she loves others.

Soma sometime called me and waiting for me when I came back from school and Witting at by room windows but I should not understand that she may things something about me but her sister Rima like by me and one days said I want to marriage with her. Rima said that she told the fact to her elder sister. Some came and asked what Rima told but I said no. Rima came back from school, I waited for her to see her face one time. We talked sometimes but she did not say that she loved me.

Jhuma came with me to visit our garden and said she likes our house too much. Jhuma was wetting on the roof when I got rest to get natural wind. She looked at me and felt something. That time remains sweet. I kissed her as she remained ten years younger and little face was too much. But when she became young, she started to love me and started to tell who would become husband once she kissed him.

It seems that Sraboni became my first attraction in life as well as meeting and remaining best friends in life. We kiss each other and she also loves me too. Sraboni is actually a cousin of Sama Rima and Jhuma. She comes to my house for school work, educational work helps and when come to meet with me then kiss her too as I Love. But her mother left her with her brother Sanjoy and started to live together with uncle Rahim. Rahim came to their house then her father sends to her mother with cousin Rahim for traveling to tourist spots or marketing and because her father remained busy working in business. Actually, it was the remaining fault of her father and when her father realized that it required to return to her mother as Sraboni and her brother are still children. After a long time, her mother returned to their house. Srboni became so sweet when becoming young but my mother dislikes her due to her mother's character. So, my mother sought her out when she came to our house. Then Sraboni starting to waiting at windows long time but I remain busy to my study too much. After all she shifts toward Joy, a young boy and later to Protim. I turn toward Rima as she attracts me by secret activity. But 10 years ago, a different Jhuma came to meet with me and little Jhuma was like a doll to me. I kiss too.

Soma likes me but Rima does activities secretly as she is attracted to me. Jhuma became young and when a love feeling started to come to her mind that I could not understand. When Rima understood that Jhuma was Loving me then she started to tell me that you love Jhuma by indication. In the end, Rima stopped talking with me.

Sight to sight

Two Building remain stand side by side;
Two candidates went far away forever.
On the both roof two candidates sitting
They remained as friends.
They stop talking for a long time, but
They cannot forget each other.
An affection and love called them and
They came on the roof again and again.
Thought previous matter of relation;
Once upon a time they remain friend;
They played together, searing happiness
And sorrow, chatting for long time,
Some of us kiss each other.
Wetting for long time sight to sight;
They went back to ground floor at evening
That might be meeting again at the same time.
The sun rises and all living beings become busy.
Everyday life remains working as per life.
Student are going to schooling, worker is going to job,
Buds form at plants and flowers blossom in time.
At the afternoon both came at the roof
As they attract by some forces to meet
For some time called love remains in mind.
The sun set give us dark night where each
The other face is not seen in natural light.
In the morning red sun rise and slowly
Bright and bright; then dull and darkness come.
Again, they came and went as daily life.

Loss life want to told something,
Bright easy want to see something,
Soft heart wants to come nearer to nearest
But something obstructs them and
Stop walking to distance forever.
Suddenly for job I go far and far but
Agnes remain at the roof for wetting for her lover
And time end forever; crying and weeping but
Good for nothing; parents arrange marriage with others.
Love and affection end forever and good by later;
The building remains as a standing structure.
-: Stop: -

Lastly, I gave them greeting cards in new years and kissed Jhuma and then met with her sister Rima but Rima said you love to someone that indication remained to her younger sister. Jhuma is ten years younger than me and I love her. She said words and stopped talking with me. Jhuma was waiting for me but I wanted to go to Rima. When Jhuma understood the matter, she also stopped talking.

Sraboni's marriage was held with a footballer and when seen, Rima thought about her. Engineering completed and training started at Gun and Shell factory and a friendship was made with Santanu. I talked about my life and showed two letters written for her and her father that I love very much, Rima. Santanu sent one letter to her father. When the latter posted to her house then called me and I apologized to her mother but her mother said it was wrong. If I told her mother as a friend then the problem was not created but her brother sought it out and told Santanu to apologize to him. Santanu was meeting with me and wanted permission. I promise to him that if and only if Rima wanted to return to my life then I should not accept her. Santanu apologized.

After three months new year came 2000 and Rime sent news through her friend to give a greeting which made stopped talking. I buy greetings and write that I want an apology form by activity.

Letter to her through in an oily capsid as the end love story as I promised and stop talking forever even Rima told me if I came, met and talked with her that all and given positive sight that she wanted to lead life with me. But I thought everything would end and I should not return to her life as promised to my friend Santanu.

After training ended, neither met with Santanu nor wanted to accept her. But time passed out and a lower level Job got in life. I thought about what should happen in life! What should I promise to break in life and accept her as I love her too much? I visited with her and she hit me with a material which kept on her hand. She called her mother and told that she hated me. Her brother came at night and threatened me strongly. That last time and as I saw a dream at morning time that became current in my life that her brother came to me and she hid from my life.

I asked several times to lord Vishnu that Rima should be my wife. And it was a dream for Rima to marry only to others. So again, asked Lord Vishnu why I should love too in my life.

A dream came and I saw that it was my last rebirth when I was Landlord and kept her at Natch Ghar/Dancing room to entertain her by forcefully returning to me in this life. She was my Malini who neither accepted nor tolerated me in her life. She rebirths as Rima and it returned to me as an insult.

I left my locality and suddenly met with Sipra who remained in a relative's house. She called me and met with me as a friend and other times remained at Club at the nearest colony. Mitta, Rita, Sita became students in life as students as Exercises learn.

Devoted to lord Vishnu

I prayer to lord Vishnu that
I want to marriage with a girl
Who likes it the most in life?
It became feeling that without her
I could not lead life as attraction
Attraction Increased major and more in life.
I got sleep after meditation to lord Vishnu
A dream so that most like girl
Marriage happened with another person.
I should care about the dream that
I believed it might be real in life.
I gave a statement to again and
Again, I want her by heart.
But day by day crack the relation
How much I try to bind her up by heart.
After all, break the relation and
I again meditated on lord Vishnu.

I asked again and again what was caused.
I saw a dream at night that
Lord Vishnu sited with goddess Laxmi
They laugh at each other when they see me.
In the morning, I understood I was wrong.

Sampa became one of my friends and she remained the sister of my friend Staytanath. My friend Saytanath got a job in a private company but I am trying for a job in railways. Sometimes I meet with his father and mother and get news about my friend. One day his sister called me and said she is also my friend and hence I can share my sorrow with her. I feel happy that someone gets that I may be relaxed enough to talk about my life. Sampa's sweet face became my friend and I shared my life story when I met her. I gave her a friendship sculpture to remember me forever. I feel happy but remember about Rima who hates me too.

Rebirth and meet once again

She loved to me at beginning,
Later she started to hate me.
Rima called her name by other,
But I told her as my wife in my life.
She talks and smiles all time,
Later stop talking forever in life.
I thought that why she hates me,
I asked lord Vishnu for meditation.
A dream came at night when sleep,
A girl captures me and impresses her.

I remained a land lord and was rich man,
I liked her too much in that life.
I forcefully kept her in a house for ever,
Her dance impressed me in that life.
She hated me in that life as I love her
I should not marry her to give social life.
She hated in that life and rebirth again,
We met once more to chat once again.
-: Stop: -

Time passed and Samir became friends but Father of Samir expired and new business started. Clube left as the situation changed.

I Joined at IGNOU and several friends came in life again some remain meal and some remain female again. Dilbara Blikis Islamic community. Drabandra, Jogandra, Shalli remaining Punjabi.

I avoid friendship of Dillbara Blikis

Suddenly a girl meets with me,
She said her name is Dillbara Blikis,
She was student of same class,
And introduced as a late admission.
She slowly makes friendship with me,
Later some time came to my house also.
Some time talk and discuss about any things,
Friendship is entering deeper from both sides.
I had not any confusion about her friendship,
She believes her faith is by birth a religious matter.
Suddenly a madder case happens in our area.

News came to mass media as Hindu Muslim affair,
I feel some things she is Islamic by religion,
They had a relationship, marriage and a different system.
If remain Hindu convert to Islamic
Then she should marriage with me,
It remains a general matter as they remain conservative.
Love and like had not value in that time, I remain along;
It remains better in my life to avoid her for all time.
She is a good girl, nice in nature, beautiful sight,
Good looking, good behavior and bright eyes.
But she is Islamic and I am Hindu that make problem,
Obstruction in life; we separate from each other.
Social system, religious system is manmade,
But others might not see realism as conservative life.
-: Stop: -

Life lost importance to lead and I believed Lord Vishnu in prayer to Lord Vishnu again and again to save me. But some time I thought if Lord Vishnu met with me then what I should do with him as believed to be the supreme power of my life.

If Lord Vishnu come nearby me

The life become with tension, fast traction;
I became angered again and again.
I believe Lord Vishnu is my power,
Who gives everything to me if I want?
Oh Lord! My life destructed in every point;
I miss every target whatever I attempt.
What I wanted should not be filled.

What could I do? What have you done?
My Lord, My Power, I became sad.
If I get you nearby me than bit and
The aggression of my mind should cool.
I pray to lord Vishnu and sleep at night.
At night at dream seen Lord Vishnu,
Idol of Lord Vishnu came to my palm of hand
And body became idle and powers less;
I am unable to move any more than the idol finishes.
When I became free again idol seen to my palm;
Again, I had become powerless more and more.
The whole night passes out like this and
I rolling in bed in dream that to bit to teach him
But I could not do anything near him.
I defied and became sorrowful, then he blessed me.
The morning Sun rise in red color,
I got up; then remembered again and again.
-: Stop: -

Addition and subtraction in Life

In a life start from childhood
And end at any time as an inert body.
Some one end after birth just,
Someone dies at middle as young
Someone is leading life up to old age.
What do you gain and what do you lose?
Death is true where after death
Everything ends under buried of body
Or burned by others to mix with earth.

Every one calculated the profit and
Loose in life but at the end
Every calculation result become
Zero whatever ever done in life.
Zero is starting and ending point in life
Zero is most useful value in life

Sorrow becomes a part of life

What ever thought in my mind
that was not getting in my life?
What remained dream in my life
that was not full fill in life.
I lost confidence and suffer
and sometimes become sick for a long time.
Sleep long time on the bed
or sitting nearby an idol of god.
Payer to god to give me peace
and harmony in life but
I should not get peace
and harmony in my life.
I realize a person become happy
if he or she gets better things
That was not expected any time.
A person become sorrow
if most expected things were getting in no time.
A person neither become happy
nor become sorrow as he or
She knows what will happen next time.
I either became sorrow or became normal

as I fail in my expectation
Or should realize what would happen next time.
It is us really of life everyone wants to be happy
but someone become happy
someone becomes sorrow
and praying to god makes me happy.
But why such matter happened in life
we do not know that in our life
but best to try to lead a happy life.
God bless you wish by father of church
but he became father as he feels sorrow in life,
Then wish for me, by which he become happy;
good give peace to my mind and
I feel happiness that by any how life to be end
Nothing remains with me
and body to be buried to everyone
Or burn to ash as per the religious faith of societies.
Today the house name plate has my name
At past time there were my father name
My grandfather name also remains there
In future there will be by name of my son
Changing matter is the real matter of nature.
I feel sorrow become parts of life and sorrow and
Sorrow remember make me sorrow and lead life
As sorrow become a friend of my life makes me happy
Nothing remains to me at the time.

-: Stop: -

Lost the Poems

I lost the poems I wrote in my life.
The value of sorrow is most important
Then I am happy as it remains the maximum time in my life.
The Happy remain inelastic in a life
Which should be remain less time for ever
Then sorrow came again and went later from life.
Sorrows elastic are more in life which more and more
How much a person thought again and again?
Which become endless at that time and
Sometimes I feel it should not end at any time in my life.
I thought some things but got others in my life.
If a life is full of sorrow than stopped the cry
That becomes an integrated part of life.
I forget happiness in life when
Become saturated with sorrow of life.
I write the dream in a poem again but erase every time
Happy come like as full moon light but
Sorrow remain as noon sun light
Which heat up body, sweet up body and
Life is suffocating at all times.

Little heart breaks forever

My young sister death body
Lie on the floor of the hospital.
She Succeed as killed her life
The end of sorrow is in life.
Her marriage was held six months ago.

What was the sin of her life?
She was a girl and marriage
Remain statues in the common family of life.
The India a male leading society
Females are depressed from time to time.
Male gave flash statement and
His marriage is done with her.
It is not new matter in India that
Female depressed nowadays but
From the long time the stories repeated
And end beautiful roses at any time.
My sister killed her that her husband cheated
And depress life where four sights are dark in life.

Devoted to lord Vishnu

I prayer to lord Vishnu that
I want to marriage with a girl
Who likes it the most in life?
It became feeling that without her
I could not lead life as attraction
Attraction Increased major and more in life.
I got sleep after meditation to lord Vishnu
A dream so that most like girl
Marriage happened with another person.
I should care about the dream that
I believed; it might be real in life.
I gave a statement to again and
Again, I want her by heart.
But day by day crack the relation

How much I try to bind her up by heart.
After all, break the relation and
I again meditated on lord Vishnu.
I asked again and again what was caused.
I saw a dream at night that
Lord Vishnu sited with goddess Laxmi
They laugh at each other when they see me.
In the morning, I understood I was wrong.

Best on clapping hand of Mother

Little child wanted to travel mountain
And river sight at him remains at city life.
He wanted to travel and enjoy life.
He left from house for sight of mountain,
The North Bengal side had seen Himalaya all his life.
Father fed up his child should not come
Again, he led life with his life.
He took him by force with him but
He weeps continuously and saw mountain
A beautiful seen as blue in color
After rain I feel happy in life.
Little child brought up and left
Calcutta is a city of joy forever in life.
Door to door craving for a job as
Money is main things to lead life
Money provided food, shelter and cloth in social life.
For a job, for a shelter, struggle and struggle continuously but mind should not satisfy.
Little child brought up and came out from city

Where seen many mountain and river
Which give better slightness but
Mind craving continuously in life.
Young boy think it was better when
He was little child and remain on clapping
On his mother's hand; Mother saved him all the time.

*God, the power of mind *

Wherever I went for peace,
I saw same sceneries and
People were weeping forever.
I was feeling that I had most
Sorrowful life around the world
And anything I want to god,
That should not get in my life.
I went to temple of Hindu,
Meet with so many peoples
Where persons find that
They were weeping near to god,
Idols of god and goddess remain in the temple.
I went to temples of Jain,
Meet with so many peoples
Who was weeping near the idol?
Idol of Parasnath and Mahavir of Jain
I went to Christian church,
I meet with so many peoples
Whom were weeping hear to idol,
The idol of Jesus Chariest remains in church.
I went to Mosque the Islamic holy place,

The Islam is believer of no image of god
But there are seen weeping persons
Who remains like the other as sed.?
I am not only man that I am weeping
But we are all together who are sad.
When we expect some things but
Those should not full feeling as
Per expectation then we become sed.
When we should not expect but
Some things good happen than
We become maximum happy in life.
When we should not expect and
Bad things happen in life suddenly
Our mind full fill with sad and
Someone should not tolerate than kill him
Or she finds the path to the end of life forever.
Human life covers with happy, sorrow,
Filtration, tension expectation, unexpected
And many more, there have less person
Who may guide properly than?
We required confessing to some
Where do you relish your tension?
Where I confess than creeper required to us
Where we believed there has none or believes,
There have someone control to us
We explain god or goddess or prophet or guide.
We confess and cool our mind.

-: Stop: -

It was feeling that no one love me in life but in last time when someone tell friend let me Anupama telling my life story all time to her father in laws house and Surabaya remember to me as friend every one love me and as I remained free and frank as well as helpful. Hence all my friends thought about where I remain and how my life is leading. Surjatapa, when passing near my old house, thought to ask someone where I was staying nowadays. They thought but not able to meet as remained so far from them

No one loves me

So many girlfriends remain in my life,
Someone like me some one talks all time;
Chatting and talking remain a part of time.
I want someone some time who like more
And more that she to be remain in my life;
Make friendship and give a gift to a sculptor.
I practice art and sculpture wither made by wood
Or made by clay or other material shown to them;
A heavenly feeling as all remains my friends in life.
Sixteen fan remained together maximum time,
And other remains small groups and appreciated all time;
They encourage my arts and sculpture to be better in life.
Monika, stupa, soma, etc. some names remember,
But forget other who came suddenly and go back;
I feel all matters when I remain alone in my life.

-: Stop: -

Once again, remembering my life and composing songs of my life one after another.

One after another sing song about his life and traveling to meet with Sujatapa, the best friend of life and he dreamed of her last night.

Like and Love in the Life

I wish you as I Love
I wish you happy new year as I love you,
I wish you god bless you as I love you,
I wish for you as I love you very much.
Dream come to me at night as face seen in life,
Deem of family come in life as love in my life,
Deem that to lead life with you.
You remain in life and in all time a I love,
You like me as feel bright sight in my life,
You call me to meet again and again in life.
Happy new year and happy life once again,
Happy and happy you may remain in life,
Happy birth is your sight in your life.
God bless you all the time in your life,
God make you happy in life forever,
God made me happy with you in my life.

If you two sisters remain together in life
Two sisters become my friend in my life,
Love and love remain in mind for both of them.
One come to near than another goes too far away,
When two sisters like me, then why behave like that.
Both should remain in life and we together lead life,
Our happiness and sorrow are shared in our life.

Elder come to meet with me younger anger to me,
They are playing a game of hide and seek in life.
I like and love both of them in my life forever,
Then what problem do they have in their life?
Sister to sister are not able to share husband in life,
They love me but do not share with me in their life forever.

My Little Friend

My little friend come to here see toward there
There is a fair we should go to there.
My love you like to ride may go around all time,
Hurray we enjoy it together we ride marigot round.
When we meet in our life forget in life,
We enjoy walking together in this fair.
Two-time ride marigot round not to be Anafi,
My friend rode three or more times to be sufficient for us.
My little friend come to near to near in chair,
Round up Mari go around; it is lofty in here.
Free falling to downward a miracle feeling in life,
You caught my hand and kept another hand back.
It is lovely feeling in our life to talking together,
But how much time you remain here in my life.
If you go too far away from me in this life,
I cannot forget you in my life forever.

Again, and again remember you in my life
I remember you again and again in my life
A sweet face remains as bird eye view
Talking to myself that I love you all the time.

You like and love me that I can't understand
You wait for me to meet for a second
But I pass the road all the time for my work.
You sometime explain that you thought about me
I can't understand that you love me in your heart
I love you too much and I thought about you all the time.
I get study and make works of my life
You thought about me and loss your study in life
But you are unable to explain you love me in your life.
Like and love remain in mind and submerge in mind
You love me and I love you all the time in our life
I can't forget you and remember you all the time.

My friend you may be life partner in life
You were sitting on the roof to your building
I remain in my building to see you several times.
Time pass out when you were talking with me
You kiss me and I kiss you in our life
You stopped talking and left me alone in my life.
I love you and you love me in our life
But suddenly life change and you cut out relation
We become separate for all time in our life.
You small when you see to me on the way of life
I remember about you in my life all time
But talking and speaking remain constant for all time.

I unable to accept you in my life
As I promise to my friend in my life.
You say to me that we start to talking again in our life
love and like to your life and everything of your life.

But you stop talking and that not start again in our life
We are separated by events and go far away for all time.
Never we meet again and never become friend again
I become unable to accept you as a life partner in my life.
Love remain to my mind as subpar condition
I remain in mind but we remain separate all the time.

We sleeping side by side
Feel worming in our life
Back to back touch to us
Your lovely face later smile
You left the bed in that time
When I awake from the bed
You remain on the side.
You small that I remain snapping
We like to each other all time
You remain in my heart
But cannot couple to each other
I aspect you may say to me as love
We love that remain submerge
I feel and miss you all the time.
You play with me in a group
We go together in shopping
You participate in athletic competition
I pay for you to win in life.
I remain on the ground side
I acreage you by sounding
Go faster and faster to run by you
You should be first from others.
You remain in black dressing

Your aim remains to kept first position
You are my heart I fell in this time
But time passes out in life forever.
You left me and I left you in our life
Our love and like remain in mind
You meet again in my life
But you may not be my life.

You remain in life you remain in sight
We talk together and ought together
We walk together to catch our hand.
When hear your sound in my ear
My mind excited to see you for a few of time
I came out of the house as quickly as possible.
I see the dream to a family in my life
You remain in life and live in my life
But life does not remain the same all the time.
You stop talking and I write one after letters
I want to come to meet with you in my life
But situations separate us in our life.
You come to meet with me with a holy food dice
You remain to that place where worship done
I went to there and come came as you remain
I don't accept holy food from your hand.
It remains my mistake in my life
You love me and hence come to meet with me
I feel that in my life but too late I understand in my life
I become sorry when I remember you in my life.
Holy food is required to respect and you got it
I may insult not only you but also god in my life

Love remain in my heart and remember you all time
But time should pass out and not return in any life.
Even today I remember you in my life
I don't understand that you love me in your life
You observed me that I pass on the road side
I observed you as you returned from school time.
Even today that day I remember you in my life
I love you too much and express You in my life
You understand me and sometime express me
I want marriage with you in life to lead life
Your bright eye says something all the time.
Even today I remember you that time
I write several loves later in my life and tier those in life
You stop talking as I break promises in our life
I want to send letter but remain unable to do that
You again come to me but I can't understand my life.

I am waiting for you to see a view of your face
A few second see you as you go to school
A red curt and white frog wear that better
She is a young girl like a red white fairy in life.
I feel some things in mind and thought about you
You are my life and we will be happy in life
You return from school at afternoon time
Like in the morning, I wait until the afternoon.
Your long hair and bright eye attract to me
I want to say as I like you very much in my life
Like convert to love as you may feel my mind
I write poems and songs about you in my life.
You know that I love to you as I talk with you

You make friendship with me as love me
You meet again and again in our life for love to you
I feel without your life you may not lead in my life.
A red dress ware like as fairy come in my life
You come to privet treachery to take education
You become frail in my life for a while.
I feel sickness and off in education in life
You may meet with me as a friend
I don't know if I will remain alive or not.
Three months over I remain on bed as sick
You are not come to meet with me now
I want to meet with you for a while.
I recover after four months as remain in bed
I want to participate at education life
But I am unable to continue to read in my life.
I recover from sickness and meet with you I time
You become friend in my life but life risk remains all time
I make friendship and only friendship in my life.
Suddenly you feel like as me other may be friend
But every finger of hand not remain same size
Someone gets an advantage in your life.
I good by you in my life as remain unable to accept you
You remain unable to accept me as you remain wrong
Our life goes in opposite directions, friendship breaks in time.

You make great mistake in your life
We like each other too much in our life
You love me but can't say to you in life
Every word remains hidden in my mind.
You give hens but hidden all things in mind

All of you come and later left me along
Several faces remember but hidden in life
We are human locomotion and mobility are parts of life.
God remain as power of life
I face life rick that danger in my life
Every friend be happy that want all time
My love remains in my mind.
Keep you in mind but not to sow any one
Love are only feeling which hidden in mind
You remaining happy that all
I become happy about your happiness.
You remain Islamic and I remain Hindu
We remain on two opposite side in bank of a river
We are human but our believe remain in opposite
I like too you but I can't love to you
I afraid that to convert to your community
I can't leave my parent for you in my life
My parents may not accept you in their lives.
I am very much bountiful in face and name
I like you and make friend with you
You come to my house and meet with my mother
My mother like you as your behavior as good
You are belonging to a good family as your father are physician
I like you as you are like as fairy in my life
But society separates us forever in our life.

It is real life that saw David's name remaining so unhappy. In Biblical Davide struggle in his life, in devoid Cover Field it is also seen that David remained so unhappy and I remain David as unhappy. So, I was thinking when Angela Agnes met with me again and again as she remained in mind but not remained in life. Its same story is executed and at Younghood I offer a Model made by me as David Agnes to Surabaya that I know that her life is smooth but my life remains as struggleful. Sculpture making and Arts are my hobbies as plantation remains as II love nature. The sculpture was made by me as nude and others also and some friends remained and appreciated me too much. Sculpture offered to Sister in laws of Hiranya as a friend. Hiranya remained a brother in relation and I was learning music in life. Surabaya was learning singing and covered the theory of music to be heard as capturing power to learn.

Sorry and worry in the Life

I can' understand you
It is lack of knowledge of me
I can't understand in my life
You love me in your life.
You wait for me to view of face
I go to college and return to home
But a smile remains.
You smile and lovely wait for me
I am foolish that can't understand to you
You love and hence wait for me.
You visit near window to meet with me
I learn my book and neglect to you
You wait a long time and return from there.
You ask me what I have done in that time
I answer that read my book in this time
You can't say that you love me in your life.
I become sorry that become too late in life
I understand you love me in your Ife
Your marriage is set up in your life.

Mr. Tappan Ishim stands on the Arum garden where Ratnam diesel shed staff are gathering to celebrate the republic day

2005, 15 August. Mr. Kumara addressed republic day and progress of Western Railway.

Barat Barsha as Geographical area: If we enter into history then we understand that Barat Barsha was a geographical area and its foundation indicated from Hindukush mountain to iRobot where even to execute several countries. In ancient times, there were several small countries in Barat Barsha. But in Europe the Barat Barsha was indicated as Indus which turned to India by space slip to Europe.

Barat Barsha turns to Hindustan: Islamic rule enters Parashah and Persian peoples enter Barat Barsha because they also remain safe as to lead life as they believe Sun god, fire god as previous believer of natural power in Barat Barsha. Islamic peoples indicate the same land mark as Hindustan because the peoples of induces mountain was indicated as Hindu and they shift from Hidokus to Indonesia but Bharat Barsha remain as Aryabhata (Land of Aryan) and Anaryabhata (Land of non- Aryan).

The word remains as Dave as superior people and Daivari as inferior peoples and Dave means god whereas Averi means Danab(giant) Danab turns to Dabir after a long time and indicates the south Indian peoples. After long time the religious faith become submerge and as a whole called as Hindu in the whole land mark of Barat Barsha where maximum time ruled by different king of Aryabhata (Land of Aryan) and Ann Aryabhata (Land of non- Aryan) separately. Islamic peoples indicate them as a same religious group as Hindu and the landmark as Hindustan (Land of Hindu). I heard that the landmark peoples used to use milk to offer to god Siva and the milk river flowed from the temple of god Siva and the temple had a lump sum goal and money rather than greediness to give power to Islamic ruler of outer land. The outer ruler attracts to Barat Barsha and give the name as Hindustan (The land of Hindu)

Hindustan turn to India: weakness comes after a long time ruled by Islamic rulers in Barat Barsha and Europeans start to come to state commercial establishments in Hindustan and turn as rulers in different parts. Padishah ruled by the French community, Goa-Damon-Due ruled by Portugal's community and Bengal-Bihar-Orissa ruled by the British community (England-Wales- Scotland the independent three countries peoples). Bangla-Behar-Orissa became the first spot of British rule but after all the maximum part of Barat Barsha ruled by the British was either direct or indirect rule system. But the Europeans indicate the land mark as India which one called Hindustan by Islamic rulers. The European ruler indicated the land mark as France India, British India as per capture by the community.

Independent India-Pakistan: After Decolonization British India divided into two independent countries as Bharat /India and Pakistan.

Independent Bangladesh: Later in 1971 Pakistan divided on the basis of language and East Pakistan became independent as Bangladesh.

Hindi Racism: Hindi Hai Hum Hindis Hamada means we are Hindi peoples and Hindustani is ours. Hindustan means to Hindi peoples are as wool India whereas in Non-Hindi peoples indicate Hindustani means only Hindi linguistic peoples

Nowadays Hindi peoples indicate that they are superior to non-Hindi peoples where as they are at the competition examination in Hindi language which is their mother language and as well as they read and write in Hindi.

Problem to noon-Hindi peoples: Learning Regional language and only one English subject learn and participating in competition in English language.

Hindustan to Hindi peoples:

Hindi the language of Hindustan: language of Hindu peoples indicated by Islamic ruler

Political system of Barat: Social Consulate Confederation Liberalism and Non-Hindi Zone required as United Liberal Bharat as Autonomous region.

Name required of country: United Republic of Bharat

as a single name

States name required to defend: West Bengal as Bange Pradesh

Punjab as Gurumukhi Pradesh

Andhra Pradesh as Telegu Pradesh

Uttar Pradesh as Broz Pradesh

Madhya Pradesh as Brinda chal Pradesh

Demand of us required as Non-Hindi:

Birthright:

1. Mother language as Basic Educational System

2. Equality to everyone as per qualification.

3. Right to give speech in mother language or vernacular in parliament But

If vernacular not understand by other member than interpreter to requite to give translated speech in bi- lingual system.

4. Competitive written and interview Examination should be given by vernacular recognized language in the state compulsorily.

5. Within India all peoples are not Hindi whereas the Hindi leaders defend as -

a. Sara Bahasa Ache Hindustan Hai Hamada (Everywhere are good mater that is our Land of Hindu)

b. Hindi Hai Hum Hindustan Hamada (We are Hine Peoples and Land of Hindu is Only Our)

c. Bury Najjar Na hamsa Dale Saabsa Aga Hoge Hindustani (Bad view not to seek to us Hindi Speaking peoples become in top most post)

d Jai Hind (Greeting Hindu Land)

In the above case it is clear that Hindi leaders are forcefully defending that the land Of Independent India Name as Land of Hindu and only Hindi speaking peoples have right to live in Independent India. Whereas as per constitution the

Independent India has two names as 1. India in English and, 2. Bharat In Indian Languages.

Within Enter Independent India the Written Competition Examination and Interview get in Either English or in Hindi but so many Peoples are in Non-Hindi areas are getting education in there vernacular and mother language which one are State official language and under continuation that are recognized language But if Non Hindi Peoples are become unable to attempt in their own language in their own state than what valuation remain the recognize and state official language .In Hindi State Hindi Officer input Hindi language and grammar question compulsory in competition Examination and get interview in Hindi. But in Non-Hindi State there are education systems implemented in State language and English hence it is required that to be given written examination and interview either in English or state language than the actual competition to give the proper result. Others wish the system fever to Hindi speaking peoples so that they get like mother milk in their mother language. Hence after the Hindi take in Examination field and interview than the Binaries, UP's And other Hindi peoples come to the higher level in maximum number to ground leveling governmental posts. After all Hindi Racism come by the system Hence Every Hindi Speaking Peoples explain that the name of country as Hindus then and they understand that the meaning of Hindus than as Hindi land and everywhere of Independent India required to implement forceful the Hindi Language or by greediness to give awards in case by Central Government and Akhil Bharati Hindi Parishad.

In my real life When I remain in Ratnam in Madhya Pradesh remain as Parities as Junior Engineer the Senior Section Engineer Mr. Harish Chanda Panda and others said, " Why do we live in Hindustan if we are unable to speak in Hindi and when I was in Ujjain in Madhya Pradesh that time several periods were said by K. K. Mittal, That why I live in Hindustan if I am unable to properly speak and write Hindi Language and Said that I require to find out about another county. Today such words are said one after another and all states are required to implement Hindi language.

The above gives alarm that Hindi peoples want to capture whole India as Oppose that to speak in State official language in parliament and in State Assembly Hindi speaking peoples or Muslim are given statements in Hindi and Urdu respectively. After all, the Hindi speaking people support Urdu speech because both have some things similar.

I say to non-Hindi Peoples that even today we have time to wake up and be alert to save us otherwise we become baked and Hindi people say they are superior whereas they are participants in Hindi by them.

We have required to demand by revolutionary mode as-

1. Give the right to give speech in vernacular state official language with an interpreter in parliament.

2. In a State Either Central or State Governmental or public organization competitive examination and interview should talk in State official language and English.

3. Local Assembly in State should use the State official language in speech and written particular.

4. Want Birthright as our Mother language and state official language.

5. Want to demand compulsory State official language question in competition examination at list 10 percent that if a candidate remain to do work, he should able to communicate easily in working field because maximum word use by common worker as vernacular language

6 In departmental examinations, input State language as compulsory because in Hindi State there are remain compulsory Hindi Language in Departmental examination. Even in some cases the question and answer remain and getting in Hindi.

6. Every letter and notice in the State should remain in the State official Language as Hindi States.

7. Hindi Racism to mention at international level and force to implement the system and required to help the UN Department.

8. The Name of the country required to give as the United Bharat Republic because The India was given by European and Afterall the British ruler give the name British India whereas previously Islamic invader called as Hindustan because that they enter land lived the religion of Hindu

mainly and after lord Asoka ruled the landmark Buddhism start the flows in the religious under royal society but the Islamic ruler understand the land mark as Hindu land, hence the enter landmark called as Hindustan. But the real name of the landmark was Bharat Barsha and hence required the given name of the nation as United Bharat Republic for better integration of the nation.

9. Name of the currency of our nation as Indiana by which reformation of economic system required and known by every citizen as Indiana whereas at present in different state call the currency name as Taka called by Bengali, Tanka called by Oria, Rupkani called by Marathi, Toka called by Assamese and so on. On the other hand, in Nepal, Indonesia, Pakistan the currency is called the same as Rupes and hence identification of the nation requires a special as for the national integrity.

10 In the verbally Hindi speaking peoples call them as Hindustani but in Non-Hindi State the Hindustani means as Hindi speaking peoples. Hence confusion created as that defined the peoples as Hindustani, and the upper-class peoples indicate them as Indian in English but the Non-Hindi peoples indicate them as Bharotio and these indicate the dissatisfaction of the peoples. The Islamic state and Islamic community indicate the landmark as Hindustan but they indicate them as Muslim but not things as Hindustani because that Hindu is attached with the word Hindustani. After all dissatisfaction creates and terrorist increases around that part where the Islamic community remains maximum in number, hence it is required to indicate us as Braotian which

to be easy to specify us as single identity and hence the national integrity to be increased.

11. There are required by law that the name of nation and nationality should be indicated as Hindustan and Hindustani as well as India and Indian in Films and newspaper, magazine, and journal respectively. The proper name is required as United Bharat Republic and in short to indicate as UBR and nationality should be indicated as Bharotian as single unity.

12. As per constitution the name of country given as Union India and Sanga Bharat because the British India was ruled either direct ruled or indirect agent ruling and after all the religion remain as Hindu, Muslim, Shaik, Ishai (Christian), Jain, etc. and Hindustan if give the name of country than may arise problem that to feel Hindu Land but time pass out above 64 years but national integrity cannot try to increase by the identity of nation. No Liberty of tower or Liberty of statue are not created by the government and peoples celebrating independence day near India Gate and some where the India Gate make as model by the peoples but the India Gate was made by the British Ruler in Respect of visit India by the king of England George-V and he entered the Indian land through Bombay hence There also made as Gateway of India. But we become proud that we celebrate Indian Independence Day near the India Gate which indicates that we have no feelings of nationality. Hence required to make the liberty of tower and liberty of statue in respect of an independent nation.

13. The Parliament House, Governor General House (President house) in New Delhi and Right Us House Governor House in Calcutta (Kolkata) remain as the Administration purpose as Central and state of West Bengal but we do nothing after independence as our own building for local and central administration.

Area of as per language:

1. Hindi language States: Hindi used as Official language.

Haryana, Himachal Pradesh, Uttaranchal, Uttar Pradesh, Bihar, Jharkhand, Chhattisgarh, Madhya Pradesh, Rajasthan as the list of State and only union territory Delhi included in the list of Hindi Language part of India.

2. Non- Hindi language States: Indo-English use as official language.

Jammu & Kashmir, Punjab, Gujrat, Maharashtra, Andhra Pradesh, Goa, Karnataka, Tamil Nadu, Kerala, Orissa, West Bengal, Sikkim, Assam, Meghalaya, Tripura, Mizoram, Manipur, Nagaland, Arunachal Pradesh as the state and union territory Daman-Diu, Pondicherry, Lakshadweep, Chandigarh, and Andaman & Nicobar where English use as official language and the peoples of their area participate competition written examination and face interview in English and they have no other often they may participate in recognize language whereas the peoples of these area use the recognize language in study and only one language paper remain English and become weak in English and remain unknown the Hindi language which have option to attempt Competitive examination and interview. By the system Hindi speaking peoples give more and more facility and enter to Non-Hindi area where as have same qualification and same marmite as the Hindi speaking peoples whereas Hindi speaking peoples also have habit to take education in Hindi and have only one regular or optional English Language paper and they are also maximum weak in English. But in departmental and other competitive examinations one 10% question get in Hindi and become successful in the competition by the system, hence partiality created by the system and the Non-Hindi peoples become down in competition by the system.

Policy to increasing the number of Hindi States: Divide the Hindi States to increase the number as UP, Bihar, Madhya Pradesh Divided into two parts as new states form as Uttarakhand, Jharkhand, and Chhattisgarh and previously the Hindi state form by division of Punjab State as Haryana and Himachal Pradesh. The recent year when Telangana state demand and central government give more willingness to form the Telangana state than the UP Government and other political parties as majority of Hindi Peoples want to divide UP into different parts as Harit Pradesh, Bundle Khand, etc. The policy is to increase the numbers of Hindi States.

What am I? What I was? When I think about these two questions, I think about how I was brought up. Today 1st, May 2005, I am standing near the main entrance of the Western Railway cultural hall. Several people come into this program hall at 7 P.M. Yesterday, Additional Divisional Mechanical Engineer Mr. Nicoriya told us to come into the cultural hall to wear a tie. Today all Apprentice Junior Engineer and Apprentice Section Engineer who come for training at Ratlam Diesel Shed ought to wear ties. We stand with scout people as instructed by ADME Mr. Nicoriya. We are waiting and standing to give respectful salutation and welcome address to the Divisional Railway Manager of Ratlam Division.

I think that on 15th, April, first footsteps at Ratlam. My wife stayed in Kolkata. I get a chance as a Junior Engineer and training starts from 21st April. I have been meeting with my wife Santai and promised after the arrangement of the room; I should get her with me. But our child will be coming in the near future. Hence, she stayed at her mother's house. When I shall go to Kolkata then we will pass our time with joy at our house. I talk with Santai and inform that I am wearing a tie for the first time in my life.

In my childhood, I thought that I should wear a tie. Today one of my thoughts filled my life. In the near future tie will be required. I became proud that I learned to wear a tie. I also talk with my mother and say, "To day god full fill another dream in my life because if Mr. Nicoriya does not give instructions to wear a tie then I should not buy the tie @Rs.70/-. I will fulfill my dream again." Mother has become happy.

At 8.30 P.M., DRM of Ratlam came to the spot, we threw rose petals to him. Like an ancient Indian King's style, he entered into this cultural hall. I think that English people left India 55 years ago but at the officer level and other people wear shirts, pants and ties. We also wear ties. A totally English environment arises in our upper level peoples in India. We use several English words when we speak in our mother tongue also, but we cannot think like them. We see, several community peoples came in India and they ruled throughout India. Muslim people came from West Asia and Central Asia and approximately 500 years ruled by the Sultanate and approximately 400 years ruled by the Mogul. At that time Hindu peoples continue to discuss and study in their way. They mainly discussed the matter of apices and religious books. On the other hand, Muslim peoples got to study in their Mosque. Both of them did not try to develop the educational system in a scientific way. British people came into India to start their trade and business. They built the East India Company at Calcutta.

Day by day I saw and observed the weak points of Indian peoples and verified their mentality. In the war of Palasi, Nabab Sirajudulha was defeated by the British. Lord Clive became a hero and day by day British people started to rule in India. The new education system was started by Christine missionaries. David Hear, Mr. Bethune, they gave pressure to women and modern education. The system was started in a new way. In the same century Raja Rammohun Roy was born and learned English, Bengali, Urdu, Arabic, Sanskrit languages and observed that the English language has valuable books by which Indian people can learn how to lead life in new ways. They might be communicated throughout the world. English became an official and educational medium in British India. Raja Rammohun Roy supported

Lord Bunting to start English as an official and educational language.

Lord Bunting is one of the great people who tried to change the social and educational system in India, a man with a lamp who showed the way of light in Indian Civilization. Indian Hindu people had several undesirable systems at that time, one of these is the Sati system. Sati system is a system that if someone dies then by force people murder his wife to burn on his body.

With the support of Raja Rammohun Roy, Lord Bunting abolished the Sati system. It is the turning point of Indian Society. Mr. Dirozio also followed Raja Rammohun Roy and developed Indian society.

Day by day missionaries increased their activity and Christian community roles started in India. Hindu people converted into Christianity. The Catholic, Baptized Church and cathedral are increasing day by day. Many Win shops and bars are built all over India.

We copy their hobby and entertainment procedure from them. But we cannot think of doing new things.

Several British peoples came from the United Kingdom. They followed the route of Portugal, Spain and France.

Throughout the world, mainly four European countries tried to discover the world route and new communication paths found by their contribution. In several parts of the world like India, Burma, Rhodesia, America, Australia etc. ruled by them. World peoples have seen the way of world communication.

I am thinking about these matters in my mind and remain quite silent. I feel European Peoples teach us to lead our life in a better way. I am standing in the corridor of the cultural hall of Western Railway Ratlam Division.

I observe, one by one they have shown their dance performance. Most of them are officers' children. Hindi songs are sung by a group of people. Step by step the program completed then we participated at the Diner in Officer's Club. Divisional Railway Manager and Officers take part at that diner. I also got dinner and when my colleagues completed their dinner, we returned to our rental room.

From my childhood I am a different type. I got a chance in Ratlam Divisional as Junior Engineer Grade-II but I am not happy because when I am standing near Engine WDM2 which is a USA model I become sorrowful. USA i.e. In the United States of America, mainly English-speaking peoples build up this country and become free from British rule. They build up a new nation. In the field of science and technology they progress at a high level but I was born in a Bengali family hence I am proud. In childhood I tried to build up new types of vehicles by which we can travel on land, in the air, on water and into water. I am thinking about the above matter. Actually, the story of Ripon and Bunting as well as Isher Chandra Sarma called Vidhyasagar, Raja Ram Mohan Roy and Derozio story gave influence to me as wanted social revolution and independence of Ecological field through

Technical revolutions through innovation but remain unable as poor. But thinking remains as British as my dream of in my Childhood. I came from Scotland and rebirth again and again. The British give the positive side of our social and economic development where everyone gives the right to education as the candle of life in social development. Hindu save as the British took power otherwise whole India must be converted to Islamic community. Hindu Community remained a strong Caste system where only Brahmin and Kshatriya but other communities depressed by the system and Islamic community got study in Madrasa and both of these communities only learn religious text and practical depression system implementations. Scientific education implemented by British rulers and social reformers took the path of social development.

Thought about British Contribution in Indian Social development:

1. Educational development
2. Judicial development
3. Ruling system Development
4. Bureaucratic system development
5. Democracy implementation
6. Social reformation
7. Economic development
8. Technical development

9. Transportation development
10. Agricultural Development:
11. Humanity and social science development:
12. Acarological, Geological, Botanical, Zoological and human study done and one after another department development done. Department, Mining college, Marin Engineering college, development done.

In the meantime, my previous life's story was suddenly remembered by me. I was born in a poor family. I had two older sisters and one older brother. The eldest sister's name is Mukta and elder brother is Pintu. Sibani was my elder sister. I am the last child of our family.

Before the birth of my elder brother, my father had a dream at night that two monkeys named Ram and Shyam came near him, who can speak in a human voice. They said, "May we enter into your house." Father asked them, "Who are you? Why you come?" Both answered, "We are two brother Ram and Shyam and we agree to enter into your house." Father again asked them, "Who take responsibility of my family?" Shyam answered, "I take responsibility." Shyam entered the house. But Ram was quite silent and entered the house behind Shyam. Then my elder brother was born, then sister Sibani, then I.

We were very poor and had a small hut which was made of bamboo fiber. We resided nearest to Dumdum Junction Station at Roy Mallick colony. In the sense, "I was and I am." It is totally different.

An underdeveloped colony called 'Roy Mallick colony' sometimes called Kundu Bagan, each and everywhere have small ponds or muddy lanes. Another colony was also founded in 1948 after the division of India. Before the foundation of those colonies the total area from Airport to Dumdum Junction Station was covered with jungle and nobody came here after evening. I heard from my father that after the division of India so many Hindu peoples came from East Pakistan. They also had properties in Pakistan and they left all by their fear that Pakistan would build up for Muslim community and that period communal harmony was destroyed because India divided according to community in 1947. Hindu Muslim riot holds on. They came to West Bengal in a helpless condition and they were so hungry. So many people came to Sealdah station and got to a nearby vacant place. They tried to live together, although one and another know nothing about them. They became refugees and got shelter at a refugee camp. The government declared that all refugees might be sitting temporarily in vacant land. In this period so many Zamindar (Land Lord) had so much land which was covered with Jungle. Hence refuge captured the vacant land and cleaned the jungle. Like the same, peoples of the colonies at Dumdum build hut temporarily by hogla(Long Grass) leaf's which were available nearby Bagjola channel. The peoples are given the colonies name according to the name of the landlord, e.g. the name of colonies is Mallick colony, Roy Mallick colony, Seth colony, etc.

Now come to our family matter Mr. Nabakanta who is my father came to Calcutta in 1948 for his work. He was working as a carpenter with his elder brother who lived in Chiriamore where some rental rooms were available.

At that time Jibon Krishana Talukdar came to meet with Rakhalchandra. He is the elder brother of Nabakanta. Mr. Jiban Krishna Talukdar said, "Rakhal, we may capture vacant land at Dumdum, I heard some colonies are capturing and setting up at that place. If we live together that will be better to us." They came all together that night, and sat on the land of Jaminder Shasticharan Mullick who got land from someone Mr. Roy. A group of people came and sat temporarily to build a small hut by hogla leaves and given name Roy Mullick colony. At night they captured land and the whole night they were staying without sleeping. The mosquito was biting them again and again. First, they indicated their land by some thread and bamboo, then early morning they went to a low land which is near the Bagjola channel and they collected hogla leaves then temporarily built up a small hut at Roy Mallick Colony. Then their mother Sukhuda came to Dumdum after one year from East Pakistan. They lived a little bit of happiness. In this period, night school started at Calcutta. Nabakanta worked as a carpenter at day time and got admission at Raja Manindra Night School. By hard and solid work, he tries to stand on his own leg. After returning from night school, he studied until 10 o'clock and sometimes more. The whole night passed through study, then in the morning I got some food which I prepared last night. But he tried to study continuously. He returned from night school by walking very fast. Hence someone laughed at him and told horse run on the road. But up to class ten he continued his study. In 1958 he got Railway service at the post Khalasi (Helper). He joined Loco Shed Kanchrapara.

In Loco Shed Narendra Nath also worked at different sections. One day, Narendra Nath saw a beautiful young man with bright skin. He asked the name of the young man. The young man proudly answers that his name is Nabakanta and expresses his work at Tool Room Shop. Then Mr. Narendra Nath asked the residence of the young boy. The young boy answered that he resided at Dumdum and came from East Pakistan in 1948.

In the same way at returning time from the workshop, sometimes Mr. Narendra Nath visited with Nabakanta. Then one day he tells Nabakanta that he has a daughter and he ask to make him his son in law. Nabakanta has a good behavior that when we meet with Mr. Narendra Nath, he solutes to him (Narendra Nath) in the style of Bengali culture and says Namaskar. Narendra Nath becomes satisfied with his behavior. In last year Nabakanta's elder brother Mr. Rakhal's marriage with Sova Rani-I who lived at Baranagar. Hence Nabakanta has no problem with marriage, he is the youngest brother in his family and only he remains bachelor.

On the other hand, some clashes took place between Sova Rani-I and Rakhal. Sova Rani-I went to her father's house by quarreling with her husband. She said that she could not cook food for Rakhal's brother and mother. She agreed to live with her husband only. Eight months passed and after eight months Sova Rani-I returned to Dumdum but she remained in a single family.

Nabakanta gave a proposal to his mother and elder brother, that some one person named Narandra Nath have a daughter and he wanted to make him son in law. Nabakanta's mother and elder brother go to Kanchrapara and meet with Narendra Nath. His brothers and others go to Kanchrapara with Sukhuda. Narandra Nath and others come to Dumdum when the mother of Nabakanta agrees about the proposal of Narendra Nath.

Nabakanta lives in a small hut at Dumdum and they have no smooth dice by which they can host hospitality, offering food to Narandra Nath, his brother and others. His brother and others oppose making relations with Nabakanta but Narendra Nath likes him very much.

The marriage holds on after three months of joining. Nabakanta's marriage was held with Sova Rani-II. Narendra Nath lived at Kanchrapara. He has only one daughter and three sons. Narendra Nath gives brass and bell metal utensils in the name of Nabakanta because Rakhal's wife's name is also Sova Rani.

In this stage Nabakanta only earned Rs. 75/- per month and Rakhal always say, "Nabakanta, this money is insufficient to carry out family to maintain foods." Rakhal works under a conductor and has done windows or doors in airport. He earns more money, hence Rakhal is not agreeing with the joint family and on the other hand, Nabakanta hands over full payment to Rakhal whatever he gets money from Railway service. Rakhal's two daughters were born, he gave names Anita and Dali. In this time Nabakanta's daughter Mukta born and Nabakanta make a policy in a Bank to deposit money for his daughter and think when his daughter will be young then the deposit money will be useful to him. He will be free of tension.

When the matter flashes out to Rakhal, he quarrels with his brother and ultimately Nabakanta tears the paper of the bank. Nabakanta is a very hot-tempered person and when he becomes angry that time, he forgets any importance about the matter. After all, cancel the deposit fund of his daughter. But the peace does not remain in the family. Rakhal quarreled with Nabakanta about deficiency of money.

One month later, Sova Rani-II went to her father's house and remained at Kanchrapara. When Sova Rani-II returns from Kancharpara, she may not understand that Rakhal and Sova Rani-I become separate by quarreling with Nabakanta and they prepare foods separately. Her mother in law Sukhuda expressed the matter and gave instructions to prepare foods. Nabakanta handed over his income to Rakhal but after quarreling, Rakhal might not return money to Nabakanta. Hence, he remained under great problem and land money from others and then carried out his family maintenance expanse. Part time he did carpentry works to earn extra money. But time might not stay for a while and human life passes out with joy or in struggle. Sukhuda joined with her elder son Rakhal to take her food.

Nabakanta is doing daily passenger in every day for his service at Kanchrapara. He decided to stay at Kanchrapara with his family to avoid a train journey. He shifts to the Railway plot at first and then gets a rental room near his father in law's house. Two years pass with a happy life. In this time Rakhal got a chance in group-D post to do work as a carpenter in Durgapur steel plant. But before getting the job, Rakhal said to each and every body at Roy Mallick colony, "My brother fills up my application form, he may not fill up properly, otherwise authority of the DSP Company calls me." But the company called him and he got a job. Rakhal goes to Durgapur. His mother becomes alone. Relative and other say, "Who get responsibility of Sukhuda." One related elder brother Jogendra gives a letter to Nabakanta that his mother is very ill, he shall come to Dumdum for hospitalization. Nabakanta comes to Dumdum when he gets the letter and takes care of his mother.

Then Pintu born in 1964, Rakhal started to say that Nabakanta had a son and he had only daughters. Rakhal's third daughter was born in 1965 and the word repeated again and again that Nabakanta had a son whereas he had no son. In this time Sukhuda becomes brain shorted and continues talking about anything whichever comes to her mind. Son of Rakhal born after a long time of Rakhal expectation and he became happy in his life but Sukhuda wanted to see the son of Rakhal once. Rakhal neither came to Dumdum with Ranjit nor took Sukhuda with him. He talks to others that his mother becomes mad and if he gets his mother with him, his position and priestess become hamper at Durgapur. Then

Rakhal's second son is born. The second daughter of Nabakanta Sibani was born at this time. Sukuda becomes so old and always becomes angry if anything is not shut to her. Sukhuda died at this time. In this time Nabakanta's eldest brother is also present at Dumdum with his one eldest son Anil and five daughters.

Eldest brother of Nabakanta, Raicharan had come to Calcutta in 1965 to produce the letter which was sent by Nabakanta to tell him to come to India. Raicharan had given a letter to Nabakanta that he wanted to come to Dumdum from East Pakistan. Nabakanta gave a response letter to his eldest brother that he should come to Dumdum with his family. No body of the family of Raicharan have done work with Sova Rani-II and tell others why they have done work with Sova Rani-II but they get food in the Nabakanta room. In this way, how much time could a man remain silent? Hence quarrel exists. Raicharan say, "I should try to do such things that you should leave this land as before which I had been done at Pakistan, Nabakanta." Nabakanta reported this matter to the colony committee. By the help of colony committee registration name of land change from Sukhuda to Rakhal and Nabakanta by who land captured when the colony set up in early stage. In this time period Ishim Kumar born, last and youngest son of Nabakanta. Mr. Raicharan calls him 'Dog of Bhadra' because Ishim Kumar was born in Bengali month Bhadra. Mr. Raicharan used to say that the Dog of Bhadra might not be a batter in his life. After six months Ishim Kumar became sick and the physician also could not detect what diseases attracted him. Nobody says that he may become recovered in his life and be brought up. Mr. Raicharan says, "What is profit for treatment to Dog of Bhadra, he might not be alive." These types of words are heard by Ishim Kumar's mother and father but they become worried and quite silent.

After all, in 1971 India Pakistan war was held and so many refugees came from East Pakistan and East Pakistan became an independent country to get the name Bangladesh. Naxalist (Terrorist group) started hooliganism activity in West Bengal. In this time violence of law and murder started by the Naxalist. One day Raicharan hears that land is to be capture at Madhugar at the bank of Bagjola channel. Raicharan goes to that place by capturing some part of land and then goes to Madhugar with his family.

Ishim Kumar heard the matter from his mother. He also heard that when he was born, a nurse gave one teaspoonful of water which he did not take. Then she gave water with sugar to him. He took sugar first and then took water. In his childhood he might not get cow milk without sugar. Day after day he was brought up.

At the age of four, he had been suffering from fever some times. Again, and again he was suffering from different diseases. Then one friend of his father Dr. Sama Pada Aich suggests, "He have tonsil problem, so it is better if operation have done." Father Nabakanta gets him to B. R. Singh hospital. 30 injections were given to him then multiple tests were done. The operation was done through his mouth and for that region four teeth were removed from the front side which are called milk teeth. The Aryabhataperation became successful. He became happy.

After cure, it become the nature of Ishim Kumar that he is thinking all the time that he should have done some things that people don't forget to him. When he was a child, he was thinking about how a poet writes a poem. When he was admitted in class as an infant from that time, he was thinking how sculptors are able to make a sculpture. Day by day he tries to build up some figure in clay medium. He does not get such tuition for Arts and also in his school have no such things according to the syllabus. Only his mother has some knowledge by which his mother tries to teach him and guide him, what is wrong and what is right.

But father told him the story of Bengal Tiger ``Ashutosh Mukherjee" who was very intelligent in mathematics. Ashutosh Mukherjee had the ability to solve a sum of arithmetic into different methods and in his childhood, he also had done a sum in different methods in school examinations and he got more marks. Due to hearing the story by Ishim Kumar, he also tries to do a sum in a different way. But he is very poor at solving mathematics and gets a number in the mathematics subject as zero in class IV by applying the different methods in a single sum. But all the time he thinks about how he became a great man.

It is also his nature from childhood that he became angry if someone forcefully told him to do something but if politely command to do something then that should be done by him.

In his childhood they had used a toilet which was built by some corrugated tin and one well was used for dropping the stools. They were poor but were happy. A big pond was near their house. Sometime from that pond someone caught fishes by Nate. In his childhood he had seen the ponds were covered with hyacinths and when the hyacinths became large in size, the pond was cleaned to collect hyacinths by some people for feeding their cows, which they pet. He was a child and hence, he was jumping on the hyacinths like in games. Sometimes his elder brother and others made vala which was like a boat. By hyacinths they used to make Vala for riding and they enjoy the games that they might ride a boat. But generally, Ishim Kumar wanted to remain along

At the age of seven Ishim Kumar was sitting on a bench nearby a tea stall of Jitendra Roy. Someone named Gopal was playing cricket with some other and was beaten by him. Suddenly the ball came near him. Gopal ordered to give him the ball. But Ishim Kumar was stool sitting on the bench. Suddenly Gopal came and pushed him to the ground. The bench falls down to his finger and thumb. Ishim Kumar's right-hand thumb became injured. Three months were taken to recover his finger. Actually, Gopal was born in a rich family and felt that his order should be carried out by others.

In Ishim Kumar's life, so many years were passing over at Kundu Bagan in the Uttarayan club. In his childhood Nihar Ranjan Das ruled the club. Gouranga Nag, Shyamal Barman, Shyamal Das, Jaydab Das and Krishna De and Madhu Das were guides to his group. Folk dance and pair practice which are called brotochary. In the struggle of Indian Freedom fighting, Brotochary had an idle activity in Bengal. Ishim Kumar and his group were gone in a semi island ground called Kundu Bagan Math. They practice dancing with the song of the Brotochary. Generally, boys used to brand. Kamal Da Barman, Kamal Guha were joined in the colony committee, they also started interfering about the matter of the club. At that time all drainage and lanes in the colony were not made of cement and brick. So, in the rain session all the place became full of water. At Dumdum road, people are frequently doing tailoring work and shopping. Ishim Kumar's mother made two or three dozen i.e. 36 pieces of blouse in a day and got six (6) rupees per day. Through hard work, she tried to make up for the family expenses. Some time ago, she was getting mud from the pond and making fire wood dust cake. The wood dust was getting in chief rate and tried to decrease the family expenses. By coal dust she also makes the same types of cake for firing.

Within this environment they try to bring up and try to stand in their lag. His eldest sister appeared in matriculation and then passed also. After matriculation his eldest sister took admission in higher secondary course at Khudiram Bose College near Haduya Park in Central Calcutta. At the same time Sapan whose residence at Kharagpur was teaching to Ishim Kumar and his elder sister Sibani and both was learning to Sapan. At that time Ishim Kumar was learning at class IV and three times he was in the same class. In that time his father told some Mathematician's story. That story was rounding in his brain. He tried to follow the story in class IV. Because of this matter, he failed the examination. Then changed his mentality and then the third time he passed in the class IV exam. Up to class IV he was in Kumar Ashutosh Institution but in class V he got a chance to take admission in Adarsha Vidyamandir at Shet Bagan which was not so developed at that time. At the same time his father suspends the private tutor Mr. Sapan because his father suspects that his eldest sister tried to make some relation with Mr. Sapan. One day he was gone at Dakshineswar with his father and mother due to prayer by goddess Kali. On the same day his eldest sister gave instructions to him that he should meet with Mr. Sapan and told him to meet with his eldest sister. Ishim Kumar also did the same and went with his mother and father.

From that day, the eldest sister's love affair started and she also started a quarrel with his mother. But my younger sister has not had such a relationship with anybody. His father used to go to Kanchrapara Railway Workshop in the early morning and return at 5:30 or 6 P.M. His father is a very angry man, so everybody in their house is afraid of him, but they make some mistakes. His eldest sister is making such a mistake.

At this time, according to a Bengali poor family, a young boy came to see his eldest sister for marriage. His eldest sister has not agreed to marry another. But his father worried about the marriage of his sisters. All that time his father is talking, "In my head I have two burdens. I have two daughters and in marriage how much money are necessary only, God know." His father always used to think that his daughter had to be a government servant and educated groom. So, try to do so.

But Government servant people have so much demand for dowry Rs. 50000/- and more. They have no such ability to give dowry. For that reason, every arrangement break, either in the first stage or second stage.

After all, eldest sister 'Mukta for a while becomes married when two years pass without meeting with Sapan. But suddenly younger sister Sibani meets with Mr. Sapan and informs her eldest sister. At the same time Mukta's marriage was arranged by her father at Semurali. The person has a poultry farm and was a worker in a private company which was locked out at this time. Several time Ashim Kumar was gone at Semurali which place are at a distance about 23 Km. from their house and that person's face also not so good but he is agreeing to marriage with Mukta for that reason their father agree in the marriage, the candidate want 10,000 rupees cash and ornament at the stage of marriage. In this time Mukta meets with Sapan again once more and asks him to get the address of Mr. Sapan's sister. Then Mukta and Sibani both go to meet with the sister of Sapan whose name is Moni.

Then express the details about the relation with Sapan. Although Sapan is Brahmin, he speaks the truth. His uncle comes to meet at Mukta's house and speaks with her mother, "Whether you are scheduled caste and we are brahmin(priest) that does not arise any problem but Sapan now has not any good job. Only work as priest and doing some tuition so if you give Rs. 10,000/- cash Sapan can do something in near future." Mukta's mother agrees that the marriage may be arranged with some program. But her father is thinking some things differently and goes to the Sapan's sister's house. He is thinking that his daughter will head to Semurali where he will give his word and that will break. Then he agrees that he paid 15,000 cash and the marriage will be held at Kalighat at Calcutta Kali Temple. It is a custom that love marriages are happening at Kali temple at Kalighat. Mukta's father's decision is executed, so others can do nothing. Her mother and elder brother all become silent then make some decision that they arrange some dinner at night that comes as a guest. At 4 P.m. Everyone went to Kalighat and the marriage was held on. The group has gone by two taxis and on the same taxis all members come back to Dumdum. Ishim Kumar is not agreeing about the system but he can do nothing. He is thinking that their house peace may come in the near future. The next day the bride and groom went to Sudpur to Sapan's uncle's house. Ishim Kumar's mother and sister are crying but Ishim Kumar is thinking, "It is the real fact, previously mother and eldest sister were quarreling all time to each other. Sometimes the elder and eldest sister fight with each other. But today my eldest sister has gone to her husband's house and house become cool."

On the other hand, elder brother Pintu stopped his study at class IX. So, their father and mother break their hearts. In their house Sarasvati (goddess of education) Puja is held every year but when Pintu ends his study at class IX, parent stop the puja. Then father is thinking, it is better that Pintu may be engaged with some work. It is better to join in the work but without work, an idle mind may do something wrong. So Nabakanta goes to Bulgaria to meet with related brothers,

Paras and Narash. Nabakanta's maternal uncle's son introduced him to a small Industrialist. Pintu started to learn the lath work. But after some years he starts night duty and associates with hooliganism, then starts to talk loosely. Sometimes I sighed unnecessarily. In this environment Ishim Kumar continues his study and gets better results. Some times Pintu heard the song on radio or in tape-record but Ishim Kumar silently read at night from 8 P.M. to 2 A.M. But sometimes he is sleeping on the chair by the support of a table where generally he is sitting to read the books. Father does not see the matter, but calls him in the early morning i.e. at 4 A.M. So, any things he can't read at that time but feel disturbed and again sleep on the table. Day by day he started to progress in his life.

In the meantime, when I (Ishim Kumar) am in class VII, I get attacked by T.B. in the chest. For two months I was in bed. My mother is so worried about my sickness. Then nearby Furniture shop owner Mr. Santi Ranjan came to my house. We call him Santi uncle. He used to come to our house. Sometimes he makes some decisions also. At this time Santi uncle told my mother that we should consult with a Homeopathy Physician, Dr. Subrata Saha, nicknamed Gopal. So, I called Gopal Kaku. In Bengali Kaku means uncle. Gopal Kaku started my treatment but I was not so worried. So, one day Gopal Kaku asked me, "Do you know, what happened to you?" I answer, "I know, I attacked by T.B. and it may cause to death myself but it is curable diseases." Days are passing with tension. This time my elder sister Sibani's marriage will be arranged. My elder sister Sibani is young. She is talented. She knows timbering and wavering of woolen cloth.

Father becomes worry about the marriage of Sibani. Now she is studying at class XII. Our relative come and tells to my mother, "One educated boy working in municipality, if you agree then they may come to see your daughter." Someone is maternal uncle of the candidate who use to song of god and goddess in a festival who come to our house. Mother believe god and think that person may be good. Then, one day they come to see my elder sister Sibani. In the mean time I become ill again. My mother becomes worry. Then my mother tells to my father, "You may leave the matter of marriage." My elder sister love education and love to see movies at T.V. or in cinema. But my father thinks, it is not good, so creating some restriction. She tries to break that restriction. Whether the candidate of groom in short height and thin but my elder sister agrees because she know that our father may be roaring to her and applied aggression and another thing that is, in our house have no T.V. and tape recorder, hand pump etc. but their house have T.V., Tub well and hand pump etc. Also, the candidate is educated. I give some suggestion to my father, "She is your daughter, so you hand over to some groom who have ability to do some work and you verified him, weather he speaks truth or not." My father has not any doubt because they also are same district's people, same caste and someone relative get this samondha (relation of marriage). That time I am in bed. Three doctors (Physician) became failure. Several blood tests have done and X-Ray also etc. be taken. But result becomes nil. Then Dr. Sunil Kumar

Datta (home physician) sends me to meet with his professor Dr. D.K. Ray who lives in Crick Row. My elder brother first meets with him. Then, my elder brother, my mother and Susanto get me for check up by him. Dr. D. K. Ray asks previous record and how I feel my body condition. Then tell me, "You have done some blood test and mulatto test then after seven days you come for checkup." He prescribed some medicine. I was on bed for about three months but by his treatment I recovered and after seven days I went to Dr. D.K.Ray's house without the help of others. Then he got all the reports and he suggested it to me. He told me, "You are attracted by intestines T.B. which may be affected by your large intestine. But you are lucky because 95% case may not detect in early stage, only 5% get their life, you also one of them." Then 90 injections are given to me one day each.

From my childhood I may get 200 injections because in my childhood I also had been suffering from fever due to tonsillitis and at the age of 4 years, my tonsil operation was held and at that time several injections were given to me. When just now I recovered from disease my father arranged the marriage of my elder sister in 1988. My elder sister's marriage held on. After her marriage the auspicious occasion was held at her father in law house.

My elder sister becomes unhappy on the auspicious day when she is gone to bed at night. Every female may be unhappy if her husband remains ill and cheats on her. Her husband also does this. He is not B.A. or B.Sc.; he is only a higher secondary pass and he is not working in a municipality. Only he has gone some time to municipalities to pay the tax of the other and get commissions. He has done tuition up to class X. He has major operations in his lung and he is less strong.

But my father is agreeing about this relation with that person without his knowledge. So Sibani think that in my father house we also crying for T.V. and cinema. Hence, I have freedom to see T.V. but human feeling cannot get satisfaction. Then some time cried and told me, "One day you will come and you may see I hang to death." I also afraid but do nothing. In the meantime, at March 1989 matriculation examination held whether I was in bed about three months but before my sickness I completed my syllabus and I had confidence that if I appear in examination, I should stand at 1st division. At the time of sickness, I could not study the books but appeared. I am waiting for result. Up to 5th, May 1989, I was in my maternal uncle house. My father come on returning time from his working place at my maternal uncle house and meet with me. I go to my sister Sibani's house with my father. Elder brother of sister's husband starts to sought when we enter into their house. Now days Bengali people start to wear Turidar Kurti or Nighty who is married but previously Bengali people was not like to do so. So, I report that Shari, turider Kurti and nighty all are dresses. Whichever is good looking that may use by girls or women? My father also become against to wear nighty and turidar KLurti, he supports to them but father is not thinking that they cheat with us and my sister is crying in her mind that her husband is not physically fit. We come to invite to my sister and her husband to join in Jamaysasti (Son in law festivals). But then I and she support about nighty to wear in modern period. My father tries to bit us. I suddenly back to some distance but my sister can't move. My father bit her and sought, "I don't think that due to my daughter someone insult me and tell me some things wrong." Sibani tell, "I also could not think that any further can arrange his daughter marriage with a liar person." Then Sibani start to cried and start weeping. I enter into her room and telling her, "What can we do? You know that our father is like this." Father is not entering her room. I am calling him to come here. At the same time, rain suddenly started. After some time, we will go to our house. I may not solve the matter. I can say the matter to my elder brother Pintu. After the rain stops, we start our return journey. Before starting of our return journey, I meet with my sister and tell her, "We now going to our house, you and your husband must come to our house." She asks me, "If you have done arrangement of my marriage in late then my father money might not be finished." I tell her, "I only can give decision but cannot execute my decision because I am youngest in our family." After all, we return at 10-30 P.M. to our house. That night was a dark night for us. My elder brother also comes to our house too late from work. When I was talking about the matter to my elder brother, suddenly the tenant of my sister's house came and told me that my sister had become seriously ill. My father and my elder brother immediately go to Bulgaria but everything finish. My elder sister suicide hang to death. A shadow comes to our house.

Next day, wife of Naras uncle come to our house and tell me, "You come with me." She asks me, "Whether you come with your mother also.'' I say, "You tell everything that will be better to me." I ask, "What happened?" She tells me, "Your sister suicide by hang to death." Then I become hard in my mind and make some decisions. I told this to my friend Shamal. One worker of his house came with me. We went to Belgharia to my uncle Narash house with my mother. My mother stays there. My friends and I went to Dashpriyanagar where Sibani's husband and his elder brother cried. I sought to them, "You are guilty because you don't give peace to my elder sister and all of you also told everything flash." Then we went to Sarada hospital where my sister 's dead body lay in the morgue. Police come and asked that who is related to her. I said, "My own sister sir" Then asked for my address. That day, I also learned how to write proper addresses, that is first to write my name, then post office, then police station, then pin code. I signed in the police file. I went to Belgharia police station with sister death body. I saw all the people sitting there. My maternal uncle also comes to the police station. Santi Kaku also comes to the spot. Everybody saying that we cannot write such matter i.e. FIR, whether my maternal uncle or my related uncle have the same behavior. Then Santi Kaku made a decision. My father wrote the application and Santi Kaku directed it to him. I could only tell that his expression is right. Then we go to the morgue with the dead body at Barrackpore and the police go with us. After some time, I returned with my friend to Narash's house.

Narash uncle's family and my mother, all come to our house by a Taxi. Mother understand that her little daughter suicide and lost her life. We were not telling her any matter but by situation she knows that everything is finished. That time Sanju Taluckdar's mother one of my neighbor tell me, "You get some food." But I can't do so. Then she gives a glass of milk. I get that and wait when others came with lash. At 5 P.M., they come with a death body. Then according to Hindu tradition, the dead body gets to the burning ghat. This is the first time that I went to burning ghat.

I think the matter is that my father made some misbehavior. When we were getting ready to go to the burning ghat, he said that he was so hungry and told us to do everything as quickly as possible. Then someone next door gave some food and my father ate that nearby the lash. I feel sad because after all she was his daughter, so how could he aet in that situation? After burning the dead body, we return from the burning ghat and do something such as touching fire and eating neem leaves after taking a bath into Ganga River.

Days are passing with sorrowful mind. In the meantime, that twenty days pass out that my elder sister died, that is 25th May, my matriculation i.e. Class X final examination result publish. I was appeared the examination in last March. My elder brother tells me, "You go to Salt Lake and meet with my factory's owner." We called her Didi, which means elder sister. I go to that place but I am feeling that if today my own sister remained alive today then I must meet with my sister 'Sibani'. But she goes far away from us where we can't meet with her.

Then my father's rules and regulation were broken by me. I am thinking the suicide matter of my sister. If fathers are not so restricted then that type of things may not happened. At the same time, I take admission at class XI in Adarsha Vidyamandir School at Shet Bagan where I have completed up to class X. I have one friend, Sanjib Gosh, who is an English version student. After his completion of class X, he took admission at Scottish Church Collegiate School near Hedua Park.

One day Sanjib came to my house and asked how much percentage I have in matriculation. I got 62%. He discussed it with me and my father. He tells my father, “Your son will get admission at Scottish Church Collegiate School. He gets better marks in the Matriculation examination. You give him admission at the Scottish Church Collegiate School. Only Rs. 50/- taken per month and Rs. 250/- taken admission charge.” Suddenly my father tells me that I can bear this charge. My friend asks me, “Do you have any shoes and good blue pants and white shirt?” Then I tell him, “I have all these things.” Then he told me, “The class is scheduled from 4.30 P.M. to 7 P.M. You agree to take admission in the school.” Then I say, “Yes, I have no problem.”

Father pressures me and gives money. I take admission to Scottish Church Collegiate School. That is the first time I have so many English medium school friends. I am in Bengali medium but Scottish Church Collegiate School has both mediums. In my childhood, I was worrying about the style of an English medium school! When I first go to the school to take admission to higher secondary i.e. class XI, I wear a full pants, a shirt and natty boy shoes. Those shoes may be the first shoes in my life which I bought from the local shop due to the Adarsha Vidya Mandir School's Headmaster giving pressure to wear shoes when I was in class VIII. But the maximum time I used to go was to wear chappals or Hawaii. I was angry about my father because when I was ill, he was bothered about money but now he can bear such money for my studies whereas we are poor. How can I maintain the experiences about the school status? But on the other hand, I feel happy in my mind that now I also take admission at one of the most popular schools in Calcutta. I go to Scottish Church Collegiate School with my friend Sanjib. He is habituated with such a school because he completed class X at Cossipore English School. From his childhood he learned through English.

Now a days sometimes father tell me, "Sanjib know very well to speak in English." He sometimes says that which is good for someone, you should follow that matter. I have no proper environment but I try to learn English again and again. I think a matter that after all you may heard that great Sanskrit poet Mr. Kalidas told, "A stone also change its shape by friction with other material, so man also do some things if he tries to do the thing again and again." First day I went to Scottish Church Collegiate School and tried to see every part of the building construction and design. I follow whether anybody laughs at me or not. I took admission at Scottish Church Collegiate School and I am feeling that it was in my mind, I shall study in a great school. Today is that day when one of my dreams fully fills in my life. I feel very happy in my mind.

From this time period, I used to go to my friend Sanjib's house. His father is in a higher post than my father and he is the only son in that family. So, our lives are struggling and their lifestyles are totally different. When I go to Sanjib's house, his mother gives me some food. Sometimes tea or sometimes biscuits and other foods are given. But we have no ability to do so. So sometimes I feel very sad. But life may pass through struggle. Same way like a river where sometimes some obstruction comes and sometimes can flow easily.

In 1990 Sanjib passed higher secondary i.e. 10+2 but he failed in chemistry. So, his optional subject biology became the main subject and he passed. This time, give priority to the chemistry subject if anyone wants to pour science or Bio-Science in a degree course. But he fails in chemistry, so it is a problem to take admission in the Graduation label with a Science subject. Then he takes the decision that he returns his result in the council of W.B.C.H.S.E. and also tries to apply for scrutiny. One person makes a decision that it is better to accept that result. So many candidates he has seen in his life who refuse results, he might not succeed in his life again. I am with him and trying to realize his position. After all, he took admission in B.Com. At Umas Chandra College he takes admission through his uncle's recommendation. Next year 1991 I passed a higher secondary examination. Sanjib and I both apply for polytechnic course i.e. Diploma Engineering Course. In 1991 when the Joint Entrance examination of Polytechnic results was declared, Sanjib and I both passed. Sanjib thinks B.Com. The course may be better. This time, he gets interest in commerce subject.

Previously I had been suffering two times by T.B. and at the time of matriculation, my mind become totally breaking in condition. I am also thinking the death of my elder sister Sebani and I become angry about my father behavior in this time. I feel unsuitability in my mind. In the same time, I make friendship with several girls who use to take tuition in the same Cochin.

But previous girl friend is not forgotten by me. I think the previous friendship that was closer to me. Surjatapa was one of my best friends in that time when I was in class X. In surjatapa's house several girlfriends came to chatting and discussion done about the matter of the course's subject. I was only meal person within sixteenth female members group. All female candidates were study in Adarsha Vidhya mandir. They made friendship when I was in class X. In the same time, I was used to practice Arts and got admission in an Art School at Tala Park. Art teacher also have two daughters. In art school, I make friendship with Shukla and also make friendship with Nandita. Nandita is the daughter of my Art teacher. It was my habit in that time that I used to go on sun day morning at Art school and at evening went to the house of Art teacher. Several portrait and poster I had done at art school. Several drawing and printing had done at festivals in the area of my art teacher. I attended once time in sit and draw competition at Sangamitra club and got third prize. Then I sent three printing on the different matter in Camlin Company through my art teacher, also got first prize from Camlin Company in North Calcutta division. In the same time, I became sick. Hence it came to my mind that if I died then my dream should be finish. I was travelling several times at book fair and flower fair which mainly held at Central Calcutta and in Tala park area. In that time several female friends used to come to my house. Hence some known meal persons in our locality who are more or less same age as same as to me, they feel jalousie. They had some other type of intensity. I only made friendship with them but could not love anybody. I didn't know that whether any one might think about me or not. Like as Shri Krishna I made friendship with all. They should entertain and enjoy with me in a group. That time I had attraction on Surjatapa.

I liked Surjatapa very much but didn't flash out any word of my mind to her. When I remember that time, I feel that Shri Krishna also was the same. Every female was attracted to him by his speech at Brindavan. In my life, Seth Bagan was like as Brindavan. Not only had girl friend who was reading at Cochin with me but friend's mother also become like friends. They also some time speak their personal life, when they were passed out their school life or college life and some boys indicate some intention to them. Maximum people knew that Surjatapa's father was my uncle and my house was situated at sheet Bagan. In shet Bagan, I used to participate in Sarasvati Puja and other festivals. Maximum time I was playing with my friends and sometimes sleep at noon to my friend's house Dabobrata Datta at Shet Bagan.

Dabobrata Datta is the son of J.B. Datta. Maximum people know in this area to J.B. Datta and his wife both are employee of a bank. So, their economic condition is far better. Dabobrata and his elder brother were mainly stay in their two-storage building. Their maximum room was vacant. Rajib Saha and I went to their house. We were discussing our study matter and sometimes entertain, sometimes went to Surjatopa's house and his neighbor Sudip's house.

My mind is not feeling freeness when I got the chance in a polytechnic. That time I was thinking to change the place. Previously I went in Nepal with my elder brother Pintu. I had no knowledge about traveling by train. That time we went to Golgolia by Darjeeling mail and return by Kanchenjunga Exp. So, I was thinking it might be that, only two train travel in this rout. I only had little idea about Jalpaiguri and that time Gorkha National Liberation Front (GNLF) was creating problem in hill region to demanding Separate state. Just passing agreement to sign Hill Council, hence created problem by GNLF at Darjeeling become reduce. In Malda where I can stay? That time I had no idea about hotel. So, think that it is better to choose Jalpaiguri because there we have relative and at the last time of Nepal traveling, my elder brother and myself went to Siliguri and Jalpaiguri to our relative house with sister of my father's son Dhiran. My final choice became the study center as the Jalpaiguri polytechnic. This time I had no idea how I could find out an address. I was thinking that polytechnic may be known by everybody. Jalpaiguri are a small town, so it might be easy to find out if ask to some body. In the voucher of Admissions, only gave the stamp of Jalpaiguri polytechnic but it was not asking, that how we can reach at Jalpaiguri Polytechnic at interview board. In the Syllabus book there also give the name of polytechnic only.

I go to Jalpaiguri with my father by Darjeeling Mail on a general compartment. In general compartment has no rash. So, father may easily sleep but he feels very much tensions about me because if I may not return to the house or make love affair with someone at that place. But my mind always goes to outside of my house. He goes to Jalpaiguri with me only. I know the house of my uncle named Uasananda. He has two sons and three daughters. Two daughters were married and his elder son Anil has two son and one daughter but younger son Sunil have one son only. Their house actually situated in Jalpaiguri district but at Udla Bari nearby railway Station. Total four train run from new Jalpaiguri to Udla Bari in a day. In morning one up and one down train is available. In evening one up, one down train also available. We think Jalpaiguri polytechnic may situated near by Jalpaiguri station. So, catch a train from New Jalpaiguri to Jalpaiguri and get down at Jalpaiguri. Then several times ask to several person, "Where are Jalpaiguri polytechnic?" But no body answers properly. Days have been rained frequently. At 12 noon we get lunch in a small Restaurant. Then there have no train toward Udla Bari, hence we catch a bus toward Maal. Someone told the polytechnic may be in between Jalpaiguri and Maal, but Rain dropping frequently. If we become late then also, we face some trouble to find out the relative's house. Hence when we traveling by the bus, we decide that it is better to go to Usananda uncle's house and we do so. We go to Maal and from there catch bus toward Udla Bari. At 5 P.m. we enter into our relative house.

In my mind have some interest to see hill area by which attract to me to come again at Jalpaiguri. Previously when I came at Udla Bari, that time we came from Nepal. First cross Machi River then came to Bihar Bengal border then caught bus for Siliguri and meet with two sister Vaggo Laxmi and Haro Laxmi. Who is the daughter of the sister of my father? I and my elder brother Pintu follow the rout with the elder brother of them. I am remembering all this thing that was the matter of the sister of my father, whether they are leaving in a hut but in the backside of their house is like as natural forest. Two or three time I also climbed up and down on a tree again and again. Seven days we were staying at Nepal and nearby my Ante's house have a cinema hall which made by corrugated tin. In our town we see cinema hall are built by cement and brick but roof made by corrugated tin. There is use only corrugated tin in everywhere.

In that time 'Love Story' film of Kumar Gaurav is signing condition. One day saw that film then came at Siliguri. One-night stay at Siliguri. From Siliguri, we go to Udla Bari through Jaldhapara reserved forest. Mountain scenery is sowing from my uncle house from far away. That was the morning time when we were traveling from Siliguri to Udla Bari, so I was feeling very enjoy and bus entirely pass through the road of the hill side. That time I was feeling very glad and saying in my mind I should meet again in this place. Then saw tea Garden near the uncle house also. Thista River crossed by our bus. I was feeling that I might enter into haven and from those view, I wanted to pass out my whole life at Jalpaiguri. But father cannot understand that matter. In my life I love natural beauty. Father afraid that if I stay permanently at Jalpaiguri or may make any love affair with local girl. Then if I should not return from that place.

I remember that time period when first I foot stepped at Udla Bari. I cannot forget that time when I stayed at this place. A small park is situated on the side of railway line. Hill is seen from my uncle house. On the tea garden have a river which flow on and meet with Tista River. We took bath on that Small River and travel at the tea garden. Tea flower are same as guava flower. I collected leaf, buds and flower of a tea plant. One day we reached at that park which is situated on the side of rail line. By walking we reached and visit the park. A heavenly feeling came to my mind. Flower covered in every tree. Back side of the park boundary wall, hill seen clearly. I thought that I came at the heaven. So many children were playing on a slip which build as an elephant and used that again and again. Train were coming on the rail and passing into a cave. I sited on a tool which made by bricks and cements but the sites are like as Tung of a tree. A miracle dream covered my mind and I thought that I should visit the placc again or otherwise reside in this place in my life. At night; I told a story to my nephew. They thought that I read that story in a novel. But I composed that story like as "A robber killed to other by using an axe in a forest. He also sold fire wood. If any unknown person entered into the forest, then the unknown person killed by him and he got everything which ever had to that person." My nephew feels enjoy to heard the story. After three days I returned to Nepal. From Nepal we were returning to Calcutta. By walking we crossed the Mache River and reached at the Golgolia station. We were waiting for a mail or an express train for Calcutta. At mid night Darjeeling Mail came and my elder brother called me but could not enter into a couch. I had seen peoples sleep on their berth. I thought in Darjeeling Mail have such type of arrangement only. In this period, I had no idea about sleeper couches. Whole night we remain at the Golgolia railway station and previous day early morning we caught the Kanchenjunga express and reached at Calcutta.

Now we stay one night in our uncle house. Uncle and other talking with my father that people go to Calcutta for their study but your son come here for his study. It is not good. Here have jungles, sometime forest elephant come here and that time we use dram or dice to obstruct elephant by the metal sound. They lighted by fire into woods. Then elephant left locality. Sometime destroy house parts. In last year two people killed by elephant, my uncle explains.

Father afraid and tell me, "I may be sick, you go with me at Calcutta." Then I say, "May I stay here for four or six day." Father tell, "I may not to give admission in this place and it is necessary to return with me. By forcefully he gets me from this place. Two days rained. Then in the early morning when sun rise, I see the mountain becoming bluish colour. I learn arts but neither seen like this real fact nor some time seen mountain become colourfull like as arts. I return with my father but I weep silently that I leave a beautiful place where I want to stay. I tell to my father, "I may lose in my life." But my father is not hear my sound. He tells me that if I get chance in IIT or in B.E.J.E.E. then what I shall do but I am not getting any chance among these.

Father doesn't admit me to Diploma in Electrical Engineering at Jalpaiguri and he is not trying to find out where that polytechnic is situated. I become angry in my mind when father repeatedly tell me, "Sanjib can speak in English but you cannot do so." I try to learn English and start to read English newspapers, journal and Magazine. I read all these but sometimes understand and sometimes cannot understand.

I pass Higher Secondary examination in second division. I take admission in B.Sc. Pass course at City College at Amass Street. I start to learn in English version and think appear to IIT entrance again. I also buy several books for IIT entrance and try to learn chemistry, physics and mathematics. I have started reading in English version. I cannot take any tuition in the early stage for entrance examination. Then I observe that I can understand through English but I have no ability to write the answer in English version. I take tuition at Maniktala Bag Mari in meddle of 1st year B.Sc. Someone becomes my friend at this time. One person starting Cochin in his father in law's house and there have some vacant room by which he continues use as Cochin. One teacher of Kalyani University in physics and another person who start Ph.D. course in chemistry at Indian Science Institute teach to us in the Cochin. It was my deficiency at this time, I cannot expose in English version. But I am trying to do so. The B.Sc. pass course of Calcutta University is two years course. In 1st year I pass very marginally. One chemistry teacher tells that previously whose version is in Bengali and in graduation start in English they might not complete B.Sc. in Calcutta University. After declaring the result of 1st year B.Sc. that teacher gives instruction that you try to give heavy pressure to reading. But my decision is not good at this time because I also take admissions at Marine Radio officer course from Hyderabad, Kochigoda through corresponding. I also read that study material. I apply for 1st semester examination in Marine Radio officer course but in my application form I make a great mistake. Witness and surety both given by professor Dipak Das. There is given instruction that give two witness signature and address. I give one witness. This time I cannot think that it is not real procedure and I also cannot discuss with my instructor of the institution. For that region I cannot appear at marine radio officer course in 1st semester then left the course.

Then apply for B.Sc. final exam and appear. In the same time, I apply for IIT entrance exam. Due to disability of my writing capability in English, I become failure in the all field. I become upset but I should not break my heart. Life becomes under struggle. People of neighbor laughed at me. I have knowledge about art and sculpture which mainly learn from my mother and I observe if someone draw some thing or if someone do something whatever it is. When carpenter make a coat or chair or table, I also observe how they start and finish. I learn wood cutting and start to make wooden sculpture. Several sculpture I make in wooden medium. First, I make bird or same symbol. Then I start to make human figure mainly. I have interest about female nude model. So many couples produce in wooden medium and shown to my girl's friend name as Sabani, Sama, Sujata etc. One day Rima want to see a model and I hand over a nude couple which builds in wooden medium. Rima return the model quickly and tell me you have done such type of figure that she cannot be sown to other. In the ancient India at Konark temple have sexual related sculpture. I have seen the picture and getting interest about this mater previously. I visited with someone artist in my childhood who was drawing scenery which he has seen. He became my friend where as he was 55 years old and I was only 12 years. He discussed about nude model and sexual related figure. I had habit to make some fruits or bird or animal by clay or some time try to draw which I had seen or try to copy of portrait and picture in my childhood. By this way I learn drawing and in the same way I try to learn sculptured making. I start to understand English but cannot getting clear conception in the matter of study. I passed my time for doing sculpture and art. I also make a drawing book which matter is science and development of weapon. I give the name of the book science and war. Then I try to make other books Pallei Bangaler Abosta which mean Rural Bengal Condition but does not completed. I try to write several stories. Five or six story completed. In the same time, I start to write my auto biography in Bengali.

Life becomes struggle full. I lost all. I become failure in the B.Sc. course and cannot pass in IIT entrance. Actually, it is difficult to pass at IIT entrance. For success in IIT entrance it should take preparation form base, but my base was so weak by which I cannot stand for IIT entrance. I was in Bengali version but IIT entrance book are in English version and syllabus also totally different from West Bengal Council of Secondary Education and Calcutta University. So, I have no such ability and collapse all. Then I learn taxi driving. Father is talking me, "You are pass H.S. standard and now you start preparations for your competition examination and it is impossible to complete B.Sc. by you." I become angry because he had not given permission to take admission at Diploma in electrical engineering which I got chance through polytechnic entrance at 1991. So, I am thinking that due to father I cannot stand on my own leg.

I am quarreling every day and night. I am thinking all the time that it was better to took admission in polytechnic. Father are quarrelling with me that I get education up to H.S. and I should require trying for government job. But present situation is not like this. In British India it was easy to get job. But government job recruitment is corrupted. In west Bengal private work also are not available because maximum private companies are lock out. Several people are becoming jobless. I see one of such candidate Dhiran Roy who was working in a private limited company, but now a days his company become lock out and he became jobless. He has one daughter and one soon. So, it becomes hard to carry out to maintain his family and also difficult to get new job. Only he has three ball press machine and side by side he used to do umbrella cap by the machines. Now it is only the strike to stand on his life. Once up a time I also work under him and get Rs. 200/- per month which expense for myself. Hence many questions are coming in my mind.

I am thinking that it is better to join at Govt. Organization at grass root level. In the mean time I get decision that I again appear in polytechnic join entrance examination. B.Sc. was not completed in the last year, so again appear. I appeared in polytechnic entrance examination, but I cannot pass B.Sc. examination. I leave it from my mind. I take admissions at O-level computer course at St. Xavier's computer center which is situated in the campus of St. Xavier's College. Once up on a time, I think that I get study from St. Xavier's College. But I take admissions at St. Xavier's computer center. Class has been held at St. Xeviers College building, so god full fills my willingness. Polytechnic join entrance results declare. I become success and take decision to take admissions at The Calcutta Technical School because this institution is nearby St. Xavier's College.

I appear to selection board and express my decision. Selection board interview held at Jadavpur Painting Technology Institutions. When I appear at certificate verification, Verifier talk to director that one month before my age became over to take admissions in diploma course. Director tells him that up to interview board he comes, so give him admission voucher. Then they tell me, "You give some letter." The director tells me that am not necessary. Today my father comes with me at the interview center. I also have tension. Then I get permission to admission at polytechnic course. I come out from interview board. I talk to my father that there is no problem but cannot express details. Father returned at Dumdum to our house. I go to computer center. I get admission to The Calcutta Technical

School. In previous year when I attended IIT entrance that time thought that elder brother of a friend of Sanjib are studying Engineering course at night in this Institute, if I get chance in this technical school to study that ought to be better to me. In this time God again hear my sound and I start Diploma course at The Calcutta Technical School.

I remember that days when many people hated me because I mainly pass out my time through reading or doing some sculptures in wooden medium and leave the chance in Diploma Engineering at Jalpaiguri and fail in B.Sc. second year in 1993. I try to forget previous matter and try to observe Rima's figure. When I am observing the figure of Rima from far away, I am thinking about her and remember that day when I was used to site for observation to her. I saw her face and figure when she was returning from her school. I was used to seen her like that I could able to said when she used which dress, I could easily grease. One day I was gone to her house at evening and it became habit that I used to go at her house in every morning or evening time. I remember one specific day which day was different from other days. In that day, I went to her house and went to first floor. In that time her house was like as that one room built once side of the first floor and remaining part remain open. I suddenly went to open roof. That time just darkened the environment with shadow. Just I went for cooling my body through opens air. That time was hot summer. But when I went to roof, I saw that Rima become necked body and took bath in the open air. That time becoming darkened so I just came near by her and asked what happened. She was sitting in condition and told, “May you go.” So, I ask, “Why?” She answers, “You see to me and observed my condition.” Due to darkness, I feel that she was unconditional. But why she has done like this. I don’t know. But common people say something may have done for create attraction in my mind. Day by day I become attracted more and more to her. Her face is not so good. Mainly that time her face was covered with pimple so her face was becoming dual. But why I was so attracted, I didn’t know. One day when she is standing nearby my house street I say, “I observed you when you return from your school previously.” She tells me, “Yes, I know.” Then I tell her, “One young boy when observed a girl and why a young boy done so, you should understand that.” She answers, “I understand.” Then I tell her, “I want to marriage with you.” She tells, “You are good student but I failed at class VIII and class IX several time. You get first division at matriculation and second division at Higher Secondary. You are good student but I am not like that. So, you may get better girl for marriage.” Then I ask her, “Weather it is possible to marriage with you or not?” She answers, “It is possible but, it is not the place of discussion.” In this year she becomes again fail in her class X examination. Then I tell again, “Don’t worry, you may marriage with me.” But she again tells, “That will be good luck, if I become house hold wife in your house!” This type of talking again discuss with her now. I am remembering the time period when I asked her to kiss once time but she denied my offer. I am thinking that day when she took bath in the evening in a condition of necked.

She became happy when she passed matriculation in 1993. After three year she passed examination. Then she gets admission at higher secondary course and get some Higher Secondary arts books from me. Arts books remained to me as my elder sister got study in the arts course. Then several times, I am talking with her that she may marriage with me. Rima try to study hard and soul lobour. Her elder sister tells me, "You are educated person and hence required to get study by her. She has necessary to pass Higher Secondary minimum. You are engineering student." Sometime Rima and her sister Soma asked me, "Whether have you seen blue film or adult film?" I already saw that. Hence tell them, "Yes." Rima immediately tells me, "How you control yourself? You are sexy." I remember the words and I see to her face. I think if she became my wife then how much time we pass with entertain and full of joy. I think that She become able to discuss everything where as I remain unable to tell her. I feel in my mind but cannot express to her.

Diploma course start in the month May. In 1994 I make friendship with Samir pal who get rental room to our neighbor house. October month Durga puja held on Calcutta as like as held on in every year. Previously several years I travel throughout Calcutta in Durga puja Festival. So, I discus Samir that in this year we travel through South Calcutta and enjoy Durga puja Festival. In the meantime, Rima tell me, "I agree to go with you." Her elder sister Soma and her younger sister Jhuma also agree to go with us. Maternal uncle of Samir agrees to go with us. One related nephew of me Minuti who is friend of Rima also joins with us. We start our journey by metro Railway. Fare is given by Samir. Samir give nick name to Rima and Minuti as like as Agni and Roti respectively. Rima and me get down from train at Bhavani Pure station but other remain in side due to gathering. Rima tell me, "you and I travel at Durga Puja, it will be questionable." I tell her, "I try to do some things for them." I catch hand of Soma, Jhuma and pull toward me. Train is full rush but they become able to get down by the help of me. In Durga puja Festival at Astomi trithi (eight day of new moon) transport system continue in whole night. So, we start our journey from Bhavani Pure metro railway station and we travel Jatindas Park, Jodhpur Park, and Kalighat. South Calcutta almost travels by us. We observe pandal (temporary temple by bamboo and cloth) and idol of goddess Durga. We take soft drinks. Rima and Jhuma are not take full bottles. So, I am not wanted to destroy the drinks and take the remaining of the drinks. Samir tell to Rima, "You enjoy to travel with Ishim Kumar." Rima tell him, "Yes, but what happen." Then Rima remain with her sister Soma and friend Minuti. Whereas her youngest sister Jhuma travel parallel to me and chatting continuously. I also offer to them to round up on merry-go-round. Rima refuse because she is afraid to round up high merry-go-round but I try to give pressure to her. I think if she became afraid then at the highest point when merry-go-round's sit start to move downward, she will catch me. I see the dream in my mind. Then return by taxi. Fare Rs. 200/- are paid by all together but I only expanse Rs. 50/- for return journey. Next day I understand, Rima and Jhuma give me a name 'Jalal'. In

Bengali 'Jalal' is big burned clay jarred and we are using to kept water.

Minuti understand the situation that I and Rima have some interest or have some relation. When Minuti asked me, I clearly tell her that I have some attraction to her and she also has some interest about me. From next day, Rima stop to talk with me when she understands I flash the matter to Minuti. I use to go to her house but her younger sister, elder sister talks with me. Her younger sister Jhuma is becoming nearer to me. Some time she standing nearby my window where I am sitting for study on my bed. One day Jhuma directly tell me, "I am standing for a long time but you may not take care to me." Several times she tells me that our house like very much by her. I detach with Rima and attach with Jhuma.

Once up on a time we quarrel with her family because they capture six-inch land from us. Actually, it is the fact, at the age of my grandfather, his grandfather captured the land of my grandfather and police case also hold at Dacca court due to nonsense activity of his grandfather Jiban Krishna. But they create the problem and they was attaching with our enemy. So, quarrel started. But again, meet and quarrel become dissolve. Rima stop to talk. I cannot concentrate my mind in my study.

In the meantime, i.e. 1st January 1995, I offer to give greeting cards to all of her sister. First, I give greetings card to Jhuma. She became happy because when I ask to give greetings card, she tells that what necessary to ask her. Then next greetings I give to Subani. She is daughter of Rima's uncle. Subani's mind is fresh whether she become young and have attract to young boys of our locality.

Subani became along when her mother left her and gone with her uncle. The son of maternal uncle of Nyati is handsome and Nyati no doubt a very good person but had not been given much time with his wife. Maximum time pass out in his business. In this time his maternity brother got advantage. His maternity brother Haran came frequently to his house and pass out time with Naiti's wife. Naiti's wife is very beautiful that she is soft minded and young lady. Day by day young mind came to nearer to nearest and she thinks he is better than Naiti. She left his husband, daughter and son, and tried to build a new family. But society could not tolerate this matter. Every one discusses that she is not a good lady. Time pass out. Her son and daughter become young. Her mind become change and she understand how much good her husband Naiti. Subani and Sanju get her mother again. Naiti apology his wife and welcome to his life again. Actually, he understands that it is his fault, he didn't try to give time to his wife. So, someone get advantage and his wife had done something wrong and went with his brother.

Subani very beginning told me, Rima are different type of girl but I cannot control my mind so again and again I tell her that I like her very much. Actually, I wanted her own speech that she agrees with me. I am thinking when I shall become establish I may marriage with her. But she does not understand my words. She thinks that I have something wrong in my mind and hat me very much.

In 1995, 4th January I go to her room and try to give greetings. She shutdown door and on my request, she open the door after thirty minutes. I hand over greetings to her hand. I write something on the greetings that 'Wish You happy new year with love.' On the word 'love' she strongly opposes to me. She tells me, "If you behave like the same with me, I shall not talk with you again." She totally stops talking with me. Days are passing with my study and making some nude model. One day i.e. 17 Sept., in Bengali culture we payer to god of work called Vishwakarma. Nearby Santi uncle's wooden shop they payer to god Vishwakarma.

That day Rima are arranging holy food for the god. After payer to god, Rima distribute holy food (pashadom). First, I go there but I see Rima distribute holy food and I returned to my house. She observes me that what I have done. Then afternoon, she come to my house with pashadom (holy food). She wears Red color Shari (cloth). I open the door but I am not talk with her. She feels uneasy and asks to my mother, "What I have done now." My mother repeatedly tells me, "You get pashadom. Every day you go to her house and now you have done acting." But I answer, "I cannot do so because she is not talking with me." She feels uneasy and asks to my mother, "What have to be done now by me." My mother gives instruction, "You put pashadom on the table." She does the same. I get holy food when she gone from our house and eat something. Some amount of food is given to my monkey Rani.

Rani my monkey, my elder brother gets her from Sham bazar@ Rs. 50/- from temporarily market called Hat. So many times, I pass with Rani my pet. We went to take bath and swim on a pond at Mallick Bagan. Rani swim into water in every day but some one lady make objection that monkey cannot take bath in the pond water. She tells me, "Here person take bath but you come with monkey. Next you should not take bath here." We go to Kundu Bagan pond and she takes bath. In the early morning I walk on the road and garden with Rani. Rani becomes angry if anybody touches to me. After traveling I lock her on a rack which builds up by me in the front of window. Peoples give to Rani as banana or fruits. In this time Jhuma tell me, "I get smell of monkey from your body." I think her word. Time pass with Jhuma. Jhuma get study at class V. I kiss her when I meet with her and vice versa she wants to kiss me. One day I kiss six or seven times to her. But when she kisses me once time, I try to move. She tells me, "You kiss me how much you want but when I kiss you only one or two times, you leave the place. It is not good." Then I stand near by her and she kiss me again and again that how much she wanted. I return to my house and think that Jhuma become at the door step of young age. She feels sexual life and loves me. I try to avoid her because I want to build up relation with her elder sister Rima. I start to think both of Rima and Jhuma. I walk on the colony road with Rani. On the other hand, Rani bit to them who touch my body. I lock Rani at inside of our house and she takes bath on tap by the help of me. I observed that Jhuma try to indicate some things other. She touches her body from top to bottom when she passes by the side of me in a vacant place.

Rima start to hat me too much and actually she proudly tries to live in society. We try to lead our life in simple way. So, we live in different pole in the life. But I cannot control my mind, and I am thinking about her that she to be my life partner and think deeply about sexual life. She has doubt that I have love affairs with another girl. At B.Sc. level I used to go to Surjatapa's house at Shet Bagan. But when Surjatapa's mother suspects that I have some other relation with Surjatapa and told me "You can go anywhere with my daughter but don't talk with other girl." I answer, "I have no such relation other than friendship with your daughter." She told me, "You cannot make jock or relation with other girl." That time I was afraid to accept her offer because in the beginning with Surjatapa's friendship, I attracted with T.B. in second time. So, I am always worried about that matter. When Surjatapa's mother gives instruction and indicates that I can make relation with her daughter, I write down two letters to Surjatapa and send by post. Surjatapa's sister returns me the letters. But third letter everybody of her house read that which already send before returned the two letters. I wrought, "I live in the dark world of life so want to go far away from everybody, so I cannot able to make relation with you and your family." Before two year I leaved Shet Bagan. But I cannot understand that why I have attraction to much too Rima.

Life is under trouble by sickness and situation. Day by day I try to observed her and thinking about her. Some time making some sculpture or nude model made in wooden medium by chisels. I attracted to Rima and she also is creating some activity to attract me.

In the meantime, Rima's younger sister Jhuma become developed and she try to do some things that I shall be attracted to her. Due to detach with Rima, I becoming attract by Jhuma. Jhuma try to build up relation with me to love. Her study also hampers. After failing in two times, she leaved her study at class VI. So, I worry about this matter. When Jhuma realized and hear that I have attraction about her elder sister Rima, she stops to speak with me.

Both follows me that what I have done. Mainly I sit down at my bed nearby my window to observe them one time minimum in a day.

I start diploma mechanical engineering at the age of 24 years, so I also worry about the matter, that if I carry out first chance that when I had gotten the chance at diploma in electrical engineering, my life should change and I should become established. God don't give any peace to my mind. I continued study but thinking all the meter of my life.

In the time 1993 December my father retired so our family income become reduces. I also think about my tuition life. In that field I also could not continue and student was not getting better. Once girl student got who showing her breast when she got teaching on their bed by flatten forward. Another student who are my friend Partha's sister. She also not serious, she might think about sexual life so when I asked her, "You explain Bowel's law in physics." She answered, "Breast may increase if someone presses on that part." I left the tuition. Her father several times came to my house and had meet with me but why I left the tuition of his daughter, I caught not explain. Only explain that she was not serious. Hence totally I become dependent to my father.

In the meantime, my elder brother has done love affair with Jolly. Her family has some dispute. My mind actually cracks at that time when I re attracted by T.B. in second time. When I try to lead live with love to Rima, she refuses my offer. I am always thinking that what I have deficiency that Rima are not like to me. Day by day study hamper. Some time I am thinking that should better to take admission at Jalpaiguri, my life style might change. But past is past and it bit me again and again. Several times I am quarreling with my father.

In 1996, May 15 my elder brother left house by quarreling with my father and telling again "Jolly must not come to your house." Then he goes to Allahabad bank and get 2000/- rupees by withdrawal from his account. Three days over, Sagar his friend suddenly meet with me on the Dumdum road and inform Pintu get marriage and stay at Jatinagar. Next I meet with my elder brother at Sealdah Baw bazar where he has been working. His company owners tell me, "You can adjust with your father and your elder brother." But I think if I adjust now then again sometimes quarrel may held in between them, then both may tell me that due to myself they come to the house and then arise problem. So, I become neutral and tell him, "If they want to come at house then I have no objection and if they are not wanting to come at house then I cannot request them to come in the house."

Then I come from his company. But he continuously remains outside.

In May, 1995 I had examination in diploma course. Before examination in the month March, our house construction works started where as I gave instruction that after examination it was better to do works. But father ordered to start works and I got responsibility to maintain the work of construction. My first-year result was becoming hampering. I get 68% in the exam. But my father was not happy.

In second year 1996, father eye condition deteriorates by formation of cataract. Hence his vision problem arises, he cannot see clearly. Father's left eye operation held on but that day I have an exam. Some problem arises at the stage of operation, doctor call relative but mother also can not present due to late to leave our house. Lance cannot set up but operation become success. By the decision of doctor, the case handled. After one month he gets power by spectacle. Next eye operation held on after six month that also becomes success

I success in the diploma mechanical engineering and apply for job. In the same time start Lipoma treatment to my father. Ayurvedically medicine is given for eating two times daily and every day warm that part with hot water i.e. Therapy should do by means. Hot water with some medicine warms up in the morning and evening by my mother. After one year some chemical treatment has done on affected portion as external use. First time, half part of Lipoma destroyed. Then some medicine use to build up new skin and start chemical treatment. After six months again external chemical use to remaining lipoma, then that became pick formation and father feel tension. My father become worry about that he may not be cure and suddenly become sick. Due to high tension, his blood pressure increase. In the mean time I have gone to Bhubaneshwar for Railway Recruitment Board Examination for the post of Junior Engineer Gr. II. So, I also meet with my elder sister at Kharagpur at returning time. One-night stay. At night I have seen a dream that Rima tell me, "You immediately come to your house." In the morning I say to my elder sister Mukta that I have some necessary to go at Dumdum. Father condition is not so better. I start my journey at 11 A.m. but reach to our house at 5 P.m. I see door are locked, and then ask to our neighbor, "What happen." They give information that my father is admitted to B.R. Sing Railway hospital at Shealdah. Immediately I go to hospital and meet with him. I know that if my father seen to me, his mental tension may reduce. Due to hart problem, he was admitted to cardiology department but in back side, nearby back bone his shirt become wetted with blood and pick. Physician asks the matter and sends him into surgical department. Next day operation held on and when Doctors send him to bed, he crying again and again because he is thinking death may come due to this operation. I tell him, "Father you don't worry. You should be cure." I consult with physician; they give decision that if operation part start to cure than there has no necessary to test Biopsy. Biopsy means cancer conformity test. I am worry about this matter and weeping in my mind. But they get seven days for taken decision. After seven days they clearly tell me, "Don't worry about this matter because it starts to cure." But skin cream has some deficiency in Railway hospital. Only at the Hospital dressing have done in a day after one day. Then dresser give suggestion to my father, "You get release by yourself and take care on your house." Father get release and we consult with a compounder. From hospital some medicine has been prescribed and again compounder have seen the condition, he give some discussion and tell me some eye drop which are to be use for increasing cell division and tell me cream create skin formation but not use to create marshal. Then according to his decision, we arrange medicine. Within 5 days he becomes totally cure by applying eye drop which prescribe by compounder. Skin formations start on the affected area by applying cream. He becomes cure.

But one thing that Ayurvedically have better treatment about cancer which we have lost due to neglecting of that type of treatment. Who have done the treatment of my father's Lipoma? Do you know? Yes, they have no degree or diploma. Both husband and wife use to practice this treatment which they learn from her parent. She is better physician named Rakha Kabiraj.

In India much other treatment procedure lost due to getting secret and has no written formula. Someone invents the procedures or therapy or some medicine, but due to without written material we cannot use that after the death of the inventor. Someone doesn't know English so have no scope to write and send to get paten. There has maximum chance to cheat with them; hence they get secret the matter till their death.

I give mental strength to my father and tell him, "If no body come to meet with you don't worry but I am with you, so you don't worry about this meter. You have no risk. I discuss with doctors and they give instruction that you have no risk."

Within this period of time I have already pass diploma examination in 1997. I start to applying for post in signal Maintainer & telecommunication maintainer Gr. III on the basis of class XII where H.S in science with physics and mathematics is one of the requirements to apply in the posts. On the other hand, I have completed diploma in mechanical engineering. I am applying for the post of junior engineer also. But now age become 27 years so I worry about the matter whether I may get any services or not. Another disadvantage come to myself, eye sight become short distance viewed. So, I cannot apply for Asst. Driver post in Railway where medical standard wanted A1, i.e. eye sight require 6\6 without glass.

I have seen in the employment news and find out medical standard like as A1 should be 6\6 i.e. normal eye A2 up to - 2 and B1 up to - 4, etc. Who can say that my distance vision may not be cure but that is possible by Liassic operation? For Liassic operation require Rs. 20000/- which I have no ability to expense. My distance vision becomes - 2.5 in left eye and - 2.75 in right eye. Hence, I cannot apply for the post of Asst. Diver.

After Diploma I have register may name in Engineer Institution (India) from where someone can complete equivalent degree in engineering i.e. AMIE.

In parallel way I am thinking that my father telling me that I may not complete B.Sc. Previously, I heard about IGNOU i.e. India Gandhi National Open University from where B.Sc. be possible to complete. I take admission in B.Sc. at IGNOU on dated 11 Sept., 1999. I am thinking that in the same day 11 Sept., I had come to the world and saw light of the sun first time in my life i.e. my birth day. So, B.Sc. should be complete. In the mean time I have been attracting by jaundice two times. It is true fact some things happened all the time in my life and life become tough.

In my life, I start to appear Railway examination in the outside of Calcutta. First time Railway examination attends at Patna. Previously I heard that in Bihar local people create problem if someone come to appear competition examination from outside states. Bihar people appear competition examination in all over India. I heard that they sometime bit who come from outside of Bihar. So, I am worrying about this matter. I get call letter. I am SC candidate. So, I get pass for free travel. If Railway Recrement Board are issuing pass, it should be use for reservation. Father have no experience about the matter but sought first time, so he tells me that it is not possible to done reservation. My elder brother left his study at class VIII. He cannot try to appear at any competition examinations. I am the first candidate who wanted to go too outside of Calcutta for appear the Railway examinations. Hindi is not my mother tong and also is not my subject at any stage in Matriculation and Higher Secondary etc. Up to class XII I took study in

Bengali version, but one English language subject to read as second language.

In class VII and class VIII, I had one Sanskrit paper, but I have no base in Sanskrit. One day I had set down on bench near a footpath stall. One Hindi speaking people came and asked some things but I did not understand any things. I was feeling something pain in my heart. Next time I wanted to read Hindi. Father has one Hindi book which is learn through Bengali. In my life at first time, I used to read that Hindi book and used to practices letter script writing in Hindi. Then start to read Hindi newspaper. Day by day practice Hindi from 1993. In this time, I buy some Hindi books to complete my journey. I start to read magazine and competitions master in Hindi because it is my first time that I am going to Patna for competitive examination. This time outward Journey ticket given by reservation on free pass which given to me as SC/ST candidate. I heard that in Bihar, there is also strong casteism. In T.V. screen several time I see Ranbir Sana and Bhumihar are fighting with each other. In my mind I am thinking all the matter silently. My reservation ticket is in RAC. I am worrying about this matter, weather my ticket becomes conforms or not. Gourango, Malay my friend comes to meet with me. Before starting my journey Rain start, so Gournago gets a taxi for me. I get an Alfa VIP suitcase with me. Reach at Howrah (HWH) station by a taxi. I see someone telling berth number and coach number at the point of RAC and waiting number chart. I can't find out my coach number. So, I get help from that man. He takes 10 rupees from me and find out couch no. and berth no. I try to learn that how he finds out couch number and berth number. I find out that at the left most number RAC / 43 that is actual position of RAC and by this number he finds out statues of the ticket from W/L (waiting list) chart

I take berth and train start to move. I request to some one passenger that when Patna junction shall be arriving, then please inform to me, then go to sleeping. Next morning, I get up in the early morning. First when I have seen Patna Bihar station is coming, I try to get down. My suitcase remains on my hand but nearer passenger informs me, Patna junction station are the next coming station. He says to me, "Maximum 30 minimum taken to reach at Patna junction by the train. When Patna junction enter by Danapur Exp., I become ready and come nearest to exist. The train stop, I get down at Patna junction. First time, I ask to a ticket collector in which side has any hotel. He guides me to go to right direction. When I come out from the station someone Rickshaw puller tell me, "Here have only two Hotel, one has rent Rs. 100/- per day for single room and another have Rs.150/- per day for single room. I believe him. Rickshaw puller calls me with him. Then I sit on the rickshaw and I reach at that hotel. @Rs.150 for single room, I get a room at Jaisalmer Hotel. Rickshaw puller get Rs.20/- from me as a fare. Next I go to platform for reservation. I submit requisition form for my return journey ticket. Reservation clerk ask S.C. certificate xerox copy with requisition form. I already get SC certificated with me. From opposite side of the station, I take a xerox copy. But at Patna, xerox call photo copy, so first time I become confused. But when I remember similar word, I understand the matters.

I get reservation ticket in waiting list. Then three days pass out. Today, I become ready in the early morning in Sunday after taking bath and breakfast. I pay rupees 500/- total whereas room rent given 3*150=450 rupees and rupees 50/- taken for foods. Only my suitcases left to hotel reception counter by me. I leave room for saving my money. I go to exam center. It is first time that I am outside for examination. So silently take set and appeared the examination. After examination, I am coming toward the Hotel. In the way someone candidate ask me, “Where your house situated?” I tell him, “My house is in the Calcutta city.” He tells me, “The Calcutta, there are many facilities to you. So, why you come at Patna for examination?” I answer to him, “If Bihar people may go to Calcutta then why we are not come here. Problem may arise but what happened?” That person becomes silent. I come at the hotel and get my suitcase. I go to Patna junction station. Some time I am walking here and there and sometime sitting on suitcase and observing Patna passenger train platform. The station part is most wasted. I am thinking, “How people are living here?” Time pass out. At night one hour before of the train arrival, I go to nearby ticket supervisor room, then check ticket. Ticket is not conforming. Some one ticket collector writes some number and tell me you take sit at general compartment. I understand that I am talking in wrong way i.e. I mixed up Bengali and Hindi. Hence, he may behave like this. But why he behaves like this? I am not understood. I am thinking that he may be higher cast and seen that I get SC candidate pass, so he may behave like this. I talk with a potter and agree to give Rs. 50/-, if he gives single sit at general compartment but he places my suitcase in general compartment when Danapur express enter into Patna station. But the potter cannot give me any sit because total couch fully pact up. I sit down on my suitcase and next morning reach at Calcutta. Without sleeping night pass out.

Days are passing by applying in several RRB i.e. Railway Recruitment Board for job. I start to study Khurmi's objective mechanical book and several general knowledge books. In this time Ram Bilas Paswan become Railway Minister. I heard that if someone gives 1 lac 50 thousand rupees in the wrong way then he may get Railway job. I am thinking that I have no such amount, so what I shall be done for me. Several time I appeared in written examination at Bhubaneshwar Railway Recruitment Board, Calcutta RRB and other RRB. I cannot pass the examinations. My brain is not working and I am thinking that what I will be done the works in near future in my life. In my locality several people are talking me, "Now your father is alive and he get pension. So, you are getting food. When your father will go to haven, you may not carry out your life by yourself income." In this time central government are leading by Janata Dal. Ram Bilas Paswan becomes Railway minister. This time Janata Dal government i.e. actually Yaukta Front government are ruling India by B.J.P. support from outside to the government.

B. J.P. Party support withdraws from government of Janata Party after one year and ministry loss their majority. Then six months temporarily ministry lead by I.K. Gujral. The Government support by Congress party.

In next election B.J.P. get maximum sit and build up N.D.A. In N.D.A. Government Mr. Nitish Kumar become Railway Minister. Vigilance department are started to checking files of recruitment and in the case of recruitment only written examination start. In this time Railway Minister abolish interview for recruitment. By vigilance enquiry several duplicity cases flash out on the head line of National newspapers. Maximum examination of RRB becomes canceled and reexamination starts. In this time retirements age declare up to 60 year. Ministry declare due to reduce of expanse money; they stop recruitment for two year. In the mean time I become under tension in very much. My mother becomes worry about my future. In this time, I go to an Astrologer chamber and shown my palm. Then I give my date of birth and birth place. He makes my horoscope. Departmental friend of my father Durga uncle who have knowledge about Astrology, he also told the same things which he describes in my horoscope. Both of them say that I shall be far away from my family due to my job. I shall travel several places and several countries. At 2003, I shall be independent. In May month, 1998 there are a job opportunity but that may be stable only 3 or 4 months only.

Mainly I worry about these things which told to me by the Astrologers. In the beginning of 1998, I send my bio data to a consultant but on May month, Dumdum Valves & Bearing Pvt. Ltd. Company calls me for interview. I have sent my bio data to several private concerns and I also attended so many interviews. In polytechnic replacement instructor, I submit my bio-data. Replacement instructor Mr. T.K.C. sends my bio-data to The Corporate Engineers Company. The company calls me for an interview. I attend to the interview but not get any opportunity.

In the meantime, I attended interview at Dum Dum Valves& Bearing Pvt. Ltd. Company. Only they want to pay Rs. 1000/- per month for one year and if next year extent, then in second year pay Rs. 2000/- per month. I agree to their condition. They tell me, "We think about you because you live at Dumdum."

Previously I have attended two or three interviews, but not get any chance. In this case I get letter for appointment through courier service. I attend next morning at the office of Dum Dum Valves & Bearing Pvt. Ltd. That day give appoint order on which condition are given that up to one year get @ Rs. 1000/- per month, and the extend another one year of payment Rs. 2000/- per month, then they may be considered for permanent staff. I get the appointment letter and go to Kaykhali at their factory. I meet with General Manger. He introduces to other worker and works Manger' Ramalu. I was thinking to learn about CNC machining. There have CNC machine i.e. Computer Numerical Control Machine. There are one Milling, one Lathe, two Boring machine which control by CNC. I become happy. The General Manager tells me, "You learn the works and make note in every day." I have two exercise books and I start to make note. With every machine, manufacturing company give manual. One is operating manual and another is maintenance manual. I get operating manual. I have started to read the manual of the all machines and make different note for milling, lathe and boring to operate the machines. Maqbool also get same opportunity in the same company. We are the friend of The Calcutta Technical School. We studied the course diploma in Mechanical Engineering on that Institution. He is Muslim but I have no such feeling that maximum Hindu think not take any food from Muslim shop like these. Maqbool eating at Muslim hotel and I also get food from that hotel. There also makes beef curry. Maqbool tell me beef curry have better than mutton. But I tell him in Bengali culture Hindu people do not take beef and they telling if Hindu take beef, he destroys his culture and religion habit. Maqbool also tell me you are Hindu. So, don't take beef. I only take vegetable curry and two paratha and eat that. When I pass through Raja bazar nearby Shealdah station I have seen several times such type of paratha in Muslim hotel. Some time I want to eat that type of paratha. Today I get like the same type of Paratha and become happy. My father and mother used to habit to go at Ramakrishna Mission in my childhood. Actually, they are member of Ramakrishna Mission. Several Ramakrishna Mission's books are collected by my father. In that time, I also went Ramakrishna Missions with my parent. Sometime read The Gita and Hindu sastra i.e. Chandi, Bhagavat Gita and Mangal Chandi, etc. One of the commands of Shri Krishna in Bhagavat Gita is like as "To day which you call yours, once up on a time that was to other and in future that will be to other." I also read Ramakrishna Katha Mitra. I several times remember the word of Ramakrishna "Amra Jatra Daler Sang Saja Ashache Nachbo

Gibo Tra Par Chalazabo." that means we are actor at a stage, we sing a song and perform dance then we will be gone. Inner meaning, we come in the world and we act as actor then go to haven. Sometime remember the song of Rabindra Nath Tagore "Jadi Tor Duk Suna Kaw Na Asha Taba Akla Chalo Ra, Jadi Kaw Katha Na Kayaay Taba Akal Bolo Ra." i.e. if you call someone to walk with you and he may not response then you walk along and if anybody are not want response to your sound then you should speak along. From my childhood, I have varied few friends who give accompany with me. Friendship circle change day by day. So, take both these rules.

I am talking with Maqbool and taking paratha and vegetable curry and thinking about Ramakrishna and Vivekananda. Once up on a time Ramakrishna wanted to eat beef and wanted to payer on Mosque (Masjid) to wear lungi and Kurta i.e. Mohammedan dress. But Mathur Babu was not give beef to him and Ramakrishna payer to masjid in Muslim manner and payer to Allah. Vivekananda use the huka and get smoking to all religious usable huka and test whether he have changed any religion. I also eat at Muslim hotel but not change anything in my mind. Previously I prayed goddess Laxmi and lord Narayan and today I payer to some goddess and god. Then also I have done work but Maqbool behave something like selfish. We are two friends so thinking we should learn CNC by help with each other. But he tries to learn from me. Which he understands, he is not explaining to me. Maqbool house is at Kharagpur, he goes to Kharagpur every week and sometimes coming late by one day but when I get leave one day for my personal work Management create objection. He is not coming some time without information to management but one day I have done like this. Management sought to me. In that time in my house have no telephone. But Manager tells me on telephone you should inform us. In the early morning I go to duty. Maqbool also come that day in the early morning. Telephone ringing repeatedly than I receive the call and understand some girl dials wrong number. Till that time, I am afraid if I dial the number and if something become fault. Manager may seek to me. That day I learn that how to dial the telephone and I use telephone freely and talking with Maqbool. Maqbool get information about rental room. So, I also go with him at Kaykhali to find out where rental rooms are available. We meet with a young Muslim person who's native at Malda district, tell us previously he was thinking Hindu's behavior are not good but now a days he gets rental room in Hindu locality and he satisfy. He feels Hindu Bengali culture is better than Bihari Muslim or Malda Muslim culture. So, he gives suggestion to Maqbool. "You previously live with Hindu friend at Sanarpur, so you get rental room at Hindu majority area." Nearby Dum Dum Valves and Bearing Pvt. Ltd. at Kaykhali, several Muslim houses we have gone to find out the rental room. After all he finds out along and gets a rental room near by the factory. So, he starts early coming in the factory. In July Works Manager tell me to do work in a sun day. I presence at work shop and have done work with works of Kirloskar Company whose come for repairing work. That day Maqbool is not present. Next day Maqbool come on duty in right time but I go on duty at 2 P.m. Maqbool sought to me that why I come too late in the factory. I say, "Yesterday I have done my duty." Maqbool tell me, "Why you are not informing to me?" He sought to me that he has done work along. Generally, we work done together. Today is Monday and he have gone to Nagerbazer to contractor company where small scale work done. Hence, he sought to me. Before two-week Works Manager and General Manager send us out side where the company gives order and takes rough machining job on laths. We measure specific dimension and DDV seal on work piece and sign on paper. Then send the material by them. Dum Dum Vale and Bearing Company also have two other factories. One is at Nagerbazer and other are at Nasik. Nagerbazer factory name Dum Dum Metal where casting work has done. So, I have interest to get knowledge about casting. We go to Nagerbazer but cannot enter into Metal Factory. Outside job is interesting, three hours works become competed within one and half an hour then go to our own house and get rest. But party send information to our company and General Manager Send one person to verify and outside work started to done by other. We remain inside the factory.

On 16th Sept. 1998, all worker become busy to clean their machine where as I have done work on milling machine. Within two and half month I learn CNC Machine operation and if machine repair work done then I also done work with repair man. That day all worker is cleaning their machine on which they have done work. In milling machine, maximum work pieces given to machining. Owner of the company give newly casting bearing which is heated. What I can do? I carried all newly casting work pieces nearby machine. Mind is not wanted to do so. Suddenly main operator of milling machine goes to toilet and request to me to do work. Two- or three-piece bearing shell has done already but running piece is not touching by the tool. Hence, I want to change tool position. Previously I have done such type work and gets experience. Today also try to do so but have done some mistake. Stop the machine in intermediate position and change the operational distance of the tool. Then start the machine through computer program. But machine was in tool changing position, so magazine holds the tool. I have no such knowledge that if the machine is in tool changing position then by manual operation be done that first magazine should be remove from tool, then start the machine. I have done mistake and tool post come with magazine when I start machine. Machine started to move downward and magazine band by pressure. I forget everything that in such a position requires puling emergency button. I push hold button again and again. Machine tool position holds for a few seconds and starts again then move downward. So, machine tool comes at bottom position. All ready magazine damages. I stop the machine by off the main switch.

General Manager come to the spot and sought to me. Executive Manager, i.e. factory owner is not to give permission to touch the machine. My face becomes dull. In my first job I have done accident so want some punishment but General Manager is silent. Everybody ask me whether I make any mal operation. I say no, I have not done so.

Actually, tomorrow have Vishwakarma puja (payer to god of work) so I have work done quickly.

Next day 17th, Sept. Vishwakarma puja and management may take decision against me. I attend at puja and get holy food then get lunch. I come back to my house.

In this period Mona become my friend who is the wife of my friend Shamal. One-year pass Shamal marriage by love affair. In Calcutta now a day love marriage held maximum. Shamal and Mona were chatting at a dark corner at the stage of love affair at Seth Bagan. When I was stay at Seth Bagan and meet with Sujatapa. Surjatapa remained with her sister along, because her mother became pregnant and staid at her mother house. In that period Surjatapa's age became 18 years above. Neighbor were chatting that in these ages i.e. 45 years, and 55 years ages of mother and father respectively not required to do that. They had 18 years and 16 years age daughter but had no feeling that daughter becoming at required to marriage. Surjatapa prepared food item and both sisters eaten, then she went to college. Ishim Kumar came as before but within 16th friend remains only three friends. Maximum friend's marriage was held on. Only one friend left her house with her maternal uncle's son. But why Mala had done such relation? We didn't know. She is very beautiful name Mala. Face cutting also better. Mala also a friend of Ishim Kumar but suddenly heard she left her house. Her father economical condition is also better. But she builds up sexual relation with her maternal uncle's son whereas he also married. They left Calcutta and went to Mumbai; Mala became pregnant hence left her house without given any information. Then neither got any information from her nor was communicated by us.

On the other hand, Surjatapa cooked and some time she feed to me by her hand. One day she explained, "If someone loves to other then how she explains?" I said, "She may directly tell him that I love you." She told me, "It is not possible." Time passed in this way. Her brother born but her father was not given permission to touch her brother if she or her sister came from outside. If required got her brother then required to wash hand by soap. I made a modal of Agnes and David which I wanted to give her. In David Cover field Agnes and David was friend. But their marriages were not held in their life. I had feeling that our condition also be same. Surjatapa wanted a handmade sculpture. I gave the modal of Agnes and David to her, she became happy. In that time, we passed our time with new member of their family. When her mother bounded to me under restriction, I told her mother that I only make friendship with her, and then I left her house. Her Mother thought I had relation other than friendship. Whereas I know within the period of B. Com. course she makes friendship with a young boy and heard that she requires to done abortion to lead life in our society and not only that, she also explained to me that she wanted relation as brother because she was unable to cheat with me. I am different and I am not getting any advantage. I left Seth Bagan because Sujatapa's house is in that place. After two years of my leaving of Seth Bagan, her marriage held with other young man. Two times she tried to suicide due to negligence by her father and friend tontine that it was the time of marriage of her but she has a little brother. I left Seth Bagan forever.

Shamal and Mona lead to marriage life with their daughter. Shamal start to sell fish on Dumdum footpath. Their daughter calls me as elder brother and Mona call me as maternal uncle. Their daughter come and see my drawing and want to sleep, walk and play with me, I also play with her as a child behavior. Mona tells me, "My daughter wants to sleep at night to your house when I sought to her at 12 P.m. and crying, Ishim Kumar is better than you." In this time, I tell my story to Mona. Mona tells me, "You don't know to love anybody." Shamal come back from his job and take rest with his family. I also talk with him. He tells me, "You try for better job, if you get that then your life will be better."

On 18th, Sept. General Manager informs me to go at office at Lack town but Works Manager give some work. Afternoon arrange vashan i.e. clay idol of god drop to river water or pond. This day my mind totally upset. I see factory owner arrange hot drinks and mutton. I get hot drinks and mutton. I join at vashan (idol to submerge into water) rally, get cigarette packet and start smoking continuously. I become out of control. After submerged the idol of god Vishwakarma, I return to Dumdum. When I reach nearby my house then think that it is better to go to Mona's house. I go to her house. Shamal is not at room. I talk with Mona and her daughter. Her daughter tells me, "Elder brother Ishim, is your health not better?" I want a glass of water, I become thruster. Mona gives me a glass of water. I think after drink I come here; it is wrong. I am not under control and in this way human being can do something wrong. I leave their room and enter into my house. My father gives me a call letter but I become unable to speak and vomiting happened when I try to speak with my father. I feel that I will be removing from service from Dum Dum Valves and Bearing Company.

Next day when I take breakfast that time my mother asks whether I took drinks win yesterday. I say real fact and promise that I shall not take win in future. After breakfast I go to factory and General Manager tells, “You have not required going at head office; tomorrow you should meet with me.” I understand that I cannot work here. Today is last day in this factory but what I have done in future. I should try for government job. But due to tension I drunk win too much and smoking continuously yesterday.

I meet with General Manager as per his instruction. General Manager tell me, “You will not come from tomorrows.” I answer, “I obey your word, and you should give me certificate and give me payment in this month.” He tells me, “How I give your payment?” I answer, “If it is not possible then kindly you will send the payment to my house. I don’t want to see your face again. I obey your word. You also send money by any how to me.” I hand shake and tell him, “Thank you.” I come in ground floor.

Maqbool also call by G.M. and he meet with him. G.M. tells him that he also may remove from service if required.

I am feeling that it is like as a work as general shop that someone take servant to maintain their shop and if require to remove then tell him, “You not come from tomorrow.” I get last lunch at Dum Dum Valves and Bearing Pvt. Ltd. Before two month ago I got a dice and a tumbler on which I mark 'N' by chamfering. After lunch wash the dice and tumbler and pack both. I am thinking one day I came here and got these things for a long time that may be minimum two years that I stay in this company but today I leave the company.

After getting meal I meet with G. M. and tell him, "Please you give me certificate." At 3.30 P.m. he hands over the certificate. I hand shack with GM and good bye to him forever. I meet with every employee in the factory and good by all of them. So many peoples tell me that certificate have no value in future. But what I can do. I get dice and tumbler with me. I come at bus stand and cutch bus '30B'. I think horoscope also matches some times. It is my experience this time. In my horoscope give instruction that maximum three month I may continue my job in this period that becomes true.

I become jobless and try for Technical Apprentice Training and meet with Board of Practical Technical Instituted authority. It is rule that if anybody when not get any job and anybody not get any chance in any factory then government give three chance of interview within some industries through B.P.T.I. If anyone select at interview then he/she will get practical training.

First B.P.T.I. sends me at a chemical and metallurgical factory at Khardha but I do not get any call letter for interview. I contract with board office. Authority tells me, “You get another chance.”

After three month I get a letter for interview at Calcutta Term Corporation Workshop. I attend at interview but Works Manager chatting and tell me, “It is not better to accept.” I am not select for practical training. I think political influence may require. Once up on a time I thought that through political influence may I get service in Term Company and I get call letter for interview but not success.

At Vishwakarma puja festival Guranga, myself and another visit the workshop of Staxman. Someone gives name and mobile phone number and tell me to meet again. He tells me, “I should try to give chance to you in this workshop.” I think if I get chance to this company by his influences that will be better. Gouranga already get a chance and select at a chemical factory and get one-month payment and get another chance at Dumdum Instrumentation factory. I meet with that person who promises me but he talks with me, “This is not possible to me. Now a day’s staff recruits through union.” When I told with him at Bishakarma puja that time he drunk win and now he is normal condition, hence word become change. I understand that.

In this period tension increases into my mind and read the study material of IGNOU to complete B. Sc. course. Time is passing but I cannot concentrate to my study. So, some time go to the house of Mona and Sama. They become friends hence I discuss my life story. In these time sisters in law of Mona become closer to me. Her name is Laxmi and she has no child whereas Mona is younger but have a daughter. One day she asks me, "So many years pass after marriage but I have no child. I payer to god to become a mother and go to so many temples but god also are not hear my word." She also calls me maternal uncle. I give suggestion to consult with a doctor freely. There has much system to modern science. I explain the procedure of test tube baby. In these system animal and human process are same. By suction system ovum collect from ovary through uterus in case of female candidate. On the other hand, by mechanical process sperm collect from meal candidate. Then sperm keep at Zero degree Celsius on which temperature sperm become into sleeping condition. As requirement ovum get into test tube and 30-degree Celsius sperm get under activation condition then by simulating drop sperm become excited and artificial fertilization be done. Then fertilize ovum set up into uterus by injection process. In case of cow have same process but, in this case, testis collect from butchery and sperm collect from testis then same process follow as human being. Common people think that by injection calf born. But without ovum and sperm baby are not born. Laxmi ask then about clone system. Ishim Kumar explain that clone system is different in this case germ cell have no requirement and from any cell colon can be form. One cell of any part of our body activate by using stimulate and nucleus change in divisional mode by which cell division start. By cell division an embryo form which set up into uterus by inject into a female candidate. Female only require if daughter born but for son require meal and female both because any cell collect from meal candidate but after an embryo formation require to set the embryo in uterus to a female candidate. After setting of embryos at uterus then require nine months to delivery or otherwise reacquire to surgical operation and baby born. Laxmi discuss their matter with a doctor and become pregnant. Her son is born by surgical operation. Her son keeps some time to me and she cooks.

In these time period Shipra come to Laxmi's house that is her elder bother's daughter. Shipra some time talk with me and one day we exchange our telephone number and start to talk on telephone.

Once up on a time I was play in these houses. All the two houses that is the house of Mona's mother in law and the house of Sama's father cannot distinguish by other. There had only two small huts but today family member increases due to their marriage held on and third generation come in the family where as in my childhood we played hidden into secret place. So many events passed in my life in this house. I remember one event when Umaa's husband died to drink win. Umaa is sister in law of Laxmi. Her husband was working as security guard and was drink win every day. Her husband came to Dumdum to his father in law's house. At night he drunk win with a known young boy and got sleep. In the early morning his mother in law went to called him for bed tea. She saw that Mr. Singh body became strife. She called other and got Mr. Singh at R. G. Kar hospital. At hospital doctor declare Mr. Singh became expired. Weather he became died to drink win then police case be held. From hospital inform to Chetpur Police Station. Laxmi's house at Dumdum which is under Dumdum police station but hospital is under Chetpur. Hence, they required to get certificate from Dumdum police station not to as murder case. Umaa came at Dumdum from Kalyani with Mr. Singh's nephew. Mr. Singh's nephew and Umma gave declaration to Dumdum police station that Mr. Singh had habit to drink win every day. Previously two times fell on the side of railway line. They got no objection certificate from Dumdum police station to taken over lash. I went to Chetpur police station with Umaa's two brothers. Police got the certificate but want money Rs.500 to relive death body from the morgue. Death body got from R. G. Kar hospital to Nilratan hospital because at Nilratan hospital has postmortem facility. They send me to their house to get money otherwise money may be short. I went to their house and got money from Laxmi. We went to Nilratan hospital by a taxi after given Rs.500 to police. At Nilratan there also required money to remove lash and lash was to be carry at Kalyani, hence required to arrange vehicle, flower, garland cloth, etc. We arrange all material and pay money to morgue. Only four persons remained to go up to Kalyani, we arranged a matador too went at Kalyani. After hand over the lash to us we started our journey toward Kalyani. Rain started with storm and vehicle run in high speed. In that time back side of matador broken and we were feeling insecure but reach at night. On the other hand, local peoples of Kalyani came to Kolkata at Dumdum. They returned at 11 P.m. Up to these time peoples cried to saw him. Relative and as well as neighbor all were crying, I tried to maintain them and lash covered with a new cloth because lash wetted on the rain. Lash was postmortem case, hence after rain blood also wetted. In that time another matador arranged and relives the previous vehicle. We went to Halishar burning ghat and fired the death body into electric furnace. That time Mr. Singh had little two son and one daughter. They lost their father due to drinking win. We returned to Kalyani at 4 A.m. Next day I returned to my house. Mr. Singh's two sons and one daughter become young and talk with me when they come at Dumdum. But I drunk win and promise to my mother that I should not drink win again in future. I try to obey that and think poor person are not require to drink win because win rate also high.

Suddenly I get a call letter from Staxmam Company through B.P.T.I. and attend at interview. I face a great problem that I have gape in between H.S. and D.M.E. In every interview selection board ask same question to me about the gape. I cannot give proper answer and I become failure. In this time same things happen.

Within these periods I am attended several Railway Recruitment Board exams. I payer to God, I shall success in a governmental organizational recruitment examination. Every week I am getting Employment News and All Indian Appointment Gazette a biweekly publish. I am applying 17th RRB all over India whereas all over India have 19th RRB. I also send application in other organization like Atomic Resource Center and Aeronautical Center.

In 1999 March I get call letter from Gun and Shell Factory the oldest and biggest defense factory in India which founded by British govt. of India before Independent. The factory is under ministry of defiance I appear at interview. Morning eight o-clock I meet with security at main gate and write name and purpose on registered book. Then someone tells me to sit down on a branch in left side compound of this company. Another candidate also sits with me. We have instruction that we sit there and wait for a while then they call us. Up to two o-clocks we stay there but nobody comes to meet with us and call for interview. I ask to someone about interview then get information. They say now it is lunch time starting, after lunch they may call for interview. We take lunch at outside and after complete our lunch we meet with Works Manager and Asst. Works manager and inform, "We are waiting from early morning. Nobody can express where we may wait for interview. You are not arranging any proper system." Then they tell me to cool because I sought to them. They tell me, "You wait at computer room. "Four or five candidates are already staying there. One by one call for interview. I understand that sometimes ago I sought to whom they taken our interview. One by one interview face in a series, I also face interview I see Works Manager, Asst. Works Manager are sitting on their chair and introduce with me, e.g. Ask my name, address and family back ground. Then ask about previous experience. I answer one by one. They ask general knowledge, "Who is chief minister of Madhya Pradesh." I cannot answer then ask about current affairs. This time Atal Bihari Bajpai are prime minister and on his minister atom bomb and hydrogen bomb test at Pokhran, they ask on this tropic ask about fusion and fission process. Then come tropics about lathe and milling machine. I answer about CNC machining also. Then they satisfy and after interview I return to my house at Dumdum.

After four months call for medical test. 2nd Aug. 1999 I attend at medical test in Gun and Shell factory. I pass medical but I am afraid that if they take X-ray of my chest and find out some things wrong then this chance also misses in this time. Gun and Shell factory's medical officer of health unit check only height, weight, blood pressure, urine test then gives fit certificate.

From office given attestation blank form and bond form to fill up and given seven days to submit them with complete procedure. On 8th Aug. they give appointment order by submission of all paper with two granter signatures. I join as Apprentice technician. First, we start our training at Tool Room section. Severally ITI student are also getting one-year practical training. They get training for three-year Apprentice. I hear that previous all apprentice candidates were absorbed but now a days no body absorbed in Gun and Shell Factory from 13th year back. My father is not understanding that after one year completing of our training Authority give certificate and then we cannot enter into factory also. I have seen that after 13th year some apprentice candidate joins and they also get job after hunger strike. We are Apprentice Technician. Hence have no possibility to get appointment at Gun and Shell.

Dipankar, Shankar, Sanjay, Paratha, Sharna all become my friend. In the same time, I follow that when I am going to Gun and Shell Factory Rima may stay at a water tap which are behind of my house or at the corner of my house but not talking anything. I talk story of my life to my friend.

In 1999 eldest sister of Rima, Ms. Soma becomes married. Soma's husband works in a jute mill at Naihati but she may think that if her marriage held then she may get normal life. Some time when she looks at me, I think that she has attraction to me. Her brother Subrata is a tread apprentice at Gun and Shell Factory. So, some time talks with him. After some month I follow that Rima follow me, what I have done and whether I also follow her or not. Previous year when she come at tub well and used hand pump and gets water in such a way that I might not see her face. But from January 2000 she behaves deferent. She observes me directly.

In this time, I apply for group-D post at railway and also appeared at preliminary examination in 1999. Today I cannot forget honorable Railway Minister Mr. Nitish Kumar declares that Group-D recruitment should be done through Railway Requirement Board. On the written test basis recruitment, be done and abolish interview. I think that I may get government Job. Mainly I think that at list I may join at Railway. In the mean time I have gone to Jaipur for RRB/Ajmer examination at the post of Junior Engineer and think if god gives chance at Group-D post, I will be happy. After Mr. Nitish Kumar declaration a Nitish declare at Employment News, Chennai Railway Recruitment Board that they want Group-D Khalasi in Southern Railway.

I applied and also appeared at examination but when I started journey from my house, rain start and in radio, television declare that cyclone was coming toward West Bengal and Orissa, costal where be alerted. Super cyclone came immediately, I had waiting listed reservation ticket at

Coromandel Express which departure time at 12.15 P.m. Due to warning of whether department the train diverted its rout and rain already started. Trains at the root of Bhubaneshwar diverted to Tata, Rourkela up to Vishakhapatnam. My ticket was not conforming, hence I thought, first I reached at Howrah station and verified ticket then got decision but ticket became conformed. In super cyclone, maximum ticket became cancel and on the other hand train rout diverted, so Bhubaneshwar, Palasha passenger remain at Howrah. In this time, I have no telephone at our house. I try to talk at a shop of Loknath who is my friend but could not get any link, so I phone to my friend Prasun's house whose house are so far away from my house. I started my journey.

Once up on a time I wanted to see that in the western side of Purva Ghat Mountain and thought that there is any rail route or not. God fill up my offering which I thought. Train reached at Vishakhapatnam after 28th hours. I got some light foods. This time I had no idea that train to be reached at Chennai after one-night journey from Vishakhapatnam. I reached at Chennai in the day after tomorrows in the early morning. In the early morning I reached at examination center and waited up to 10 A.m. In this time, I went to latrine once more. I appeared at examination. I payered to god from the beginning that I should get chance in this post, promise in my mind I should attend Puja (offer holy foods) to god and goddess at Kamrup temple, Kanyakumari temple, Meenakshi temple at Madurai, Mahalaxmi temple and Mumba Dave temple at Mumbai. I paired to god on the train. On Supper cyclone I was not afraid. I thought there were alternative route to go to Vishakhapatnam. I was thinking competitor would be less but every candidate might be thinking so. After examination, I meet with Bengali people who came in same situation. I understand that Bengali economical position become down and now a day in West Bengal every privet concern becoming lock out. Due to infiltration of Bangladesh peoples in India, Indian Bengali peoples face more problems. Now Bangladesh becomes the name of East Pakistan after independence at 1971. At the stage of India, Pakistan division in 1947 maximum Hindu peoples came in to India. In 1947 when Pakistan declare for Muslim peoples, riot start and several Hindu peoples murdered by Muslim peoples without any cause and fired on their property. Hindu peoples became afraid and took entry in India

In 1971 when independent movement of Bangladesh (Bangladesh Mukti Andolon) hold. India-Pakistan war started. India government supported to Bangladesh Mukti Morcha. That time many people came from Bangladesh and they start to live in India. At present infiltration are continuing. Some time they come with their passport and visa but when they start to live in India, they through passport or some time they come in wrong way, i.e. at border give some money to security and pass the border. On the other hand, communist party is ruling at West Bengal from 25 years back. Maximum peoples are communist minded. If some things wrong with a worker then all workers protest against owner by unity.

In the British period Industrial production start in the bank of Hugli River Industrial areas but after Independence of India jute producing area became under East Pakistan whereas industry remains under India. So, jute industries hamper after independent. Hamper its position. After independent West Bengal other industrial condition also remains in better position. But factories are not modernizing whereas modernize machine invent day by day. Old factories productions become less. Factories management wants to stand in previous record. Union wants their own position. Day by day peoples get more facility through union. But other state have no such union and they are weak too walk. Company owner think by same investment get more money from other state because they are not united. We are not brothers about that. Old factory back bone broken and due to fairness of tread union; Industrialist is not getting much interest to found new industries in West Bengal. Bengali peoples come out from West Bengal.

At 10.30 P.m. I Caught Chennai Howrah mail from Chennai railway station. I took bath at sleeper class waiting room at afternoon and got dinner at a Bengali restaurant outside of Chennai station. At 10.30 P.m. train started to move and goes to sleep on my berth. Next morning, I saw several candidates are with me. Krishna, Maher and other become instant friend. It is my character if time not passing then chatting with other. First ask, from where they come and then make friendship to getting phone number, etc.

In return journey train also run in the same diverted rout. So, Chennai Howrah mail got 12 hour more to reach at

Howrah. Hence journey became 32+12=44 hours. We passed out our time with fun and joy. Another passenger also joined with us. One old lady with her granddaughter was traveling by the same train. They joined with us in Antakshari i.e. sing any song of the main paragraph, the song one after another start with last alphabet of previous song. Then I requested to her. Old lady sung a song of Rabindra Nath Tagore. She sung, "Purano Sai Dinar Katha Sunbi Kira Aay Osha Shuka Dukhar Katha Kabo Gan Sonabo Tai, Maora Vorar Bala Phul Tulachi Dulachi Dolay....." Meaning of this song "You want to hear the song of previous period; you come and hear. We pluck flowers and wavy movement be done on a hanger.

When Ishim Kumar hears the word 'Phul tulachi Dulachi Dolay' he remembers lord Gopal. We kept lord Gopal into a small bed at evening and next day pluck up flower in the early morning and awake up Gopal (childhood name of Lord Sheri Krishna). In our Bengali tradition we payer lord Sheri Krishna of his childhood, Bal Gopal (child Gopal). We think God also sleep at night and take food in the morning, noon and after noon. So, at night our idol of lord Gopal set up on a small bed then next morning awake up from bed flute shankha and kasi band in the early morning. We take bath then pluck up flower from garden and then sound of bell and dice (kasi)we get the idol from bed and set the idol at sighasana (sit of god). The old lady sung the song than we sung other song.

Time passed out we may not feel boar. My new friend Krishna prepared mixture with fried dry rice call muri and onion, chanature (fried dal and nodules mixture), pickles and chile. Chile got from his bag and I explain, Krishna got his Chile and cut into small pieces. My tone became difference which meaning also became deference. Every young people laughed and enjoy. In the meantime, a gang of young girl came to our compartment when train stop at a station. Train started to move. They told us that they are player of Volley ball. They came for tournament at Raurkela, in the state of Orissa but programmed became cancel. We consider them to adjust within us and distribute the mixture to all which prepared by Krishna. Everybody enjoys with us, day after tomorrow at evening train reached at Howrah station. We hand shack each other and leave Howrah station.

At 6 P.m. I reached to my house by bus from Howrah to Dumdum. My father and mother might not get any information from my friend. They had seen television news and got information that Coromandel express run into diverted rout and Madras mail late by 12 hours to reach at Howrah.

I heard my father word and thought that my elder sister Sibani like to observed TV. Television is not only for entertainment but from T.V. we get information and it is one medium of education. But my father was thinking if he gets a T.V. then our education might disturb. Several years pass out my elder sister Sibani hang to death. Then FIR applied at police station and case continues about six years. Several time my elder brother and myself had gone to court and meet with lawyer and got return gift like almirah, coat, and other material to our house by court order. My elder sister Sibani liked to see movie at T.V. to her friend house and for that region, father several time bit her by groom. But due to her interest we have buy black and white T.V. in installment by the help of introducing with her husband friend. Today Sibani is not alive but TV. Serve continuously and we observe that. Her case become final and proved that due to aggressive she suicides hang to death.

In 1999 I was feeling very bad. In my horoscope have declaration that I will be independent at the age of 33+ years and time will come in 2003. After join at Gun and Shell Factory I try hard and soul to get a job whatever it is. Some time I am observing Rima who come to collect tap water and sometime come to get water from hand pump. When some candidate come to seen her for choice to marriage, she is not look to me but when candidate refuse her or give negative answer, she again observes to me. When I understand the matter, my mind starts to think I like her too much and she will be married! I like her too much and want to marriage with her but she hats me again and again. Why she hats me? I do not understand the matter. Mainly that maybe I talk too much, some time there are no necessary to that matter. Another thing I cannot tell her my internal words. She is not telling me any things of her internal words. Days passing, I also write a letter to her in October month but cannot hand over to Rima because she stops talking with me. After some days I think it will be better to tell to her father that I like too much, Rima. Rima's father Sukumar also frankly speaking with me; I think that may not be arising any problem. I know that if my father and mother known the matter then they sought to me. So, I write, "Please do not inform to my parent" on both letters. Both of these letters I keep to my purse.

Within three month I become popular to Gun and Sell factory. I have done decoration at Vishwakarma Puja. Then section change one by one from tool room to fuse, from fuse to shell, from shell to maintenance (MM). On the starting fourth month I start MM section and I select at group-D Khalashi helper post in Southern Railway. In G-gang department some one name Heranmoy a well-known person sown to me short gun function and component of that. Several times I use to go there and one tread apprentice name Susanta become my friend. He is also a friend of Subrata. One day Susanta is chatting with me and suddenly he gets my money bag open from my pocket. He finds out two letters which I write to Rima and her father. Three months over I wrote the letter but I could not handover the letter neither to Rima nor to her father. Susanta get five rupees from my money bag and he buy one envelop from Cassipur post office and write the address of Rima. Then drop to post office box at returning time. Before drop the letter, Susanta ask me he may sourly drop the letter or not. He drops the letter. I think whatever may happen, I should solve that. Either the relation builds up or otherwise relation to be finish. I use to go to her house at evening. I calculate that within three- or four-days letter is entering to her house. On fourth day the letter already enters to Rima's house. In the evening when I go to Rima's uncle room, Rima's brother Subrata call me and sought to me and tell me that he may create problem to Susanta. Rima's mother tells me, "If you like so much to my daughter then you tell me clearly and I also behave friendly with you. You have no problem to me but you are talking the matter to other person. Why you behave like these?" Hence, I confess to her that I have mistaken and I am sorry. Then she tells me, "Rima may come to home after some time, you go from here otherwise she feels disturb." I come out from their room and enter to her uncle room. Rima's mother starts to sought, "If you are not confessing me and are not want apology for your sin then I might be given punishment to you or inform to police." I become quite silent.

Next day Subrata go to Gun and Shell Factory and threat to Susanta by grouping with his friend. Susanta become afraid that if they bit him when he returns to his house. He come at my section and meets with me. He tells me, "Subrata threat to me and they may bite me." I tell him, "Don't worry about the matter, I shall talk with them and you will be with me." Susanta tell me, "I should get apology to him about this matter but you promise to me that you neither talk with Subrata's sister nor marriage with her." I promise tell him, "They create problem now, hence if they agree to my offer in near future and call me to discuss the matter or if Rima come tell her word than I shall not accept her offer."

When Subrata's gang comes in the way, we go near by them. I tell him, "That is my hand writing on that letter then you tell me what you want. But why you threat to him. He will get apology to you for his sin". But Subrata tell me that it is not possible, after all he become agrees to me." Susanta gets apology to him and mutual the matter. I promise to him that neither I accept any offer from them at later period nor I speak again. I become silent forever. Within two month I write the poem in her topic. After some day's one friend of Subrata call me and say, "You want to discuss about the matter of Rima. She wants to talk with you. After some days new years are to be start kindly give a greeting and meet with her." I buy a greeting and become prep ear to go to her house. I enter to her house after two months. Her house door is close, so first I knock and enter to room. Her mother asks me, "Why you come again?" I answer, "I want apology from your daughter so I come to your house. Last time I got apology from you and the matter are related with your daughter. Hence I come to meet with Rima."

Rima tell me, "You come to my house that become good because I am not thinking that you will come to my house again. You are not thinking about the word of my mind and it was necessary to do some things by discussion. You get better decision to discuss with me. It is enough to meet and come to my house and again you come to meet with me that it is better. I do not want any things more." Then I try to give greeting but she refuses to accept. I tell here, "I come and get it to give you so I keep it at Dressing table." I return from her house. After three hours called by Kallay who come to my house and ask me to come outside from my house. Subrata and Ganesh are standing in a distance place. Subrata return which I give to his sister and tell me, "Rose is the symbol of love. You give rose to my sister." But I give a flower bunch to Rima on which Rose and Chandra Mullica flower attach. Subrata ask me, "Why you give her Rose flower?" So, I ask, "Chandra Mullica is not any symbol which indication anything about love. I was given two Chandra Mullica and one Rose." So repeatedly asking, "What indicate by Chandra Mullica?" Then quarrel for a while and I return to my house with that greeting and change the topic. I modify the greetings and send to Somnath one of my friend.

I remain silent. I think that from several months my father is suffering from hart problem. So, in January, father check up by a heart specialist. ECO also have done and sometimes he faults down unconsciously. So, Doctor thinks that it may be happened due to hart block. So, Doctor gives suggestion, when my father goes to latrine than he should open the door always. Days passing like this. I become worry about this matter. In this time several problems arise.

On February 15 that may be, I am in the house. Suddenly father become unconscious and become seance less. Immediately I try to phone to that physician who treat him. But I am not getting any link, so call to young boys Sankar and Bhambol. Bhambol is not serious so, I tell them, "You go to your own work." I call to Ranjeet and his sister who are my father's elder brother's son and daughter. Daughter of my uncle come to their father's house for pass out holiday of their children at Dumdum. Immediately call Dr. Sunil Kumar Datta. When Dr. Sunil Kumar Datta comes he suggests getting the patient to a hospital. I am not west time, run to main road and call a taxi. I get him to hospital of Railway at Sealdah. My mother and Ranjit come with me to B. R. Sing hospital. I express whole situation and doctor tell me that immediately pacemaker should be indent because operation is necessary and to be fit pacemaker to him.

Savarkar Datta, my friend at Gum and Shell factory whose father 20 years before put-up Pacemaker. Several time his father fault down at road. His father works at Tata Finance Company in the Cashier post. I asked rough idea about pacemaker at earlier stage of my father illness.

Savarkar Datta tell me in the back side of our hurt have pacemaker and it work to create hurt beat but when our pacemaker has been arise fault, our hart beat decrease. Flow rate of blood become slow. Blood supply oxygen to all parts of our body and act as medium. When flow rate of blood become slow, oxygen supply become less. Due to deficiency of oxygen human sense is not work and human being automatically fall down.

Pacemaker machine cover the deficient of our hart beat by parking inside hart chamber. Pacemaker machine generally set up right side near the hand junction. But his father case is different. First time pacemaker machine set up on right side but not success so again operation held on and pacemaker set on left side.

On producing hospital card indent become ready by the doctors. Doctors give date of operation. But suddenly fever come to my father hence operation date extends. This is the month of February, maximum day my friend punches the card at punch card room of time office. In and out punch of the attendant card in the Gun and Shell Factory is done by my friend Savarkar. Otherwise punch to be done by Saurav. Actually, we are apprentice diploma, so administration is not bothering about that whether we are physically present or not. Same case has done by permanent employees by their adjustment. Then why we worry about done like the same. I tell my problem to my friend and friend help me. We have no telephone in our house or have no mobile phone to me. But Savarkar's house and Saurav's house have land phone, so I inform both of them on telephone to card punch and sometimes go to factory.

One day I go to B. R. Sing hospital at cardiology department at 5 P.M. from Gun and Sell factory by bus. When I reach at cardiology department, seen the bed where my father was in the yesterday, he is not presented there. My mother is standing nearby ICU (Intensive Care Unit). Another patient informs to me, "Your father is at ICU and emergence pacemaker put due to seriousness suddenly. I meet with my mother and she tells me only one person is allowed to meet with him. I go to ICU and meet with a nurse. Nurse informs me that only one person can meet with him and be silent please. Nurse gives me a sample of emergency pacemaker battery and tells me to buy from a shop. She tells me that pacemaker with a battery have set up to him already. It has only one-month life period. It required to other as extra piece and give information to get fat less Sugar company's milk powder. I get all requirements which instruction given by the nurse for my father from Sealdah market and hand over to nurse. Then nurse give permission to meet with my father. I go to nearby his bed and seen that father lie on the bed unconscious. A machine given an indication that my father is alive by shown a graphics of red sign. After three days operation may be held and every night either my elder brother and other or I alternately remain at hospital. One day morning my elder brother Pintu meets with father, he winds up by thread due to faltering on bed. After four day's operation held and success. Doctors give me all necessary paper i.e. Prescription and pacemaker manual then release him. I see the pacemaker are made in USA and understand India till now in backward position.

USA a great nation where science and technology developed in high level and so many inventions held on encouraging by government and peoples have scope to resource work where as in developing country are busy to political profession and fighting divisional group and sub-divisional group with each other. They have no national feeling that how they develop their nation.

It is better that USA develop a good quality pacemaker and my father's live become save and after 15th days father returns to house. I payer to god that father may get quick recovery. Father becomes afraid to touch the electric switch and to walk. In previous period pacemaker patient can not touch electric switch and he/ she might not carry heavy load. That time pacemaker had a large in size. But now days pacemaker develops in small in size as well as maximum restriction are removing by new development of technology. Previously pacemaker had 10 years warranty period where as now a days 15 years warranty period. Pacemaker battery also developed. My father was a railway employee so get total free treatment and operation in railway hospital. My father submits Rs. 3000/- to getting medical total facility in his whole life and get retired railway medical card. But now days someone get Rs. 100 /- per month for medical purpose, that person should not get free treatment from railway hospital. Retirement peoples pay only meal charge at the time of release.

I give mantel strength to my father and telling again and again, "You walk freely without getting any help from other, pacemaker set up to you to care your long life and walk freely." But my father walks very slowly and not try to walk step wise. I read the instructions of the pacemaker two or three times near my father. Then I walk in the morning with my father and try to give mental strength to speak some words.

In this time voter identity card are corrected by authority and give instruction to get corrected ID card. I have gone with my father. They get photography and load to a computer. Then tell me "You come at 4 P.M. and get corrected ID card. In this time out ward journey, we have come by cycle rickshaw but on retune journey we come to our house by walking. I talk some things about the processing of ID card. Father gets strength in his mind. At afternoon I along go to Jaipur where ID card are corrected.

One day at 12 noon go to Sealdah from Dumdum by a train. Previously we were gone to Sealdah for checking at B.R. Sing Hospital by a taxi. But today we come at B. R. Sing Hospital for checkup him by a train, he feels easy to walk and travel by train. By this way, I try to give mental strength. Actually, it is my habit to give mental strength to other. Previously I also give strength when he was not seen clearly due to cataract that time, I told him "In the world so many peoples are not seen any things who are blind and they also walk and done so many works." I also try to write in the dirk at night by the seance of touch of my finger then think it is possible but same problem face difficulty by a blind.

In these mean times my elder brother faces some trouble to his tongue. By my suggestion he makes a medical card at Nilratan medical college and hospital by paying only one rupee. In West Bengal previously government hospitals were totally free treatment but now a days get one rupee for medical card and have bed charge @ Rs.50/- per day if patient be admitted to hospital. Below poverty line peoples get everything free on producing a certificate of local councilor of municipality. My father worries about the matter and think how much money be required. I visit with Dr. Sunil Datta and discuss the matter. He gives suggestion to done operation at govt. hospital. If the operation be done at privet hospital or nursing home then charge may be 5000/- to 7000/- rupees. My brother thinks if money be requiring more than expectation then he may face problem because he don't get any medical facility. He works at a small privet organization. Hence, he has requirement of help from father, he have tension that if he cannot able to speak after operation. Then by the doctor's suggestion X-ray photography done from Theasam laboratory. After getting X-ray report detect the problem that stone formation held at Lunge Hens's gland which requires a small operation.

My elder brother is thinking if the operation are not success or tongue movement be disturbing after operation and problem arise to speak. I tell him, "There have another power i.e. God power, if he wants then there may not arise any problem. Doctor try to do success an operation which he /she done to a patient. But sometimes they become failure. They also say god has power and success is on his hand. In my life I have seen such a doctor. Dr. D. K. Ray told me, "It is your lack, I am able to detect you attack by tuberculosis in your digestion organ and 5% case they get life. Maximum case cannot detect by doctors." So, I believe god and if he wants then we get someone who can solve the problem. I try to give suggestion to create mantel strength to him. I tell him, "You payer to god, god bless you all the time."

Father tells me, "If the operation may not success and arise some problem then his wife may blame to us that on our suggestion, he take decision for operation." I also think the matter and give suggestion to take decision first. If money problem arises then I help you. That time I have no money on my hand but my father's Rs.21000/- are in my savings in State Bank of India. The account is in my name with my mother. I can withdraw money by a cheque. If father want to give money then he gives his personal cheque otherwise I apply my power. I think that but cannot flash the matter. My elder brother, Pintu are not working at a govt. organization or in a public sector. He works under a small industrial unit and he is not getting any medical facility or any leave. No pay no work base he is doing work and he get payment per weekly. He tells me if admit in the hospital then he might not get any payment. One week may continue at hospital there will not be problem to him but if he cannot able to do work in a month then it became difficult to him. I think if such problem arises then I withdraw money from account but Pintu don't know the matter of my account. Hence Pintu are not getting any confidence when I tell him to help him if problem arise and he delay his operation.

I appear for competitive examinations again and again and mainly try for railway service. Hence, I appear in the Railway Recruitment Board examination.

I go to Bhubaneshwar (BBS.) for the post J.E.II of RRB /BBS exam. On outward journey I travel by Pori exp. After examination I catch Diauli exp. I get down at Kharagpur and go to my sister house. She lives in a muddy house and she have 10 Katha lands (720 Sq. ft. Per Katha). Maximum place is cover with jungle. Her economic condition is not good.

When my elder sister Mukta's marriage was held, her husband only used to practice tuition and sometimes used to practice puja i.e. work as a priest. According to Hindu culture he did work for god and got some food, fruits and money as dakshina. Sapan is Brahmin (priest). His father also had done priest works e.g. payer to god by offering holy food, marriage and sadha.

Sadha is a system to respect to a person after his/her death. It is done by his son and he does not touch non vegetable foods up to 11th days or more. Then hair cut at river side and get bath on river. Next day prepare the foods to offer to his father or mother Spirit. In these time sons give respect to their parent as a god. Sweet also offer to parent and some gift given to priest. A priest payer to god, that for peace to his/her spirit. Daughter does such things which are calling jal dan. She does such works after four days of parent's death.

Sapan lost his father at his childhood. His mother was lead life with one son and three daughters at those times. His maternal uncles gave decision to his mother that she should pet she goat and sell milk. She followed and got money from her brother for buying a she goat she sells milk and get help from her bother. Days passed in a tough condition but grass was not necessary to bay for she goat, that is available in her land and nearby field. Goat number increased day by day. Sapan became at the age of 12, she and her bothered arrange poyta. In Hindu culture if priest son is not given poyta before 12 year than required more money to done praychata. Poyta is a system to wear a bunch of white thread on body crosswise from right to left. By a festival poyta offer to god then wear poyta to body. In these time period candidates remain into house up to 12 days and remain as brammocharya. Brammocharya is the system of monk i.e. don't see any girl face, get meals at night only fruits and hairs cut as a bell type but remain only a spot which is call tike in Bengali. After 12 day gets vikha from one lady whose name be vikha mother. Vikha mother is respect to as his mother. After getting poyta he should get anna (rice) from vikha mother. After poyta a priest have right to payer god which is call as puja. Sapan have get poyta in early age because they are poor and after getting poyta he would be right to work as priest.

Generally, priest family remains poor economic condition. They had permanent customer who is call as jagman. But now days permanency becomes destroy because his father died at young age. Their profession is call as jagmani (work of priest). Sapan practice Durga (goddess of power) puja, Kali (goddess of power as naked figure) puja, Laxmi (goddess of wealth) puja, Sarasvati (goddess of education), etc. He practices priest work as an agent of his uncle. But if he becomes able to practice directly then can earn more money. But jagman remain under same priest and his generation. Their flow continues to both generations.

Sapan completed higher secondary and joined at IIT Kharagpur as a casual clerical worker. Several people also worked as casual employee in IIT in the same batch. Someone becomes permanent employee but when he became job less for a while he could not stay at Kharagpur. His economic condition is poor hence went to Calcutta for a job and start as tuition and priest work. It is his bad luck that he is poor. He gets Salter at his anti's house.

Sapan came as privet tutored in our house and love affair with my elder sister. After all marriage hold on then after one year he returns to Kharagpur. He returns to his native place because he cannot survive his expanse by profession of tuition at Calcutta to getting a rental room.

On muddy house they are residing and have no electricity, they use fire wood for preparing curry and foods. They use kerosene lamp for lighting at night. Sapan start work in a general shop at DVC market. His shop owner name Banda Bunda. They give payment @ Rs 1500/- per month. Then lead life something better as every day they get foods. Mukta in her childhood sung a song "Dkha Jader Jibon Bhora Tader

Aber Dukha Kishar" which means whose life is cover with full of sorrow he or she have no matter to think about sorrow. It is real fact that her childhood passes out at Dumdum. That time father's income was not so good. Father was working in group-D post in railway Kanchrapara Work Shop. That time we were not getting full meal in a day; no electricity was available and had a small hut.

Sapan younger sister marriage arrange with a Talbagicha market hawker who sell under wear or T-shirt or half pant, etc. Banda Bunda gets responsibility for gust diner. Other purpose solved by relative. Life become change, Sapan tries to do better work. His sister Raba starts her marriage life at rental room because her husband actual residence is at Tata Jamasedpur. They buy a small hut at Turipara near by a forest. At Kharagpur there also forestry business starts in the waste land. But that is beyond the range of common peoples. It is only possible to carry out by rich people. Just outside of town forestry start. They use forest as the place as toilet. Generally, eucalyptus tree cultivates in the forest. Hence no body reaches to the forest. So, Raba's marriage life starts in the same as before.

Sapan start Life Insurance Corporation agent work. He left Banda Bunda general shop. His sister marriage holds on and his expanse reduce. He starts to lead life in better way. He shells 5 katha land at the stage of his sister marriage. Per katha sell @ Rs.2000/- and got 10000 rupees but expanded 8000 rupees at his sister marriage. They are poor family hence remaining 2000 rupees expanse to themselves. Now land is selling in increasing rate. At present rate @ Rs.10000/- per katha. They also use muddy house but use light and fan to pay some amount to their neighbor @ Rs.50/- per point. They have only five katha land. Hence Sapan think if he shells the 5 katha land and get one and half katha land near by Talbagicha market that will be better. He gets a redeemed one storage building. One room with kitchen is available. Total amount required Rs.45000/-. That also better because electricity also available there. He sells the land of 5 katha and buy one and half katha land at nearer to Talbagicha market.

Within this period Sapan first issue of children became death at the time of delivery due to pre-birth. So many times, pass out by weeping both of husband and wife. They are poor but everybody wants their children. Now their second children alive and give a beautifully name Somudip means always lighten. Two years pass away his mother also died. He becomes happy with his family. Now they use electricity as well as building house also buy. But god can not satisfy to seen that. Suddenly his sister's husband becomes sick. Raba's husband back bone broken. His sister economical condition is too weak to walk for treatment. Raba's have a son as same age of Somudip. Sapan try to give money to his sister for treatment expense of her husband. Approximately Rs.40000/- become shortage to submit to LIC office of the customer rupees. Customer generally hands over premium to Sapan's hand and he submits the premium rupees at LIC office. After some times every matter flashes out to customer because he cannot make up the rupees and they also want receipt of money deposition. All customers become angry and sought to him.

My elder sister Mukta tells me some things about her economical condition. My mind covered with full of sorry to hear the fact. When I have seen that they live in a small building I became happy but today I am worry about them. But I tell her, “If any problem comes nearby you then you think about your son’s future and will come at Dumdum to our house. I try to help you.” I get stipend at Gun and Shell Rs.1200/- per month, hence give Rs.600/- on her hand where as it is not sufficient. But try to give strength to her mind.

When last time, I meet with my elder sister that I see she start to live in the small building and start to use electricity. That time I became happy in my mind but this time I become hear the story from her and my mind feel sorrow. I previously expand money to my nephew for the purpose of entertainment at fair and ride on Marie go around. But my elder sister tells me, “You don’t expanse money to my son for entertainment.” In this time, I expense money for vegetable marketing and buy one kilogram of Elsa fish. I think the matter when I leave the place and travel by a local train.

Time passes out and suddenly Mukta come at Dumdum after one month by the help of a known person of Kharagpur. She come and cried, “My brother, maximum people become angry to Sapan and Sapan come at Kolkata of the fairness of customer.” Kolkata is the new name of Calcutta. West Bengal govt. changes the name the city. She wants to meet with her husband, hence meet with sister in law and explain the matter. Sister in law's husband name Gabinda meet with Mr. Tamal who is a party leader as well as owner of a hotel at Sikem and also attach with other business. Mr. Tamal agrees to appoint Mr. Sapan but agree to send at Sikem hotel as manager. In this off position Mukta become pregnant, she has a son and family maintains become tough. Nabakanta become afraid and think if Sapan go to outside then it may be happening that he may not return again. He sought to her and wants to send her to Kharagpur. In this time my training also completes and remains 300 rupees only on my hand. I have an examination at Patna in the post Signal maintainer Gr III. My father should not give permission to stay her to his house. I cancel the examination of RRB\Patna and hand over the remaining money to her and mother give Rs.300/- to her. She returns to her house where as her husband has no money at his hand because three months pass his commission of LIC also stope due to objection by his customer and he is also not submitting premium of customer. Hence it becomes require to accept the offer of Mr. Tamal. He goes to Gantok, the capital city of Sikkim State. She carries again and again. She goes to Kharagpur to her own house with her son. I go with them up to Howrah station and get ticket for them and platform ticket for me. I buy brad and fruits for them. They catch Baghajatin Passenger train. When train start to move then I leave the station and return to Dumdum. In this time, I become helpless hence I cannot help them. My training complete and income become close. Previously I got money Rs.1200/- per month but today have nothing I pass RRB/Chennai Group-D post final examination i.e. second stage examination but court case file by union at Karnataka High court as well as Chennai High court, hence appointment postpone.

I become unable to communicate with my sister Mukta. PHE-8 practical are started in puja vacation in the course B. Sc. which I start in IGNOU. In Open University system at summer vacation or at puja vacation practical held on according to program and minimum 12 candidates are requiring to give application. Then within 12 days, only 11th days practical held on by hand practice and 12th day examination is held on. Within this period candidate become busy to prepare practical work book also. In Bengali culture Dug puja is main festival and in the puja vacation period Laxmi puja, Kali puja held in the months of October and November. In between Laxmi puja and Kali puja the PHE-8 practical start. In the middle of examination that is after seven days Sapan's sister Mani come to my house and tell to my father, "Your daughter is ill you go to Kharagpur immediately." Then Ms. Moni leaves our house. When I come to my house, father tells me, "Mani tells him that I have responsibility to seen my daughter and it is necessary to help my daughter." I think in these time Mukta is pregnant hence maximum peoples tell that she is ill, it is common fact. But next day when I start to go at my practical center Maulana Azad College at that time telephone ringing and I receive. I hear sound of Sapan. He tells me, "Your sister seriously ill. You will go to Kharagpur." I ask, "What you were telling to my father at the stage when you were in our house last time." He answers that yes, he told some things. I think whether he is at Kharagpur or not. But after all, Mukta is my sister hence require getting information. I go to college and return at 5 P.m. Then I phone at Kharagpur to her neighbor house and also at Sapan's maternal uncle's house. But I am not getting any link whereas try two or three times. Then I go to my elder bother house at Jatinager to meet with my elder brother Pintu. I explain everything. His financial condition is not good. He tells me, "No body helps me, how I help anybody. It is not possible to go at Kharagpur." Then I go to our relative house and meet with related elder brother name Anil. Mr. Anil hears the matter and tells me, "You try to get actual information." I come back to my house.

After two days again I phone at Kharagpur but cannot get any link. Examination become complete I again ring up at Kharagpur. Today I get information from her neighbor. I ask to her neighbor that what happen to Mukta who are your neighbor. She answers to me, "I hear she is admitted to hospital due to pre-birth her child died before birth. Everything finishes. I previously discuss with wife of Pintu that the approximate date of delivery, but she also cannot tell me actual month whereas Mukta told every matter to her. I was helpless to go at Kharagpur and also, I do not understand the fact. I again meet with Pintu and tell him the details. He became agree to go to Kharagpur and immediately meet with my father. Father restrict to me go to Kharagpur but give money to Pintu. Pintu go to Kharagpur with his wife. Seven days pass at Kharagpur and they return at Dumdum. Next day come along at our house and explain the matter, "At night approximated 2 P.m. she got up and blooding start. She was with her son Sumbodip who's age are seven years who can do nothing but he went to their relative house and meet with one related sister of Sapen where as Sapan also is not submits LIC money of her. But she comes with her husband. Her husband tells Sapan are not done better but we are not angry to his wife and his child. Immediately relatives got her to hospital on a cycle van. He expands money and when require blood some one neighbor denote who's blood group match. Her life saves but her third child death before birth. They arrange last work of her third son i.e. buried little death body into ground. Life became under risk. Everybody of her neighbor meet with her and discuss she may not to be alive. Her son heard matter but kept silent and payer to god to cure to his mother. But she becomes cure and returns to her house. Days pass with risk. I also did the same as her son. I also payer to goddess Durga that she should get long life. I payer goddess that I was helpless hence she should help to my sister.

For any one time might not stay and that pass either happy or sorrow. Her time also pass and Sapan also earn money to do work at Gantok in Sikkim state hotel service and try to return money whose money might not submits at LIC office by installment. Someone relives to seen his condition. After three month he gets leave for 15th days, he comes with money and time pass with his family on the way of life. Whereas my father thought if he left his son and wife or if he marriage again. Outside people thought he should cheat with them but he returns money to them as much as possible.

In this time, I am jobless and father also tell me, "You should get job at Chennai in the post Group-D which you pass. Certificate also verified by RRB. You have no required applying to other RRB." He now also says same word as before as when I was at Gun and Shell factory. He told me in that time, "You give pressure to your training, here administrative give appointment in near future." Police Inspector of Dumdum Police station said same word that I get job and for that region police verification held on. I also answered to police inspector that he did not know anything. Six months over training done and after six months when training completed then gave a certificate. Then the authority might not give permission to enter into factory. But his assistant wants money about 500 rupees. He told me, "You give money because peon get less money and they handle file, they want sweet." It is known by everybody that if police verification held then required money. I gave Rs.50/- to them. They wanted more. I said, "It is enough to give Rs.50/- where as I am doing only training." Then kept silent but remain too sated on bench than asked, "Have any necessary to me." Asst. inspector soughed to me, "Whether I seen your face, you go." In these times my father cannot understand, I have require fighting at competition examination.

I apply for the post Signal Maintainer Gr III, Telecommunication Maintainer Gr. III, J.E-II, and Scientific Assistant D etc. I applied at Kalpakkam DAE department of Indira Gandhi Atomic Resource Center (IGARC) before six months. I think whether they call me at written examination or not. So many applications send at Aeronautical Resource Center but they are not call me. I am worry about my future.

In 2001 at summer vacation, biological practical start at Maulana Azad College in the course B. Sc. through IGNOU. I get physics four paper, chemistry five papers, mathematics four papers, three biology paper. Not only that I get Bengali, English and two compulsory subjects in foundation course, as well as marketing management, secretarial practice, export procedure &documentations and management system. I attend to LSE-2 practical. I test my blood group, Karyotype test, bar body test, Cell division (Meiosis and mitosis). I am not passing in the paper LSE-3, that is the subject genetics but after starting the LSE-2 practical, I realize that I should pass the subject LSE-3 which will be held at June month. After two days passing of LSE-2 practical, call letter of written examination at the post Scientific Assistant-D of the IGARC deliver to my house. I want to appear to IGARC examination which be held at Kolkata center as Bidyabharati school at salt lack area. The written examination of IGRAC is held at four noon's from 10 A.m. to 12 noon. I discuss the matter with Practical professor that I have a competitive examination at the post of Scientific Assistant and if they give permeation to appear at written examination and I should attend at second half at practical exam. They give permeation to attend at second half in the practical. First half on dated 11th May I appear in written examination in the post of SA-D as well as attend at LSE-2 practical in second half. I prepare all notes of LSE-2 practical. Then on twelfth days final examination held, I complete practical.

I start preparation for Term End examination of the June month. I get preparation for the subject LSE-3, CHE-2&4, PHE1&2etc. I also get preparation for competition examination but within two-month April and May I stop to read competition exam book.

I pass LSE-2 and SA-D both in the same time whereas LSE-2 is biological related and SA-D post examination are related with pour science i.e. Mathematics and physics. I get call letter for Signal Interlocking Maintainer Gr-III at Chennai in RRB/Chennai. I get ticket from Howrah to Chennai on date 16th Sept. On 18th September, I have RRB examination and 22nd have DAE interview at Kalpakkam. In Kalpakkam call letter they give bus route direction.

On 17 September, I reach at Chennai at 2 P.m. by Coromandel Exp. and stay at Gitanjali hotel. Previously I stay at the same hotel when come for RRB examination with Ujjal. Getanjali hotel owner also Bengali, hence if any question come to my mind for the city of Chennai then I can ask to them. In these time us also together and stay in the same hotel. Ujjal stay only for two days but I have required to stay more than two days. I attain the RRB examination on 18th Sept. and stay two days. I start my journey from Chennai to Kalpakkam by bus on 21st Sept. On call letter bus no. are given 119 from Paris corner bus stand. I catch bus 119 and get down at ECL bus stop, then catch ECL bus and go to DAE bus stand. When the bus enters into DAE area I see in every foot path concrete block have mark as DAE. At last stoppage when bus enters, I get down from bus and get small bag which I get from Nirmol who are Gitanjali hotel owner.

I left suitcase at the same hotel. In this time, I forget to take my water bottle. When I just cross bus stop, I remember I have something more and run into inside the bus stand. I find out the bus on which I complete my journey. Yes, the water bottle is remaining on the foot plat of the bus. I get my water battle but no hotel is seen near by the bus stand. I sift my bag and water battle at a security office. Security person are Bihari hence he understands Hindi where as another person cannot understand neither Hindi nor English. I find out a children school and meet with a madam. When I ask about hotel, she tells me, "It is a school." I describe I want to stay at hotel then send to DAE organization. I think here have no hotel or any restaurant. Security person also say same things and tell me, "You sleep under a statue which seen in front of Bus stand and you should submit file bag on which original certificate remain that I keep inside the office." In the front of the gate of DAE organization, I meet with a Tamil people who can speak English. He wants to see my DAE call letter to where details. After checks my call letter, he tells me to sit on his scoter and come to restaurant of DAE bus stand. I get tea and light food, then get my bag and water battle from security office. I go with him at officer hostel but have no room, then lift me to Student hostel and hostel warden want to see my interview call letter and verify then allot me a single room @ Rs.50. The host tells me that he should meet at IGARC. When he leaves then I take bath and become fresh. I get dinner at night in the student hostel.

Next day early morning I become ready to go at IGARC but travel the surrounding place and when see a temple of lord

Bishnue, I enter into the temple and payer to god that I should be reside at Chennai in near future. At eight o-clocks I catch bus of DAE. At main gate make gate pass on producing of interview call letter. Then catch next bus and reach at Atomic Research centre. I reach at IGARC main building and take sit at reception office. After some time, I go to canting to get pangol (a south Indian dice). In this time, I meet with that person who help me yesterday and talk with him about the time of interview. He tells me, "In your call letter mention interview time at 10.00 A.m. but it is not possible to call you at 10.00 am. You will see it may be at 11.00 A.m." After taken my breakfast I go to main building. At 10.00 o-clock COS call us for certificate verification. From selection list I observe that they call for interview in 1:8 ratio i.e. for one post they call eight candidates. In call letter there have mention that SC candidate get train fear on producing of ticket. I speak truth that I come on free railway pass in outward journey; I have been come for railway examination also. So, I claim return journey fear only. I am schedule cast candidate, for that region according to government act of India I get traveling fear for interview purpose in other government organization but in railway they give free pass with call letter. I am under B. Sc. course in IGNOU that become a question at the stage of interview. Interview start at 12 A.m. Up to 1.00 P.m. only four people go to inside of interview board. At 1.00 P.M. to 2.00 P.M. lunch hour hence we also go to take lunch. Again at 2.00P.m. Start interview. My number comes to enter at interview board at 4.00 P.m. When I enter in interview board, I give salutation in India style as namaskar and enter into interview board. They ask me, "How you come here? Where you stay?" I speak truth that I come for railway examination on date 17th Sept. than on 20th I come here and stay at Student hostel of DAE. Then they ask me, "When you come here?" I answer, "At 8.30 A.m. I come here. Then they change tropics. In diploma mechanical engineering I get more marks in computer science subject, hence they ask that why I get more marks in computer science. I speak true fact that I have completed one-year computer course at St. Xavier's Computer center and also appear at O-level exam. They ask, "If give charge to buy a computer then what you have done?" I answer, "I consider requirement purpose and then capacity, capability and warranty period be check done by my." They tell me some computer work quickly and someone work slowly, you may not check that? I answer, "Yes I also inquiry efficiency. Then ask summation of total number from 1 to 100. I write on the black board the formula of combination. Suddenly someone asks, "What is density? What is it unit?" I become confuse and answer volume/ mass and m3 /Kg. They ask again the same question then suddenly understand that I am wrong and give correct answer. Again, they come in computer field instead of mechanical field related question whereas the post is SA (Mach.). They ask, "If you have no knowledge about computer then how you buy a computer?" But I cannot give any answer. They say, "OK, you go." I come out from interview board and discuss to another candidate. Then I return to hostel. After some time that person come to hostel room that helps yesterday. He asks about the interview. I answer that they ask about computer but not ask about mechanical. He says that may be but ask, "What is the performance of interview?" I answer, "It is medium." When he leaves the room, I also leave the hostel and start my journey toward Chennai. I come to DAE bus stand by a departmental bus and see a bus 119 standing at that place, then take sit on that bus. I cannot speak Tamil and cannot understand that. But I am thinking and payer to God that to live at Chennai which is the capital city of Tamil Nadu." I already meet at GM office in southern railway to that person who has charge to handle my file of Group-D post which I select previously. I am thinking the previous matter on the bus then ask when the bus will be reach at Chennai. In these times some one passenger tells me this bus are not going to Chennai parries corner but this bus going up to Chengalpattu, from where you get train for Chennai Park station. Park station is opposite to Chennai Central station. I get down at Chengalpattu and see there are same as to me that another candidate who come from outside for interview. We catch a train toward beach and get down at Park station. This night I stay at Getanjali hotel and get my suitcase and return bag to them. Next day early morning by Coromandel Express at 9.05 A.m. start my return journey. On train I remember when I come at first time at Tamil Nadu, I was afraid that I could not speak Tamil language and I am very weak to speak in English. But thought that European people e.g. Portugal, English and Fence people, when they first foot stepped on Indian peninsula that time nobody can understand Indian language but they also travel India and also travel other part of the world where they had no knowledge about other language as well as culture but they come out from their mother land and once up on a time they rule the other country and now English become International language. Now a days English to other language conversation dictionary and as well as learning books also available. That time have nothing. Now communication builds up through the world. That is their hard work and to took risk by them. When they came at India and other country that time, they should face problem to speak and indicate by body language or by shown the material. Then day by day they understand other language and vice versa. Other also starts to understand English. So, I try to follows them and mainly try to follows English peoples. If require to learn Tamil, then buy Tamil learn through English book.

Several days pass but any letter might not come to my house from IGARC and four-month pass. I understand that I am not success at interview, so it is only option to try to railway job. I try for railway job. In 2001, I also pass 21st subject of 68 credits at B. Sc. in IGNOU. I try to read competition exam books and as well as study material of IGNOU.

Again, I apply at Aeronautical Research center in the post Technical Asst. but in Employment News give notice that if departmental candidate be found then they are not bound to inform to the candidate and they should not call any candidate from outside, if they get departmental candidate. I see in DAE and Aeronautical department application form have a column to give whether any relative are working in that department and relation with him asked. I cannot understand the actual matter of that. Whether they get reference candidate or through influence candidate are requite in the department. I don't know the actual matter. I realize that they may not call me at written exam. I also don't a high-level person to give reference. So, I only try to send application and appear at examination when get call letter.

Within this period Mr. Atal Bihari Bajpai is Prime Minister. The government increase retirement age from 58 years to 60 years and two years recruitment is stop, hence young generation loss two years. Government also arranges committee to activate new pension scheme. If we get chance at governmental job then we may be or may not be under pension scheme. But require to try for job otherwise have no alternative.

Day by day passing and one by one examination attend. In Ajmer I appear in RRB examination but canceled and go to again in reexamination at Jaipur city. So many examinations cancel in RRB/Bhubaneshwar. But try to appear at reexamination.

In Feb. 2002 two examinations coincide, one at Mumbai in the post of P. Way Supervisor through RRB/Mumbai and other DAE depart i.e. Cyclotron Variable Energy Center where as common people say Bhava Atomic Centre. I get call letter for written examination in the post of Scientific Assistant (Mech.)-D which departments and examination center are at Kolkata. I appear at the DAE examination on the same center. I appeared previously in the same post but in this time on the same day result of written examination be declaring at examination center. I appear the examination and wait for my result. The examination held on at 10.00 to 12.00 noon and result declares at afternoon 5 P.m. I become success and phone to my house. But give the date of interview tomorrow, it become the problem.

Next day call for interview, in the early morning I get all original certificates in my file and then start to go at Salt lack. I reach at departments C V E C. At second position I enter into interview board after verification of my original certificate. I cannot face interview in English. Up to class XII, I complete in Bengali version, then start to study in English version and due to that I could not success in W.B.JEE for admission in degree course in Engineering or Medical. I cannot speak in English within West Bengal. Nothing comes out in English. On the other hand, Hindi also was not my subject in educational life. Hence there arise problem to give answer in Hindi. But in interview either to speak in English or in Hindi in governmental service because Hindi becomes official language in 1963 and English remains co-official language. Hence Hindi speaking peoples get advantage in competition examination, Non-Hindi people face more problems, and they have required learning three languages whereas Hindi speaking people required to learn only one language which is their mother tongue. I face interview in Bengali and after interview I understand that due to deficiency to speak in English, I might not be select. India is a multi-lingual country and we cannot communicate all over India without English. British leave India before 58 years ago but without English Non-Hindi people might not get better chance. I have seen in reservation counter at Dumdum Station someone write in Hindi to fill up reservation requisition form in railway. The counter clerk tells him to write in English whereas he doesn't no English. When he explains his inability clerk tell him, "If you cannot fill up in English then you shall get help from other." On the other hand, in Tamil Nadu I communicate in English how much I can speak in English. About 99% Tamil, Telegu people don't know Hindi. I remember all these matters when I am returning to my house by walking. Interview are not good, hence think only one hour taken by walking to reach to our house and it is better to walk because sometimes pass out in my life to seen the side scenery of the path.

In the same year I pass in RRB examination at Patna RRB which I was appeared in Muzaffarpur city. Within 19th RRB, 10th RRB give Hindi language question and give copy write a Hindi paragraph which is compulsory. It becomes easy to them whose mother tongue is Hindi. Hindi people from the beginning of their education start in Hindi i.e. from primary stage to degree or diploma or Charter Account or company secretary or in cost accounting use Hindi and competition examination also in Hindi. Hindi people tell to us maximum peoples speak in Hindi. But all quality books in professional courses e.g. Engineering and Medical are in English. In higher study English language become necessary because maximum invention held on either in Europe or in America. In Muzaffarpur I have seen a candidate in railway board examination cannot write in English where as he completed diploma in mechanical engineering. But authority gave to write both paragraphs in English and in Hindi in the examination. That candidate was telling that it is difficult to write in English. Who are Non-Hindi people they also read and write in their mother tongue and hence they also face same problem but nobody can understand our problem? There happens partiality because by this system brain cannot verified properly and Non-Hindi peoples are facing difficulty in the competition examination. Non-Hindi peoples only know their mother tongue and English. Maximum Non-Hindi peoples are weak in English. So, they might not understand properly in English. Hindi people are becoming success in competition maximum in number because Hindi becomes official language.

Through all over India only Bihar, Madhya Pradesh, Himachal Pradesh, Haryana, Rajasthan, Jharkhand, Chhattisgarh are the circle of Hindi. They get advantages in competition examination. Nepal and Marathi also have similar latter script like as Hindi where as their language is different. In this way maximum latter script in Gujrati language are same as Hindi but that also different in speaking. Hence Nepali, Marathi and Gujrati peoples can easily speak in Hindi. But non-Hindi state Tamil Nadu, Andhra Parades, Kerala, Karnataka, West Bengal, Assam, Manipur, Tripura, Meghalaya, Nagaland, Arunachal Pradesh, Orissa where 99% peoples cannot speak in Hindi. They have required to learn three language e.g. Mother tongue, English and Hindi if they want to appear in a competition examination. From birth if someone learns their mother tongue then up to graduation give priority in their mother tongue then how they develop to speak and read in English and Hindi respectively.

If English be only official language then all competition examination be start in English. Then Hindi circle do not get advantage in competition examination. I am Bengali and I read in Bengali version up to class XII. Then try to learn in English version and also try to read English magazine and newspaper. In this way I come at a stage that I understand English language. When I start to appear at Railway Recruitment Board examination then it becomes necessary to learn Hindi because several RRB give Hindi language question and sometime give Hindi grammar also. So, I try to buy Hindi Grammar book, Literature of Hindi History, etc. But I do not know the author name so I face problem. Then buy higher secondary Hindi Subjective books from collage street book market but cannot find out any Hindi objective competitive examination book within Calcutta. Again, and again I read the books of Hindi which I buy from the different markets.

Several mechanical engineering objective books and English objective also read to appear in JE-II post. Physics and chemistry objective study materiel of CBSE medical entrance examination also read for attain at Signal or Telecommunication Maintainer Gr-III post. Then start to pass preliminary examination at RRB/Patna, RRB/Kolkata, RRB/Bhopal in the post of Telecommunication Maintainer, Electric Signal maintainer etc. But two times I appeared in DAE examination and passed the exam. But I am not getting any chance at Junior Engineer Gr-II post. In August 2002; I appear in the examination at RRB /Patna in JE-II (Elect.) post. I also apply in Indian Forest Service examination on the base of B. Sc. I complete 94 credit where as 96 is total credit in B. Sc. course through open system from IGNOU. Maximum time payer to God that I already pass in Group-D examination but I cannot join in that post, minimum god shall give chance to join at that post.

In this time, suddenly I feel that maximum people know that I love Rima but any how talking stop in our life. Her sister enters in between us but Rima may think about me. For that region when last time visit with her to give greetings, she told me, "You come to my house that is enough to me and you speak with me that is better to me. I don't want anything more. It is my haven, it is expectation, and it is everything in my mind that you again meet with me." I think in near future I may join in governmental organization because from 2000 to 2002 seven competition preliminary and one final examination pass but court case at the post of Kalashi may be solve. Rima is a female candidate so require thinking about her. So many times, indicate as wife to my friend. Some time she also heard that, but was silent. Once more I shall speak with her. I am observing that when she became along. I find her along when I go to meet with Laxmi, Mona and Sama. I also watch her. She comes along at tub well. I go to tub well spot and tell her, "You want to speak with me." She suddenly bit me by a porcelain cup and sought to me, "Waste boy, you come again to speak with me. I call my mother." She neither understands me nor feels my internal word. I am thinking that I tell her that I am passing in preliminaries examination and final pass in Chennai. I shall get a job in near future. But she goes to call her mother. I wait for a while and after some time she return with her mother. Her mother tells me, "My daughter hats you. Why you want to speak?" I ask to her mother, "Your daughter spite when she seen me, but why?" They both sought to me that letter was given by me, speak to her that I want to marriage her, gave greetings, etc. In the meantime, Rima spite vigorously and tell me "What you have done, I spite again." She spites again. I was agreeing to speak about my current position but situation turn to other point. Hence, I tell her, "You are a prostitute and so many prostitutes are available in a market by expense money." Then I come to my house. They are sought on the road for a while and return to their house. Once up on a time when one letter sends by Susanta to her house, in that period I was at Gun and Shell Factory and that time require to drop other letter into drainage and letter became blacken. Drainage water flooded my love letter due to her brother's behavior. Now everything finishes by her spitting and erases her name from my heart.

At evening her brother Subrata come with fifty members of his friend. They blame me that I try to do something misbehavior in the morning and touch the body of Rima. When I was spoken with her at that time, Santo who are Uncle's son of Rima were present. I say, "Santo was present at the time of speaking; you call him and ask the matter." They say that Santo does not understand the matter. I say, "He is not understanding the matter but he can able to say that whether I touch the body of Rima or not." In this time Rima's brother sought that he shoots me by a pistol or bit me by his group. My father become angry to them and tries to bit

Subrata by a steel rod. Situations turn toward father. I try to cool the matter but Subrata are sought, hence I get the steel rod from my father and say, "I see your power I bit you by this rod." Then they go outside of our house and ask, "Why you are not talk with us?" I say, "I do not touch your sister and her touchable things. If Subrata join in Puja Committee then I remain outside of the committee." I indicted to his friend that due to his presence I might not talk with them. Then they say, "We come at wrong place." They go back.

Next morning when I see Rima's mother are standing along at road crossing, I through the word, "Yes given birth a daughter and son and give education that daughter blame to other that touch the body and have a son to sought by drink win. Friend also is a drunker. Next time may say that I rape to her by forcefully to tier her dress." Rima's mother sought and goes to their house. Then come back with her son. Subrata ask me, "What you tell some things to my mother. I bit you on the road." I coolly answer, "Yesterday you spook the same word but I am not wanting to fight with you. I tell your mother that your sister next time blame to me I rape her. Yesterday she behaves like this." Subrata tell me politely, "What you think about the matter which you previously told us?" I remember the fact that I told them, I want to marriage Rima. He tries to indicate that. But so many mental tension and harassment created by them hence I say, "That is not possible." He leaves the place but his mother sought to me for a while and go to their house. I erase her name from my heart forever.

Two year pass out on tension. I tell to my mother that you should not payer god and stop yearly Goddess Laxmi puja. If god and goddess be within world then he or she will be hear my sound. After getting the job, yearly puja be done. In 2003 I feel some things in my mind that I may be going far away from my parent. In February month I become sick by cough and cold because in January month I went to Chandigarh for RRB exam in the post of Telecommunication Maintainer Gr. III then on 11th January, I went at Patna in the post JE-II. Due to cold session cool effect to me and turn into bronchitis. First, I think, I am not taking treatment in this time if death come that also be better in my life. Hence, I cannot understand that weather I go to outside of Kolkata or go to haven. Mother sought to me then goes to Nagerbazer for consult with a doctor but chamber remain close. I think Dr. Sunil Datta know the all problem of my body because he is my home physician then go to his chamber. He starts my treatment.

After continuing treatment, I become cure after one month. On 1st March I weep very much and speaking to my mind, God neither give me good health nor give me any better chance in my life. When I try to do some things, either I became ill or some other problem came to me. I face both side problem as house hold problem and personal problem. I think what happen in my future life.

In 7th March 2003 Ujjal phone to me that he receives his call letter for medical test for Group-D post which we select previously at RRB/Chennai in 2000. The court case wins the RRB. I feel tension that I am under treatment and if I miss the chance in this time then what is requires appearing in the examination for Government job. Day by day pass out Ujjal join at Tiruchirappalli Division in Southern railway. I remain in our house as King Fisher bird when the letter will come to our house. On 27th March I get call letter to my house. The Authority send pass in reverse direction, i.e. from Chennai to Howrah. In reservation counter they might not give ticket on produce of that pass. Time also become short in my hand and on producing of call letter of RRB/Bangalore get ticket but that on date 1st April. In Chennai division call me on 31 March. I think god also hear my word in this time but in near future time it is not good, I feel that. I get ticket in Tatkal (emergency) reservation on producing of my passport by an agent who get Rs.100/- from me as extra charge. On the other hand, ticket charge also gets Rs.50/- more than normal reservation in sleeper couch by railway. The Bangalore ticket remains as it is.

I start my journey on date 29th March by Coromandel Exp. I start to think "I thought in 1st March that it is the last time that I withdraw pensions of my father, I was weeping that I will go so far from my house and want to go at studio to get photo with my father but I cannot understand where I may go. But today I start my journey toward Chennai. I am going so far from my parent." I get dinner at 1.00 P.m. I go to berth.

Next day I get up in the early morning and become fresh. I get breakfasts. Total 29 hours taken to reach at Chennai from Howrah. Days are passing to see the side seen on the rail. I remember that when I came at Chennai first time, I could not speak in English and Hindi. I heard from other person that Tamil peoples do not want to speak in Hindi if he or she can able to speak Hindi. So, I follow the rule of British and think if English peoples came to India at first time then, I also try to travel whereas Chennai is within India. In the beginning to come in India by British peoples that time they faced the problem to speak and understand. That time they used to explain by body language. If they became hungry then they might show the foods item. In this time, I also cannot speak very well in English. If arise any problem to speak then apply the rule of British. I also may express my necessity through indication the things. Also, I remember that who are dram and daft they also give indication. Also think that who are dram and daft they travel on the rood and travel by a train. Hallenkaler an American lady is an example who also learned and got education.

On 30th March I get down at Chennai platform for residing at Chennai. I get room at Getanjali hotel @ Rs100/- per day. I go to Southern Railway Chennai Division on 31st March. I see a young lady clerk be verify original certificate. She verifies the certificates then give Medical memo. I become afraid because two time I attacked by T.B. One time attacked in the chest and another time in digestion system. Previous month also health condition was not so good, I go health unit i.e. NGO and meet with medical register. He tells me, "You must come tomorrow in early morning at 9.00 o-clocks." I think medical test be done in the morning.

Next day I go to NGO of Chennai division in early morning. But at 9.00 o-clock door of NGO also are not open. Then wait for a while and at 9.05 A.m. main gate of NGO open and at 10 A.m. get medical memo. At 11.00 A.m. start urine test. We are candidate so have no value to them. They may test temper of the candidate. After urine test, we wait for four hours then every candidate checks by Sr.DMO in a series i.e. one by one. In this time, several candidates also come for medical test and introduce with each other. I speak in English and some time in Hindi. I introduce with a Tamil candidate Mr. Dile Babu and another N. Suryanarayana. N. Suryanarayana can speak in Hindi. He tells me, "I am in Traffic departments and if you want to exchange the department then you be done where as in traffic medical standard require A-I on which allow up to -2 eye sight." But I have -3.75 in left eye and - 3.50 on right eye, so have no possible to exchange the department. My department is C&W mechanical hence has no profit to think the offer. He became agree to come at C&W department. We have no idea about C&W department. We think that C&W means carriage and Works. Hence, we think that we may post at Perambur Carriage and Works. My father was working in work shop at Kanchrapara in the Eastern Railway and I know that at work shop has incentive. I think C&W is better. At 3.00 P.m. the medical test becomes complete. Sr. DMO checks eye sight, chest, and blood pressure and in the morning urine test already held. I think that it is enough but X-ray of chest also require, hence send at Perambur Railway hospital. Every candidate refers to Perambur. Previously I heard that Perambur hospital is best hospital in Indian Railway. So once up on a time I also thought to visit Perambur. Dile Babu's house is nearby Perambur. He tells me to go with him because I am a new parson and I have language problem. When I ask to him that how I go to Perambur hospital, he tells me that don't worry. I go to Perambur hospital with Dile Babu by his two wheelers. We reach at 4.00 P.m., so they have not done X-ray. They tell us to come at 9 A.m. day after tomorrow because tomorrow is holiday as Telegu New Year day. In India deferent State has different national holidays according to union choice. Dile Babu guides me that how I shall come day after tomorrow at Perambur and he get drop me at Perambur railway station. He tells me to catch 'M' train from platform no 2. I learn two or three words of Tamil language like tanir means water, Aapa means father, Amma means mother, etc. But I cannot understand the meaning of 'M'. On local train when I return think 'M' means Madras which is the previous name of the city Chennai? In Calcutta use local train name by the terminal station name but here use only a single latter or short form of station name.

Next day pass through sleeping and eating at Gitanjali hotel. On Tuesday I attend at Perambur at 9.05 A.m. and become afraid about X-ray because previously I was attack by T.B. and think if any problem arises after getting X-ray. I am sitting at outside of X-ray laboratory building and waiting that when they call me. In this time, I follow someone have a bag on which have Bengali script shop name, I become conform that he be a Bengali person. I try to introduce with him. Then I ask him about his residence. He is a candidate who comes for medical test. He is appointing as Group-D Khalasi Helper -II at Avadi Division and stay at Aynavarom near Perambor loco station with his friend. His name is Nirmal and his friend name is Gabida. I want to meet with Gobida and visit their temporary shelter because they stay at railway colony of a Bengali employee's quarter. Gabida also appointed as Khalasi in Perambur Carriage and works. I understand that we may not appoint at Parambur carriage and works. Our X-ray is taken at laboratory then we go to a tea stole and get tea. We go to 4th no gate of Parambu carriage and works and wait for Gabinda. Gabinda come out at 4.00 P.m., we all together go to their shelter. Gobida find out a bangali family whose title is Bag. I meet with Mr. Bag and Ms. Bag. Ms. Bag prepares roti and vegetable curry. Roti is a process food item which made by flour of wheat. We get foods and chatting each other In my mind have tension about health that if abnormality find out then everything of my labour be wastage and it is not requiring to attain at RRB and another Govt. organization exam. But I am keeping silent and after some time I return to the hotel by a local train.

In this time, I think in my life that I face so much tension and so many times think that it is better to suicide in my life. Last January month I meet with a girl to give a handmade greeting to her. Then make a statue of Ramakrishna Paravanes and I make a valentine greeting to think to give in 14th Feb. I should hand over that but due to illness I left that. On 5th January she spoke on telephone that which I gave a handmade grating to her in previous year that keep with her as preserving condition. I thought in this year I should give a handmade greeting and think she may love me. When last time I meet with her, she again and again told me that she wants to travel with me and want to travel at a distance place. She told me her child responsibility be taken by me. How it is possible, only if her marriage with me then that is not any problem. I get medical test call letter that I inform to her through telephone. Now I think that if I become medically fit and get job then I shall talk with her that I agree to marriage with her.

At night I think the first day when I meat with her, she was so beauty but I was attracted to her figure. I thought that Rima hat to me. If she became agrees to speak with me, I may want to ask her qualification. Then so many times passed and once up on a time her father's sister Laxmi told me to take tuition of her but she resides at a colony nearby airport. Bus fare also required that not be profitable and I had no such income by other tuition. Hence, I left that tuition. But today think if that day I got the tuition then she should not leave her education at class IX stage. If I get joining then I offer to her to marriage. After marriage I should encourage that she shall start her study through open school system in central broad through English. But there is a problem that she got study through Bengali medium and she also is not able to speak in English and Hindi. That becomes a problem. I face so many problems in my life but that may be my record, if I be able to start her study and if she will be success up to matriculation. Otherwise marriage life is as it is that with child born and we pass our time as simple life.

The night passes out; I get up in the early morning and become ready to go to Perambur. At 9.00 A.m. I reach at Perambur railway hospital. I get report of X ray, I am all right. I get better report and become happy. I phone to Shipra and tell her, "You told me that you want to travel with me so far than it is better that your marriage with me. Then we travel so many places and I also try for JE-II post." She cannot understand the grade and post due to lack of knowledge and she don't know that what necessary to try again. I know that through promotion it will required to reach at the post of JE-II about 12 years but if I get chance through RRB then require only two or three years because now a days I pass at preliminary exam in different post. But she cannot understand. She agrees to marriage with me and tells me that she will meet with me when I go to Kolkata next time.

I think that my life pass through struggle and by hard and sold work I get chance in the railway job. I want to lead life in new way. But when I come at NGO health unite, they want eye power certificate and after submit of eye power certificate then they shall give fit certificate. I have spectacle due to myopia. Indian railway gets medical test with vision test but require power certificate from outside physician.

I face language problem to find out an eye specialist or a privet hospital. Maximum person may not understand Hindi or English. By mix-up language of Hindi and English, I find out a privet hospital Dr. Severna is sitting at Amrit Hospital. My name is entry on the register for appointment with the doctor. Visiting hour of Dr. Suvarna is 6.00 P.m. to 8.00P.m. So, I go to Amrit hospital at 6.00P.m. At 7.30P.m. I enter into chamber. Dr. Suvarna hear and tell dilates the necessity of me. He tells me, "I will check thoroughly your eye then give certificate because the certificated is to be put at railway." He checks color blindness, investigation of fungus within eye.

Then give some eye drops into both eyes. I sit on a bench for an hour. When eye lance expanse then checks at computer and another instrument. In these time candidates seen haziness, I also feel same and return at hotel. I have an examination at Bangalore in post of Telecommunication Maintainer Gr. III through RRB/Bangalore but tomorrow at night Doctor give power certificate. If I want to appear at the examination then require starting my journey at night, hence I cancel my programmed. I also feel tension in my mind that where my eye sight are B-1 standard or not. If I fail medical examination then there has no requirement to appear into examination then that is better to enter into business.

Next day pass with tension but some time thinks about Shipra my lover. At evening 7.00 P.m. again I meet with Dr. Suvarna and after checking, he gives me power certificated. I become very glad to get the certificated that I have -3 in right eyes and -2.75 in left eyes and I have no problem to join in railway because I am under medical standard B-1.

Sunday pass my time with dream of young life that after some month I may enter into marriage life. In my life Shipra will come and our child will come in near future. How much I kiss her that I think in my mind and enjoy by myself. So again, I phone to Shipra that I shall meet at Dumdum with her and everything will be discussing about the matter of marriage. I tell her, "I love you." I think that we will be happy in our life. In my life someone come to close too me that tell me agree to marriage.

On Monday I get fit certificated and submit at DPO office, Chennai Division on 3rd floor and ask, "When I may get appointment order." Chief office superintendent tells me, "You come after 20 days then get appointment order. Now go to native place." I had return ticket on producing of RRB/Bangalore call letter on dated 07 -04 -03 but that became lapse yesterday. Hence required to get tatkal ticket (emergency ticket) on producing of voter ID card but pay Rs.50/- be given extra.

I get tatkal reservation ticket and start my journey. On train journey, I think Shipra is a class VIII pass candidate but she is simple girl hence think when I give a new year greeting that I want to make love affair and indirectly offer to me that she wants to lead life with me. She is simple minded girl hence do not require to broken her hart. I get government service so I want to expect her as life partner. I shall meet with her.

When I return at Kolkata then contract with her on telephone and set up a place to meet with her along. I go to the indicated place at evening and see a kali temple near by the place. I visit the temple then wait for her at the temple corner. She come to wear a black trader and indicate the presence from far away by her hand, I also do so. When she comes near by the temple, we start to walk parallel and enter into a lean. We talking that the matter if our mother or father have any objection then we may marriage at a temple after court registration and ask her age but she says her age be ten years less than me. Shipra tell me, "You don't worry about my grandmother's word that the last time you visited at our house. I am sorrow for that." In this time, she repeatedly tells me, “My back side becomes wetted by sweat. I buy a new turider Kurti for you to meet first time. My face also covers with sweat.” I give my hand kerchief. She cleans her face and goes to a vacant place and tells me, “We pass our time to standing at a single place.” But I say, “It is better to walk.” Two hours pass with her but don’t touch her body. I think after marriage I shall kiss her first time. We agree to meet again and promise that we might not mind any matter about our parent and guardian. She tells me, “You shall talk two or three times with me on phone in a month.”

On that day I promise to give her some gift which made by me. I have knowledge to make sculpture by wooden medium, by stone, by cement and have knowledge about clay modeling. I already made two statues of Ramakrishna Paravanes Dave, the guru of Sami Vivekananda. When I made first statue that time my eldest sister visited at Dumdum and want that but I cannot tell her that I want to give the statue to Shipra and gave her by packing with old newspaper. My eldest sister gets that at Kharagpur and I made another one but keep that in our house. When I left Kolkata last time I think that it is better to set the statue at almirah because I am leaving Kolkata permanently and another matter that if I give a gift to my friend then relation broken, hence it is better not to give any gift and I also explain the matter to Shipra. I tell her whether it is in my house or your house that are same. She also is not telling any things more to me. Once more I meet with her again before go to Chennai after 20 days. Second time she wears Shari in brown colour and wear ornament to shown to me.

I start my journey toward Chennai on date 20 -04 -03 and think I shall get appointment order so it will be better if I reside with Gobinda and Nirmal. They also tell me to come at Perambur when last time I visit with them. I reach in the early morning at Chennai Central station by Chennai mail. I get briefcase and get books for competition examination and original certificate. The briefcase become weighty but I try to carry with me and reach at suburban station and catch a local train and get down at Perambur local station. I am not seen any auto rickshaw, I get briefcase on my solder, both solders come under pain but due to necessity I carry the briefcase up to Ayanavaram at Mr. Bag house.

In the early morning Ms. Bag tell me, "If you stay in this quarter then water problem become arise." Then I think it is better that I take a separate rental room Rs.900/- per month because last time I expanse Rs.1000/ for ten days. Gobinda tell me, "One Bihari name Rajkishar come to join at Perambur workshop, he also wants a partner to get a rental room by shear the room rent." I tell him to intrude with Rajkishar. Then go to Chennai Central. I meet with the clerk at DPO office. The clerk asks for SC. certificated in their own format. But they are not giving any format previously and after two weeks when I come to Chennai, they give such instruction. I want a pass to travel but they say, "It is impossible." I tell to the clerk, "At the first stage given faulty pass." They say that they had done mistake. All of them make mistake and harass by them. I get SC. format and come back at Mr. Bag house. Ms. Bug are present; I discuss the matter. She wants to know about my family back ground and my qualification. I explain all. Then she says, "If you come first to my house then you should be better Paying gust." In the morning she told me that find out rental room. Hence, I decide to get a rental room. In evening I meet with Rajkishar and get room at Perambur @ Rs.1600/- per month, I shear only Rs.800/- and start my journey for Kolkata by ordinary ticket. At general SLR I complete two-night journey in tough condition.

Day after tomorrow get down at Howrah station and according to Chennai DPO office instruction, I want to meet with tahsildar and find out tahsildar office at Dumdum Cantonment which working time 10-00 A.m. to 5 P.m. but open at 10.30 A.m.

It is the first time that I understand that the meaning of tahsildar. Tahsildar is the meaning Tax collector who is work under revenue office. In West Bengal Tahsildar have no power to give cast certificated whereas at Tamil Nadu have power. Tahsildar send me at Barrackpore at revenue office. The revenue officer has power to give other backward class (OBC) certificated. Only this SC/ST. certificated be given by SDO i.e. Sub Divisional Officer. I immediately reach at Administration Building and meet with Personal Assistant of SDO. PA tell me to go to ground floor and meet with inspector of SC/ST. department whereas certificated be given by SDO but require to verify.

I feel that when British rule start, they start the system to rule in the better way and start to analyze the depress community. They think to improve depress community condition through give education and help. Now become in the list of schedule caste category, on the other hand tribal is listed as schedule tribe.

Now days also call Sahab to Sub Divisional Officer. In the British rule English people are call as Sahab. We are not change the system and cannot change according to the condition of India. In India several states are Non-Hindi circle. In Tamil Nadu, I am talking in English at Chennai Divisional Office. If English not exists in India I cannot communicate at that place, so it is actually true in the modern form of India that English have a vital role. In Bengal when we go to railway reservation counter and if someone fill up the reservation requisition form through Hindi, the counter clerk sought that he should write in English, by the help of other. This has seen anywhere and I see at Dumdum Railway station, in Eastern Railway reservation counter. Hindi becomes official language from 1963 but without English we cannot establish. In India different state have different language. In Tamil Nadu has Tamil and West Bengal has Bengali. Banking system also establish by British Government. Main city also builds up at the British period e.g. Bombay, Calcutta, Madras, New Delhi. Already Indian peoples change the name of Calcutta to Kolkata, Bombay to Mumbai, and Madras to Chennai. The official works in the Non-Hindi circle are English. The Non-Hindi state are Assam, Manipur, Meghalaya, Arunachal Pradesh, Tripura, Sikkim, West Bengal, Tamil Nadu, Andhra Pradesh, Karnataka, Kerala, etc. In India 14 state within 28 states used to English as official language. In that state maximum person cannot speak in Hindi or write in Hindi. But Hindi speaking people say everywhere Hindi can be speaking. Once upon a time Muslim people rule in India, the Sultan period turned into Mogul. That time Partisan (language of Iran) was the official language of the India and born Urdu language by mix-up with Indian language so in Hindi several words of partisan are used to practice and Arabic are attaching something's with them and hence in Gulf Countries people can understand some things Hindi.

In this time, I am thinking all this matter and give application with the Xerox copy of cast certificate of SC. I wait for verify the certificate by them. At 4.43 P.m. I get the caste certificate in the own format of Southern Railway I get the certificate and phone to Shipra to meet with her because I should return to Chennai.

In the evening at 6.30 I go to Dumdum Airport Gate number 2 near the same place i.e. near by the Kali Temple and in opposite of Mosque (Masjid).

In this time, I want to see her to wear Shari (wear Cloth in Indian Style). According to my speech Shipra wear Shari in Bengali Style. She has Black skin but she wears a dip black Shari and also wears gold ornament. She became nice and catches my hand and walk with me in the side of the VIP road. Talking so many words that how much I have payment whether I becoming permanent employee of the Railway. I am getting job as permanent basis etc.

Minimum One and Half hour I talk with her. In the return time I also think whether I am in right truck or not.

But mind attack to her. In the young age it also reality that someone may be attracting towards a young girl and feel enjoy if he walks side by side with her.

I promise to her that I should remember her words when go Chennai. On 27 -04 -03 I start journey on general compartment of Howrah Chennai Coromandel Exp., 2841. I reach and get the briefcase from the Quarter of Mr. Beg. Gobinda help me by carry the briefcase on a cycle. I reach at Perambur and meat with Rajkishor and start to live with him.

Next day I submit the SC certificate but I am not getting the appointment order. The clerk tells me two or three days may be taking.

In this prior of time I expanse minimum 9000 Rupee for up down and Hotel Charge and take food from restaurant.

Day by day the clerk tells me, that tomorrow or day after tomorrow you get appointment. In the same time one RRB/ Patna also have examination. So, I ask that for fifteen day I may go to Calcutta. The clerk says, "Within one weak you may get order definitely." But what is the meaning of the word "definitely" the Tamilian may understand English, it is doughty full. Seven days pass out. I miss the examination of RRB/ Patna. On the other hand, I have no permanent address that can I applied for the post of Junior Engineer in RRB/ Patna where vacancy fourteen (14) in Mechanical has and on RRB/ Muzaffarpur have Ten (10) post of Depot Store keeper. We use all the English terms and which once up on a time start by British Government. Mr. Bug is also working from British period. The Railway start by British Govt. of India.

After 10 days of Rajkishor Medical Examination, he gets the appointment order. He come at Chennai on 22nd April and gets the appointment order on 2nd May. But my medical Examination held on 10th April and already passes 20 days. Hence, I become very doubtful and the clerk harasses me day by day. Sometimes feeling in my life harassment done by other in maximum times and mind cannot work freely. I am feeling that it may be better to death at the stage of sickness in the year 1989 but I get life again. The Physician Dr. D.K. Ray told me, "You are lucky and get rebirth in your life. Maximum cases of Intestinal Tuberculosis cannot diagnosis."

My feeling become instabilities in my life. I am thinking it is better to death in my life. The death is the true things in life and must come into the time. I think sometimes several people lead life normally and any work is not a small think to me that require leading life. From the work you get experience in reality of life. It is very difficult some times that you can observe that someone become very important personality who works in the lower level. For example Mr. Micelle Faraday, in his childhood he did work as book binder and got chance to read the valuable book and at the stage when he heard the lecture of Humph David, he send a smell note book to him and got the work of bottles washing but he was not lose his mind and try to gathered knowledge. I think all this thing and in the early morning I go to Church and payer to Mother Merry. Offer to Her that please Mother Merry give strength in my mind. Several days are passing like these. I walk around the church corridor and set down near by the Idol of Jesus Christ. Jesus was a great person in the world and due to truth, he lost his life. When Jesus alive he was not got much priority like to day and his mother have influence. Human being payer to him but nobody think that the truth of the life is the main matter of his life and for that he sacrifices his life but not bend on the force of enemy.

I may be bending but cannot break in the mind. I try to control my mind and try to improve mental stability in the life.

Many days pass in the month of May 2003. I am thinking to attend the competition examination for Junior Engineer and discussing about the matter of employment notice. Rakishor, Gobinda Biswas and Nirmal again and again telling me whatever it is that you forget, you have no service till now. You are not getting any chance in the Junior Engineering Exam. But it is in my mind that in 2001 and 2002 I passed the Scientific Assistant Examination in Atomic Research department one at Kalpukkam and another at Kolkata. On the other hand, I become pass preliminary Examination in Telecommunication, Interlocking Signal Maintainer Gr III. It means I have preparation to pass examination. I have deficiency to speak in English and also weak in the subject Heat power. But maximum question asked in Atomic Research Centre from Heat Power. I am not success at the Final Interview or Final written.

Rajkishor and Gobinda several times tell me, "You might not be success. All the life, you may be in the Southern Railway, try to prepare for departmental examination." But through departmental examination require 10 years to 15 years to become as Junior Engineer, because after 5 year you are eligible to appear for Technician or Fitter Gr III, than One-year training should be completed then another 5 years should be stay to appear for Junior Engineering Examination.

Hence, I am not agreeing to walk on their truck. I try to get a fixed room on which address I shall be applied for the post of Junior Engineer Gr II. On 24th May I get appointment order. In between this time some time I draw my picture and make flower by west paper and hear the song and every day in the morning and evening gone to Church. Payer to Jesus and learn Bible. In Bible say god is everywhere and in the same matter also say in our Upanishad and we believe. So, in the concept of our Hinduism and Christianity have no different. We payer to god that to lead life better and get something be good for me and in church I observe that young girl carried due to mistake of her in the rout of life. Some one boy carried nearby Jesus and says that his lover left him and acting with him for some time. If we believe on God and prayed to God, automatically can gathered strength in our mind. In free mind you express the all word to God and God help you. But you try again and again in your life. In this month Mr. N. Suryanarayana become friend. He is feeling I am pass maximum time along. He gives accompany with me, he come to my rental room by riding a two-wheeler moped and we both go to some times to Chennai Central of Botham Book Publisher Pvt. Ltd. In Calcutta have books market at

Collage Street but we are not seen like larger complex which I have seen at Chennai.

British rule starts first in Bengal but build main city Calcutta, Bombay and Madras in their own hand. Several building of British period in these three cities have till now. Naval docks build in British period at Chennai. Army Head Quarter builds up by Lord William at Calcutta which name change as Sahid Menara. Sometimes I remember all these things. Hence European, mainly English, French, Portuguese and Spanish were trying to find out the new routes and new land. We may be in the same land. In west Bengal maximum people do not want the come out from West Bengal and through traveling they feel fear ness in their mind. I try to follow the European and think when first time English, French people come in India they also have no idea of Indian language and India is multilingual country. I may face some problem in Tamil Nadu but should learn Tamil language. How they tackle on the environment of without knowledge of one language, I try to understand. Now a day's bilingual books are available, by which we can learn one language through other language and maximum bilingual books are learn through English. So, it becomes necessary to learn English.

Day passing in this way then I may get the order on 24th march. We go to Basin Bridge where the division sends us.

S. Satish Kumar, N. Suryanarayana and I go together at Basin Bridge and meet with Chief Office Superintendent Murli. Murli introduce with DME (Divisional Mechanical

Engineer) Ran Vijay and ADME Methide. They ask me, "Why you come at Chennai." I answered, "I cannot get any chance at Kolkata for that region I come in this city for work." They both sign on the order copy and Murli tell us to meet tomorrow at 8.00A.m.

Next day early morning we come together and discussing the matter about our current position. N. Suryanarayana complete Bachelor degree in Law (B.A. L.L.B), S. Satish Kumar complete Diploma in Mechanical Engineering, I have complete Diploma in Mechanical Engineering. M.Dili Babu complete Bachelor degree in Civil Engineering but all are joining in the post of Khalashi helper due to cannot pass in the Examination of proper post and the merit may not be use in proper way.

In Tamil Nadu, West Bengal, Andhra Pradesh and other Non-Hindi states peoples face same problem. That from the base we get education through our Mother tongue and up to class 10+2 stage, we flow the same and somewhere Degree level like B.Sc., B.Com., B.A. also complete through our own language but in the competition, examination attained through English or Hindi. Someone can speak Hindi little bit but cannot write Hindi and cannot read Hindi. Hence, we get failure in competition Exam. On the other hand, Hindi speaking people get advantage of Hindi version question. They learn in Hindi on the all stage in the education system. Hence it was better if English are only given priority and now the leading political groups are Hindi people because within 28 states there are 14 states Hindi and Non-Hindi states are not united.

By this discussion we stand on the platform at Perambur. The 'B' Train comes and we catch the train. When Vasherpati Jiva Station crosses, we understand the train is 'B' which is going towards Chennai Beach Station.

We get down from train in the next station Vasherpati Jiva and from Vasherpati Jiva we catch Auto Rickshaw and attend duty on Basin Bridge. Mr. Murli send us by the order of DME to E-Batch by which maintain work of Chennai Howrah Mail 6003/6004 be done. Washing and cleaning work given to us. First day the Section Engineer sends us together to wash the outer wall of the couches. I see all are in fresh dress and have no black dress with Greece and oil. I heard to Gobinda Biswas that his shirt and pants becoming very dirty but Nirmal get electrical work in EMU at Avadi. I feel that may be no problem to me. We are suppling water to them who washing the wall of the couches. I discuss to Rajkishar that we have wash the couches outer wall with shop solution and water. Mainly supply water to them I see the ladies people washing basin and latrine by brush and shop solution. I think they may always clean the basin and latrine and explain that other people work inside cleaning.

Next day morning we attend the duty. Section Engineer (TXR) sends N. Suryanarayana with the washing group of the outer wall but send S. Satish Kumar and me to interior. S. Satish Kumar are Tamil people; hence he is talking in Tamil language with partner and immediately start too sweeping with Bhanu Moti but I became with another 50 years old lady and see the work become latrine cleaning. I weep in my mind that God give me such types of work. By prayer to God that he should give power to control mind. It was my habit that if I see stools of human being, I feel vomiting. Two times I vomit at the latrine due to highly duty condition. Maximum Indian people are not learning how the train should be used. They travel and make dirty the train in the bad manner. Maximum Indian are not thinking after my using someone may use that and make the environment dirty as nonsense. For that reason, when train returns to a yard the trains are very dirty. They are not thinking it should be clean by some like me, only use like as uncultured peoples.

I think if I can tolerate stools of human being previously than may try for Medical Course. I heard that several cases come as dangerous condition in the Surgical Department, someone also come the burn condition. This seen is very pathetic. I cannot maintain in these movement. I am better knowledge in Biology but was not enter medical field due to deficiency of my mind strength.

This day four or five couches, the old lady washes the basin and toilet pan by a brush with soap solution. I only wash with water. But after some time, Section Engineer come and tell me you pour the gloves on two hands and rub by steel wool and soap water. I use my left hand for this purpose. S.E. tells me, "Whether you are leftist." I answer, "I am sometime leftist and sometime rightist. I have done some work by left hand and some work by right hand." By left hand I work slowly, then Section Engineer shown how to clean the pan of a toilet. By open hand he starts to rube with steel wool and soap solution. They use right hand easily but if I use right hand than I cannot eat. I start to wash the toilet pan by my hand to wear the gloves. Again, Section Engineer Uma Shankar shows how to clean pan of a toilet. Then I clean the toilet within some couches. The old lady say that we are highly educated but due to situation we are doing like such a job. That old lady is also a Christian but Tamilian.

In the evening I go to the Paramore Church and prayer Mother Marry to give me strength in my life and sit down inside the Church and prayers with other Christian to Jesus but not fill any difference concept of God. Then I get strength in my mind and have no other way to leave the job. So work is work and it should be done what it is may be done.

Next three days S.E. Uma Shankar also sends me to toilet cleaning but he is not sent another candidate. Actually, he makes partiality with me. S. Satish is Tamil and N. Suryanarayana is Telegu. I cannot speak Tamil but they can speak and hence they are not to send like this work by S.E.

Then on 3rd day I say to other that Section Engineer behavior are like partiality, I may discuss or report to DME. DME Ran Bijoy are Bihar people, hence he has also fear ness that DME may favor to me. Then See Section Engineer send S. Satish to toilet cleaning. Then on one day N. Suryanarayana get dusting, meaning to clean set and berth and we get interior sweeping. First sweeping normally then sweeping by using water.

Both start to sweep. In my life this is the first time I sweep 24 couches. My health condition become bad, my waste and back start pain but not get any help. On the other hand, Section Engineer takes inspection and tell us the cleaning are not better condition, after washing with water. Then Satish go and have done work again minimum five couches. At 1.00 O'clock pass but cannot complete. So, we are not going to take food. In the canteen get Rice with somber dal and rasom which test is not better but take that. In the beginning I cannot eat properly after doing these types of works but day by day adjust and sometime weeping in my mind. Then start to read at the Tiffin hour. I am getting some book with me when coming for duty. Days are passing and take diner at night to a hotel i.e. restaurant and in day time in the yard get meal.

Two months passing within this time another Bihar people who newly come at Perambur work shop at Deluxe AC shop name Laxman Ram who get job through officer. The Officer has power to give job in Railway. First, he working as Bungalow peon then by officer power become office peon and by officer power come to workshop within 2 years. He gets the same payment in the Railway but we come by the exam through RRB/ Chennai.

When I heard this and getting the work of latrine cleaning and I cannot tolerate that but keep salient. In the evening go to Church and weep nearby Mother Marry. Days are passing by weeping. Within this period, I try to find out rental room at Villivakkam. Near Villivakkam station again I meet with a retired Deputy Store Controller name Villivanathan who can speak in Hindi. I tell him to get room because he tells me that to give room with bed and if have any problem then pay rent after payment but when I speak with him about the matter of room, he wants Rs.500/-. He come with me and get Rs.500/-

and tell me to get suitcase to his room where as 15 days remain too due date at present room. At this time Suryanarayana enter to rental room. He leaves the room. Suryanarayana tell me, "Why you give rupees to him." I say, "I get new room to his house." He tells me, "You are new person and it is not better to do so." After sometime of the discussion about the matter Suryanarayana leaves the room. I go to Villivakkam to meet him and think if I get room to Villivanathan then may arise problem because he is a lawyer also, he remains along in his house. Suryanarayana also indicate the matter. It is requiring to get return the money from him. By walking I go to Villivakkam where as two station is requiring crossing. I meet with him and say, "I may not get your room because another friend tells me to introduce room owner of a quality room. You return my money." He says, "I already expanse money in my own purpose. You come next Monday."

Next Monday again goes to his house but he is not available. His car driver says that he has another house in far distance from Villivakkam. I learn taxi driving before ten years ago. So, I think to practice car driving if stay at his room but that may be a risky matter after all he is a rich person. Two-week pass, then one day he returns three hundred rupees but for these rupees I come to his house minimum five times.

In these periods I go to Marina beach with Rajkishor, Nirmal and Gabinda for entertainment. I have seen some one set with a computer to get finger print of palm on a white page, then by computer make horoscope and have Rs.10/- charge only. I get interest about the matter then one day make horoscope by the system. In my horoscope there are given a line that I may cheat by a wick person. I think whether Villivanathan be that person.

Time pass to draw of my own photo on a paper which I get nearby me. One day I draw picture on the back side of a mosquito coil packet. By wastage newspaper I make roll and different flower make which set up on the rack and say to Rajkishor, "Ishim Kumar died, only his sole remains and he move nearby you." It is my habit that if I have off time, I try to do some things. On the other hand, I talk to matter that Shipra will give me her photography. Next I visit with her. I write latter to her with color full design. She became all in my mind.

Then one day Rajkishor tell me, "In which house Lax man Ram get rental room there have a vacant room but that room are made by coconut levees. Rent only Rs.400/- and require to give Rs.2000/- advance money. On the other hand, if get some better room there required more advance money, like Rs.5000/- but we have no such money. Rajkishor land money from me, hence advance money is requiring too given by me and I have no interest to stay at Chennai continuously. I should try for Junior Engineer Gr.-II post; I think it is better because he leaves the room after three month and go to Bihar to his native place. He will get his wife and leave the room; I remain within the room. I go to see the condition of rental room. First visit the room and then meet with house owner's wife who get advance money Rs.2000/- from me. Lax man Ram increase rant from Rs.400/- to Rs.500/-. He is old tenant and we are new. When I tell him, "Why you tell 500 rupees per month rant?" He tells me, "You are bachelor; hence it is not any factor, I expanse money to drink win more than Rs.500/-. Why you worry about that?" I tell him, "You have money to expanse to other purpose but I have no interest to do so."

On 22nd July Rajkishor sift from Perambur to Villivakkam GKM colony. I pass preliminary examination in the post of Junior Engineering Gr -II (Electrical) at RRB/Patna. I require appearing in final examination. I give news to Shipra and tell her to get photography with her when she will come to meet with me. Within this two month I may not prepare for any examination. I read B. L. Theresa objective electrical, electronics and telecommunication book and mechanical engineering book of R.K. Join.

I get privilege pass from Chennai Central to Patna via Kolkata. I get ticket in such a way that I can be able to meet with Shipra for a while. I keep the matter as secret to my parent and think to flash out the matter to my maternal uncle Mr. Arun. I talk the matter with wife of Arun. She tells me that I am a Diploma in mechanical engineering candidate but Shipra is only class VIII pass. It is not better but I try to give priority to love.

I go to Kolkata and that day evening 7 P.m. meet with Shipra. She comes to meet with me to wear blue share (cloth in Bengali style). We walk on the VIP road and Air Port out part. She hands over her two photographs. It is the first time someone give me her photography. Next day I go to my maternal uncle's house and shown the photography to my anti. She tells me, “Shipra is good looking young girl but only one point that her qualification to require some things more.”

I go to Patna for examination and get her photography with me and shown to my friend who also pass the examination. But examination is not become good where as I was promise to Shipra to go to Goddess Kali temple at Dishwasher. But I make mistake at question booklet number and use blade for correction but that is unfair means. Hence the paper may be cancelling in my case but answer also hard. That is my coolness of my mind. Otherwise I cannot forget the matter. I inform the matter to Shipra but she cannot understand. I shall try again for the post of JE-II. I return to Chennai and buy one Electrical and another Electronics objective book of Rajput and Honda respectively. At Patna final examination they give Electronics question maximum.

I try again and start to send application to RRB to follow the weekly Employment Newspaper. I start to read again as well as start to draw Shipra’s photography by student oil color. I buy camel student colour and art paper. On the paper write in various colours “I Love you Shipra” in Hindi, in Bengali I also write the same.

In this time, I read the books also. My style is like that read main theory and read question answer of short question. In objective question have four alternative options on which only have one correct answer. I mainly mark the correct answer by a pencil then read the question answer. I repeatedly read the matter again and again. It is my habit that

I read the Sum or problem which example given to the text books but at the time of examination I directly solve the problem easily. From class VII to DME complete by these methods whereas friend surprise that how I can do so. If I have any guide than it become easy to me to understand. In diploma course when I have privet tutor at second year and third year, I only follow the sum which have been solve by the teacher on the exercise book and which given to practice. Any more problems may not solve. My friend is not believed this matter. One day my friend Gouranga told me, "We have no such capability to maintain the quality." Some time I become worry about social matter and sometime political matter. In this time, I heard that the Tamilian people marriage with their relation and mainly they marriage with the daughter of his sister. But it is genetically and in the social view not the right things. Sister daughter is equivalent to myself daughter. In the life someone plays and read with his sister then sister marriage held and her daughter born. As a child we carry in our hand. But in Tamil Nadu they have no feeling that calls Mama which means uncle they take as the Jokes.

In India English people come and at Calcutta they first founded East India Company then on the war of Palashi hold on 1757. It was the better things happened in India because after Palashi war British rule start in Indian soil. Lord Buntings comes as the vicars and Raja Ram Mohan Ray born at the same time. Raja Ram Mohan Ray was not a foolish person who supports the English language as the official language in India. He learns Sanskrit, Hindi, Bengali, Urdu,

Pharisee, and Arabic but choose English as the medium of education because in English language the people build up so many valuable books. In their life they travel all over world and write their experience. In India a multilingual country and in every Indian language have no such valuable book to get experience about the world. Actually, how Indian can be developed the educational system before British rule? Muslim ruler ruled out about 900 year. Hindu only has culture to read Ramayana and Mahabharata and with each other quarrel their Ram is the great or Maha Mata Kali (The goddess Kali) is great. Who has more power? I also believe the god and remember Gita which have true word "Koram Karo Phal Ka Bhabana Mate Show Cha." That's means do work but you don't think about the result. Indian follows the words in the wrong way they believe only payer to god and god may solve the problem. But karma i.e. works, if work has not done than how you can get the result. They cannot try to see whether we are in the right truck. They had concept that out of India had 'Malacha' mean untouchable person and if they take food from them, they become degrade in the root of their life.

Dharma is the main things. Dharma means in the Indian general seance that religious faith. Religious faith and culture generally mix up. Darmo is the great things that are you should try to speak truth and try to do good work for other. Not harm to other, but how many peoples believe and follow those, maximum peoples speak lies on the getting advantage in their life.

Actually, how Indian can develop educational system? So many people tell lie to get advantage from other and unnecessary also tell lie in such a way that other should believe that is true. I feel all the things. At British period Raja Ram Mohan Ray Abolished Sati system by support of Lord Bunting. But today I have no back support to change the system of Tamil Nadu that is the marriage system with sister's daughter. Sister become mother in law; on the other hand, grandfather become Father in law. They have no concept about the meaning of Uncle and first call uncle then build up other relation for marriage. They might not think whether that is better or not. In north India if hear such things then spite to them.

I work in Basin Bridge yard and on the rout of my journey Perambur station also there. After sift to Villivakkam I may not go daily to Perambur church but on returning time some time go to church for a while and payer nearby Mother Marry and Jesus. I get mental strength and try to follow the christen culture. At night I read books to prepare for competition examination for the post of JE-II. As well as draw the picture of Shipra for entertainment, sometime black and white Xerox also printed by oil color and dress change. Cutting and pasting be done to other newspaper photography to the painting and seen the get up.

I feel that Tamil Nadu previous name Madras state was under English peoples but the people may not revolution of their society. They have system of relation marriage. My friend Laxman, Rajkishor tell me, "What require thinking the matter." Then one day again meet with Villivanathan to return my remaining Rs.200/-. But four times require collecting the money. Once up on a time think he may not return the money but ultimately get my money that is enough. In this time, I collect several types of grass shed to make a greeting for Shipra. I make a beautiful greeting card by an art paper and other material which I collect from different place and shown to my friend. They also have seen the photography of Shipra.

In the mean time I talk with Shipra on telephone but she speaks different tones. When I tell her that I draw her photography and make a greeting, she tells me that it is not require. My parent sought to her relative whose houses are nearby my house. I informed to my parent that I agree to marriage to Shipra by a letter and what actually happened that I don't know. She tells me that they are poor and her parent are not agreeing to arrange marriage to far away. I am in emotion on her and want to lead marriage life with her. Several years pass out, several times become sick and become afraid. I cannot get proper preparation for competition examination. On the other hand, father was not agreeing to give capital to start small scale business in our house. Days are passing to our house without earning. Friends of Kolkata were laughed at me but the matter might not understand by my father. Friends of Kolkata someone start commercial art and small-scale business where as I know fine arts and also commercial arts. I made help to them at the first stage of their business but I can do nothing due to my father. He might not give permission to start business to our house boundary. I also able to build up sculpture in wooden, in stone medium and by cement, as well as clay modeling also known but I was helpless. In the field of art water color, oil color, poster colours printing also learn to seen nearby laboratory. Canvas portraits painting have done in my house. When I was joining fast time to an art school, my Art teacher told me, "You are your own master and you can find out your mistake." He was given to draw a figure of human being and natural scenery but I had done some mistake and told him that of my mistake. He was proud to me also. At class X, I took admission in art school. My art teacher gave me to draw some scenery and when he had seen that I have knowledge about color combination than call me to his house to draw his order copy. In his house I learn to draw Japan art and use Fuji colour. I choose colour according to picture and my own chose I finish the order copy but the painting was so good that he also became satisfy. He suppresses that how I learned the printing! But in 1989 I attacked by T.B. and left art school. After leaving of art school I used to build up clay modeling, wooden sculpture. Now a day's work education is up to class VIII but at our stage had work education compulsory up to class X. Paper cutting drawing was up to class VIII. We also had physical education had to practice. Yoga had done and maintains register. We draw the figure of yoga. Several friends came to my house for drawing also. Within ten minute I had done ten yoga figures in my class when candidate is not able to draw picture. Till March 2003 several neighbors came to my house for made a clay modeling for their children or drawing to their school purpose in biological subject. I also had done because some time remains free.

Drawing is a necessary activity in our life. In biology, in physics, in mathematics, in geography subject requires drawing the picture of a system to understand the subject. Now a day computer graphics and Auto CAD come into market and drawing become easy and require learning language of computer also.

In 2000 Auto CAD learned by me, I follow an American publication book of relies 12 and I try to learn 3D figure. One day instructor saw that I had done 3 D figure and he sought to me that it was advance course. Then he asks that how I learn that. When I told the real fact to read a book and try to learn. He tries to avoid guiding me where as he gives his time to another candidate. Then time pass out version also change but due to out of the field work, I also am not continuing to use computer drawing.

Now a day I work as Khalasi in Group-D category on yard and cleaning work have done by me. In Indian yard automatic mobbing system is not use but use modern chemical in the yard. Outside wall of couch washing are not improve but hand brash, bucket and by manual work washing with soap solution be done.

Actually, management system is not worry about improvement. Indian are not trying to invent new technology. They are always remaining dependent to other and get technology from foreign country. They say what have necessary to invent in our country, we have required to maintain our religion that enough and not try to change their mentality. I am different, I try to draw some figure of new system but cannot express to anybody. In the meantime, Divisional Mechanical Engineer come on our rack for inspection. He calls me as Dada which means elder brother. In this time, he asks me, "How are you?" I answer to him, "Life passes out by anyhow." Then he discusses with Junior Engineer (TXR) about roof board and panel board. In this time, I also use some painting term. DME Mr. Ran Vijay understand that I have knowledge about drawing and say, "I know that Bengali people have better concept about art and from your word it is conform that you have knowledge about art and painting." DME give instruction to make Bengali roof board to Chennai Howrah Mail because Howrah is in West. But in Roof board and panel board only write Tamil, English and Hindi. Within Tamil Nadu the Chennai Howrah Mail run only two hour and Tamil only understand by Tamil people but maximum board is in Tamil. I cannot speak in Tamil language. I generally communicate through English and Hindi as requirement. But on the body movement I also understand Tamil language some time. DME give instruction to TXR to use me for better work.

Next I get some priority to TXR and start to do some work of printing. I have knowledge about tensile cutting which I learn to my father. My father is an ex railway service man who worked at Kanchrapara Eastern railway work shop as painter Gr. I. He had done job like as latter writing and printing. In English there have five pattern of latter writing which I learn from my father. Gelation type, Italian type, Roman type, ornamentally type, ordinary type, etc. Gelation latter be maintaining in 1:2 ratio on breath and length. But it is deferent in case of 'W', its ratio is 3/2: 2. My fathers also teach me the color combination. I express all these matter to TXR. They give painting, tensile cutting work in English, in Bengali, in Tamil also. Previously I started to read, write in Tamil but left because either English or Hindi is requiring in competition examinations. I apply for the post of JE by GKM colony address. I can write in Tamil latter script. Some time they try to get work twice at a time. But I might not get more money for extra work and may not get any advantage at promotion, hence I also get require time to do that work and when I get time at lunch period, I read my books. Every day I get books with me where as that is a problem to keep, I have no locker to keep that. I use Section engineer's locker and read for require to advancement. In the morning I read books from 6.00 A.m. to 8.00 A.m. then immediately fresh to brash my tooth and face to wash by water. I come to Basin Bridge yard. At canteen get breakfast then start to my duty, at lunch hour after getting lunch I again read the book and sometime think my past matter as well as future prospect. If call letter gets at present address, I appear at RRB exam. TXR give Dearness Rest (DR) to old worker if they have done extra work but I am new person for that region he gets extra work from me but are not given any DR. Now a days they do not send to clean toilet, maximum time I have done dusting i.e. to clean set and glass window require to close or given watering. Watering that is to fill up water in the overhead tank in the couches by the help of hose pipe. By the help of two hose pipe 24 couch's water tanks i.e. 4*24=96 tanks are requiring to fill up. Otherwise cleaning work be done by Diskiller chemical on entrains of the all couches. I have no extra time to read the book. In lunch time I finish my lunch within 15 minutes then start to read where as other try to sleep for 45 minutes. I am in E batch hence if have any order couches then I finish work as quickly as possible. I have done cleaning three order couches within 3.00 P.m. to 3.30 P.m. then take bath and become fresh. I have done dusty work hence require to take bath after finishing my work. In Chennai from Perambur rental room I shifted to GKM colony but take bath at yard.

Now I take room at Villivakkam 14/1 GKM Colony, 32 streets, Chennai 600082. We give Rs.500/- per month as rent. Rajkrishor were not given advance money because on August he goes to Bihar to his native place and after returning he will come with his wife, then will get separate room. Rajkishor get incentive after one month of his joining. He gets Rs.1200/- per month extra because he works at work shop. We appeared in same examination and his ranking was beyond me but from CPO office his file sand to work shop. I observed that Laxman Ram come at 1.00 P.m. for taken lunch and may not go in second half and sometime go to at second half. Laxman Ram also works in same department with Rajkishor. They mutually punch their card. Rajkishor are punching Laxman Ram's card in morning, at launch time out and in and in the evening out also punch. I have in such a move that we have done the work in full load. Rajkishor and Lax man both enjoy. They have done in A/C Deluxe section of Perambor carriage and work. They are making duplicity day by day. Also take sleep at air-condition couch at launch hours by on the AC.

I weep in my mind but not take the job in work shop. So, I get less money and more work. So, when Rajkishor tell me, "You get better the work then me." I tell him, "If you have done sweeping 24th couches within one day, then you may understand that it is a harder works or not. Minimum 4 hours taken to sweep by a groom and bake pain happened. One day if you have done like this job then you can understand."

They are satisfied to their job but how can I be satisfying to my job. So, I buy Employment News weekly and applying by the address 14/1 GKM colony. N. Suryanarayana several times tell me to give his address in the application. Two or three application also sends by his address. I give his address to corresponding address. But seen after three-month Suryanarayana change batch by the help of COS Murli through application to DME for take more study time. His house is a great distance from Villivakkam. Two or three times have gone to his house. He changes his batch. Now coming at 3.00 P.m. and go to house 6.00 P.m. because he has known person in the yard. He is getting more time for study but maximum time pass through sleeping.

On 5th August, 2003; Rajkishor have gone to his native place and after 15 days he returns with his wife. Within this period, he is present by punching the card with the help of Laxman Ram. He saves the leaves by the help of his friend. On the other hand, I lapse all leaves for examinations. I also have one paper remain in Mathematics subject in B. Sc. course. I study B. Sc. course through IGNOU University. In IGNOU University I get B. Sc. on the subject physics (Mechanics and waves, Electrical circuit and electronics, and two practical), Chemistry (Physical chemistry, organic chemistry, inorganic chemistry and two practical), Mathematics (Algebra and Analytical Geometry and linear algebra), Biology (cell biology, genetics and one practical). In foundation course have Science and technology, Humanity and social science, English and Bengali. On the other hand, in practical orientation course get Export procedure and Documentation, Marketing management, Secretarial practice and office organization & Management all subject pass within 4 years but Linear algebra cannot pass to appear several times. In June month I also appeared in linear algebra subject at Kolkata.

When Rajkishor come with his wife get the fan from me because he buys the ceiling fan at the rate Rs.350/-. In that night how can I sleep, I worry about this. I payer to god too start rain for a while to cool weather for me. I sleep on the front side of the room to open the door. At night 1P.m. god help me. The rain starts and when the weather becomes cooled then sleep.

When come to Villivakkam first Laxman Ram give kerosene oil stove and Rajkishor buy some utensil and start food preparation by shear but Rajkishor now become separate, hence get stove and utensil and take kodum i.e. water jar with him. I buy two kodum, one dice and one tumbler. So, stop to make meals. Again, start eating in restaurant.

I draw the picture of Shipra and also understand in my mind have attraction to her. But Shipra are not thinking about me.

I make greetings and the color Xerox have done from Perambur center and also try how several changes be done by the photography without destroying that. I have two photographs and make Xerox, then by drawing and painting make several designs and take different picture by the help of color Xerox. Then again set the photographs in previous condition. Days are passing by drawing and reading, taking food at restaurant and work.

On September some order come which tell me by CTXR Uma Shankar. Then asked to COS and understand they call for Saloon Attendant. I discuss the position of Saloon Attendant and ask that I may get more time or not. I must try for junior Engineer through Railway Recruitment Board. I require to time to read the books. I appear in the interview. Before interview I meet with Mahammad Afzal who tell me that once up on a time, he was a Saloon Attendant and now he is technician group II and I get lot of time and get CR, DR if go to on line.

Hence when ADME Abdul Khadar get interview I tell him, "I know cooking like fish fried, fish finger, fish roll, Brainy and all Bengali item. Actually, I learn these things when Kanoo start a shop of Egg roll and fish fried and the Bengali dices learn from my mother.

My mother has knowledge about many items. She knows clay modeling, teach various designs by thread and needle. In our child hood my mother make shirt, pants of us by swing machine. We play with a doll which made in clay done by my mother. I remember that day I was child, at the age of six my elder brother gets a wooden lion made by my grandfather. The wheels attach at bottom part. I sat on the back of the lion and he pulled the lion by a strong thread. That lion made by the father of my mother. My grandfather Noranda Nath was a great artist and he also wrote poem which store by me but cannot published. In our poor condition our talent remains to us. We cannot expanse money in any field.

I express my knowledge about cooking when Mr. Abdul Khadar asked me whether I have knowledge to cook food.

S. Sathish Kumar also appears in interview and gives answer. Actually, we give willingness to accept saloon attendant post but N. Suryanarayana and M. Deli Babu give unwillingness and give written letter.

S. Sathish and I both are working in the same batch. In this time mainly we have done watering and dusting work. Sometimes I have done painting.

According to DME order TXR tell me to make Bengali roof board. I make tensile and also make ten boards in Bengali in the first lot, then ten Bengali boards paint complete. I feel enjoy that next my basic increase from 2500 to 2630 and shall getting some things more DA.

We are working and waiting for the order of Saloon Attendant. On November, I get the order and 05/11/03 I get the release from E- batch and join in RS batch as Saloon Attendant. S. Satish Kumar and I both get the order as Saloon Attendant. S. Satish Kumar was on leave for three days, after two day he also joins as Saloon Attendant.

Now I join in new batch and CTXR. Krishna Shame is Section Engineer. First day be introducing with me and tell me you carry out your work. I start washing work with other. After two days S. Satish Kumar come and joins in RS batch. Krishna Shame tell me, "You are Bengali person and CME also Bengali person; hence he may help you if he became satisfy and if you pass RRB written exam than at the stage of interview he may help you." I know that now a day's interview abolishes. Only single or double written examination held for selection but I kept silent because he is CTXR and I am Saloon Attendant. Then also introduce other person of RS-Batch, they tell me if CME satisfy, you may also get one-way transfer to Howrah. But I have no interest about one-way transfer. But thinks if CME or other office satisfy than may request to get work of my relative and they may join as bungalow peon. Laxman Ram, Kaniaiha ad their friends whose work as office peon in the Divisional office, they first join as bungalow peon. I meet with a parson Mr. Mahdo and his nephew. Mr. Mahdo are now head clerk who also joined previously as bungalow peon through officer and by salutation, now becoming head clear and his all nephew are working in Railway as peon and other become office peon by officer power.

CTXR Krishna Shame tells us, "You make white shirt and white pant. First, we think, we buy white shirt from footpath nearby Chennai Central station. My self and Satish have gone to buy the shirt but seen there have some more or less defect. Then carefully check those shirts and also verifies in other place, then understand that shirts are sell 50 rupees each but those are old one. They collect the old usable shirt and wash very well then get here to shell. Then decide we will buy new one.

S. Satish Kumar has a new white shirt but I have no shirt and pant. We go to whole shell market and in a shop say, we have order to make white shirt and white pant to all, there have another candidate who also will make shirt and pant. The shop keeper takes one hundred rupees per meter for pant piece. We get two pant pieces and get shirt piece free then by the help of shop keeper, we meet with a tailor. We make pant and shirt of @100 rupees per pant and 60 rupees for a shirt.

I feel in my mind after six month I can wear a better shirt and pant. Now a day we use ordinary shirt and pant. We have not required changing the dress for doing the work.

But my dream becomes only to get a chance at J E-II. CTXR send me with Damodaran in the CME carriage RA 89883. From Chennai central, the saloon attached with Mangalore express.

I become ready and wear white shirt and paint. In the other train other saloon are already gone to Madurai. Balnaroshima are in RA1 couch. Narasimha Murti has gone in RA 4153.

I am staying inside the saloon couch RA 89883 on the attendant side. CME come and CEE also comes in the same couch. I see the face of both. CME is Bengali person name Jayanto Gosh. Next day we reach at Madurai. In the morning tea prepares. When CME go to gust house V. Damodaran tell me to clean the toilet. I mob the toilet by a cloth, and thinking; now coming as Saloon Attendant. I am working as a servant in the house. Prepare tea; serve it and then toilet mob also done by me. I am weeping is my mind and thinking weather God help me to improve my position or not. In the last night I got dinner in a Bengali hotel. But today how I get meals I cannot understand. Then Narasimha Murty calls me at saloon RA 4153 and gives me food to eat. I get rice and somber but I am with Damodaran who may not call me for lunch at noon. After finish our lunch I go to Meenakshi temple with Satish. Once up on a time I promise to goddess that I offer to goddess something hence I offer to Meenakshi that only flower. I payer to goddess Meenakshi get a chance in J. E. -II at Railway. Then we come back to station and set at RA89883. Damodaran tell me, "To day, at night CME will take chicken. For CME chicken masala and paratha, be prepared at night." I also feel that if I also get chicken at night that is better but I remain silent. Damodaran prepare chicken masala and paratha for CME and for us prepare chicken rosha and chapati. Damodaran tell me at night I shall get dinner with him. I get dinner at night with Damodaran. I am not requiring to expanse for food at saloon but require to clean toilet. I think that it is my luck.

Days are passing and next GM special start to ready to go at Trivandrum. I flow a person newly come at RS room and give instruction to us. Section Engineer (TXR) Mr. Krishna Shame give instruction to do work as watering in GM special. 10 couches attach in GM special. RA1, RA90901, RA90902, RA89883, two first class AC coaches, two second class AC coaches and two SLR attach with GM special. We try to finish watering. In the meantime, new person additionally give instruction to us. He tells me, "You go and get the washing brush from the first SLR." I go to first SLR but not get any brush and see in the rack side have a broken brush and getting with me but in the middle path someone conductor person wants that brush. I have hand over that and come in empty hand. I tell him, "I not get any brush there." He tells me, "Leave it."

On the other hand, S. Satish tell me that new person gives him order to do some work but S. Krishna Shame soughed to that person and express one person cannot do two works at a time.

At night, the GM special starts at 9.30pm. Next day morning when train passes through near by a hilly area, I write two poems in Bengali. I see a small plant on the side of rail road and have a beautiful yellow colour flower. I write the poem on the matter; several plants grow in the road side. Train pass out, many people say about the beautiful flower but he not gets for offering god and the flower are helpless because he not grows inside a garden. GM special at 5 P.m. reach then again return after inspection.

In RS-batch Section engineer Krishna Shame sifted to Rajdhani batch and that new person take the charge that was given instruction in GM special.

In this time, I have no interest to go on line. But I am in the Saloon Attendant post hence it also necessary to go on line. Five times send me on line and every time cancel the program.

In this time, I send greeting to Shipra, I want her as a life partner. After 30 days the card is not return to me and then I think that she may accept. I start to draw her picture again and also make colour Xeroxes and changing dresses by printing.

In this time one day I go to Palghat with AGM carriage RA 4152. I meet with PA Nasir and peon Narasimha. Both tell me, "Next AGM wife will be coming and she select whether you become permanent attendant or not." AGM's name K. K. Panda, Hindi speaking people, hence AGM speak in Hindi with me.

The PA and peon ask me whether I have knowledge about carry making. I express that I can make chapati and other types of carry. They go to Kaveri gust house and I stay at saloon. After one day return at Chennai. In this time, I get food from Vegetarian Restaurant of Railway.

Next I again go to line with AGM carriage. The movement is done up to Madurai. In last time went to Meenakshi temple. I go to Internet center and try to find out the term End Examination result for MTE2.

Through IGNOU in the course of B Sc. in last time I appear in the same subject at last June but cannot pass. So, my B. Sc. course is not completed. But the E-mail address is change and cannot find out in E-mail address www.ignou.in.com. Then I come back to saloon. I am staying in officer's couch. Here build up a small shed and for staying build up Kaveri gust house. I travel the place and return to couch. One police guard wants a tool for sitting nearby couch. His duty is to guard the AGM and his carriage. He also can speak in Hindi. He explains that once up on a time he run behind someone but today he become Deputy Railway minister and now a day's same times he has duty to security for Dy. Railway minister and previously Dy. Railway minister was a Mafia. In Indian, it is natural seen and hence when that police person getting duty as a guard for Dy. Railway minister, he weeps on his mind but can do nothing.

I get the meal at Vegetable Railway Restaurant. The PA and peon come to carriage two times and I also clean the toilet before taken bath. In carriage, saloon attendants take bath. The toilet and bed sit are taken from carriage to gust house for AGM, PA by peon from me.

Days passing by weeping and at the time of on line I also get completive books for reading at saloon couch when get off time. I shall try for upper grade post. But at these stage Interview abolish and selection be done on the basis of final written examination.

PA and peon come to carriage two times and inform me that AGM return at four o-clocks so I also clean the handle of each door of the carriage. Inspection part of the carriage and the Denying hall door in both sides clean by me.

AGM come at 5.30 P.m.; train also change to attach the saloon. When AGM and his family come in the Denying hall, then Sr. DME of Madurai enter into the carriage. In this time AGM family and his one son and one daughter also come. His son is approximately age 35 years or above but not working and his daughter minimum age nineteen years. After some time, Sr. DME goes outside. Then they call me and take interview. AGM Madam ask my qualification and discuss in other matter, I attach mug stand and new steel mug in the both toilets. She expresses now when she takes bath, she faces problem. Then I ask, "What problem you face, you shown to me, I may try to solve." She calls her daughter who is inside to bathroom. When her daughter Poly comes out from toilet, she shows the position of the mug stand. Then I say, "In this toilet, comet position in not proper and passage is wastage. But on the other toilet mug stand position is proper because both purposes can be solving that is for toilet and bath." She explains, "We are Indian and have no habit to use comet, India become independent but system may not change. In British India English peoples use comet." Son of AGM say, "You may get chance in Junior Engineering post then leave this job but we want a permanent attendant. You may go to higher post but the process may take more time." I say, "You are right. If I pass the examination for junior engineer post, then certificate verification be done by RRB, then Medical test etc. be done by the department." He tells me, "Yes, that for time consuming matter, you carried out as permanent attendant work in this carriage." Then carriage starts to move by an engine. The peon starts to prepare chapati and vegetable soup. I serve chapati and carry to them. I feel that how restaurant boys serve in a five-stars hotel.

Then carriage attach with train and our return journey start by Mangalore Chennai mail. Next day in the early morning we come into Chennai Central station. They get down and go to their bungalow by an ambassador. I sought down the window and lock the saloon couch. I come to yard and discuss the matter with S. Satish that how I tackle to them. Someone tells me a friend come from Calcutta and wait for me in the RS room. I think that who may be come at afternoon. I was at rack and I hear that someone come at RS room to meet with me. I see that person come to meet with me who was come to Chennai to verify original certificate by RRB and stay with me at hotel. Then so many times he asked on telephone about the post and asked me about the position of court case. But I told him, "You leave it and you know that it is India. Hence court case may continue up to 10 years also. You try for other job." I also try for other job but not get any chance. He also is the same. His name is Basant Topo.

Basant Topo is a tribal christen. He can speak in English, Hindi and Bengali. His father was working at Kharagpur in South Eastern Railway. Hence once up on a time they were at railway quarter but then they came capture land of railway and build up illegal house. At Kharagpur my eldest sister lives at Talbagicha area near by Talbagicha market. We select in same examination for Khalashi but he gets appointment to late. In joint employment notice call in Employment News those are for RRB/Chennai, RRB/Bangalore and RRB/ Trivandrum. Now Bangalore become under different zone and its head quarter are Hubli. That becomes South Western Railway zone. He was given his choice for RRB/Bangalore. But due to becoming new zone; he is not getting joining in that zone. After all he was select for Southern Railway.

Basant Topo tell me story that he lost his luggage and Rs.10000/- in his incoming journey by Howrah Chennai mail. He had upper berth and he got sleep to lock his briefcase by a chain lock at bottom part under lower berth. But in the next morning seen that only there were a small chain part remains with berth's hook. He keeps money into briefcase, hence his hand become empty. He has required helping. I believe him and tell the story to other and get him with me to my rental room. I tell the story to Laxman Ram and Kaniha and tell them to inform to house owner that an unwanted event happened with him, hence Basant Topo will remain with me. Actually, same things I had seen in my life when I returning to Howrah from Chennai last time. My house owner does not understand English or Hindi, for that region I inform to Laxman Ram to tell the story to House owner and want permission to live Basant Topo with me because he has no money in his hand. Next day I also try to speak to house owner but they tell that they have no problem.

I show the drawing to Basant Topo and tell him, "I want too much Shipra and draw her photography and greetings for her but her house members are not given permission to talk with me. Last time I talk with her, she tells me that her house members are not agree to send her so far away."

One day Basant Topo find out a Demonia book which given by E-Batch CTXR to me and see the necked picture of women and read their hip size, breast size and waist size, etc. He read the sexual trips which given in that Demonia. I have no interest to read that I also see the picture of necked women figure and try to dress up by printing. It was my habit to seen the picture of necked women and I was trying to make node model figure by wooden medium or other medium also used. It was my habit. So many friends came to my life that they buy Demonia or Fantasy on which books have necked figure of women. Basant Topo start to read the Demonia book. S. Satish some time come to my room to read the Demonia book. They have interest about the matter of sexual question and answer. In Demonia they find out those pages where some stories about extra ordinary have. It is reality that if anybody thinks about sexual matter in his life in maximum time, then human being cannot control his /her sex. Then there may be happened accidental event and relation build up with someone which is unacceptable by the society. At the age of fourteen-year interest grown up about sexual activity and increase day by day up to thirty-five years then decrease again day by day and sometime someone have exceptional case. I have been seen that at the age of fifty years also habit to go in the red-light area. But if you try to control yourself then it is possible to control by human being. By yoga you can control your mind and if you involve on the creative work then your mentality may divert into another field. Then automatically it is possible to control your mind. If any matter comes about sex to discuss by your friend. Then you discuss the matter freely and not think deeply. After discussion, you don't think that matter repeatedly then you become free and easily control your sex. It is also my habit to change the picture. I start to draw the dress on the necked figure and print out that but Basant Topo tell me that he has interest on naked figure and it is an art that he describes. Hence, I stop the printing on lDemonia book.

I also draw the picture of Shipra and discuss the matter of attraction on Shipra. N. Suryanarayana, S. Satish Kumar, and Basant Topo tell me again and again that I should require forgetting Shipra and marriage with another girl. They tell me, "You are working in railway then you will get many girls if you want." But I cannot control me. Then one day I send all drawing by speed post on a big cover and think if she cannot accept that then I may participate in Christian missionary and work for social and world development. In India and other developing country beggar number are maximum and poverty are increasing day by day. I shall try to develop through missionary. In Hindu organization have no such influence like as Christian missionary. I have required participating in large organization. In our country several peoples say that priest of church gives some facility to Hindu people who convert into Christian. I had seen that from God of Assembly Church the member distributes sweet and hotchpotch to bagger and poorer to poor. I feel if economically weak person converts into Christian to get some facility and get education then they may improve their life style, then what problem to us. We cannot help to them who are under poverty line. In my life I have interest to do social work whatever it may be. I am not bound my religion aggressiveness and think that if I have no idea about other religion then how I am able to say our system is better than other. I already go into Church, Cathedral, Mosque and Temple etc. and meet with Father, Muloabi and Monk respectively. I observed that in everywhere there you have seen that the people are weeping or crying nearby their god and want relive from their problem.

In this time, I also read the objective mechanical, electrical, electronics and general knowledge books. One call letter comes from RRB/Mumbai suddenly. Examination is held on 18 December for the post of Supervisor P. Way.

Before one month some candidate went to Assam from Bihar for Railway Group-D examination but local people were betting them. Then anti attract to Assam people done when Assamese travel by a train and pass through Patna. Bihar people are not only bit them but also done help to Us to ladies' candidate. Then riot start at Assam and start to bit to Hindi speaking people. Railway examination be postponing all over India. In Mumbai the people of Maharashtra are demanding their work for Maharashtrian only. Generally, RRB cancels Group-D examination. I think for Supervisor post may not be canceled, hence RRB send call letter. I get reservation ticket with N. Suryanarayana.

On 17/12/03 we start our journey in the early morning by Addra Exp. N Suryanarayana complete his night duty and come at Chennai Central earlier than me but I reach at 6.15 A.m. at Chennai Central due to mistake to catch 'B' train from Villivakam station. 'B' train go to Beach station, hence I come in round up rout by two trains. He gets foods item from his house and he tell me that he gets down at Guntacal station. But I shall continue my journey. At 3.00 P.m. when train enters into Guntacal station my friend gets down and I become along.

Next morning train reach at Dadar which is in Mumbai city. I go to my examination center first. This time center is in

Malad west. I reach at Malad by a local train and first enter into a temple which is on the road side and I payer to god for success in the examination. But when I reach at examination center then hear that examination become postpone and reexamination will be arranging in near future. Then I walk here and there and some one candidate tells me that on the Employment Newspaper on dated 17 -12 -03 given a notice in a small part. That examination is postponing due to uncertain problem. I buy Employment News and verify the news and seen the notice. I go to a temple and take set on a bench. In this time Red colour apple are given by a priest. I get holy food and think that it is my luck that I get holy food and get rest for a while.

Then what can be done by us, all condition return to Mumbai CST. Previously came at Bombay VT which given new name Mumbai CST. We visit Gate Way of India; I sit near by a wall and telling to other if they become interested to go to Elephant Island. But nobody agrees than I go to Jahangir art gallery and see the exhibition on art and sculpture. I understand what ever oil colour picture have done on paper and paint on canvass. In case of sculpture, I also understand how that made and what material used on making the sculpture. I meat with artist who's picture also publish on the newspaper and the newspaper part also pine on a broad. I see some work have done on hand made paper and some work have done on other types of paper. She says that it is Arches paper. I also see some work have done on multimedia and indicate all medium. The artist asks me that whether I travel and see exhibition in different city. I answer that I know art and sculpture making but I have no degree or diploma in the field of arts and sculpture and my financial condition also very poor to carry out the exhibition. I come here to appear Railway examination in the post supervisor. I used oil paint, water colour, I work on wooden medium and stone medium, I make Ramakrishna Paravanes and Jesus Christ on cement medium etc., and I have diploma in mechanical Engineering. Then try for job and life become struggles.

I go to Mumbai CST and wait for Mumbai Chennai Mail. I take dinner and I enter into the train when train comes in the CST station from yard. I take my site and train start to move at 11.30 P.m. In my life it is the second time I return without appearing exam and both time exams cancel. I return from Mumbai and take decision to change room. In my room have no sun light and I want a big room where enter sun light into the room. I think, Basant Topo and me both start study for competition examination and it will be possible to discuss about general knowledge. Times pass in the morning and I return to my rental room and in evening two house visits to minimum for taken a new rental room. I continue read the books. I also get books with me when go on line or duty. I get time and try to get study.

In 18/01/02 have an examination. It will be held at Ahmedabad. I get the call letters for written exam. One for post of Junior Engineer GR 11 (C& W) and another Junior Engineer (Mech./DSL). In C & W have more post then Mech. / DSL. So, I get ticket to show C&W call letter and in Mech./DSL call letter my seen the picture wavy pattern.

I start my journey on 16-01-04 by Navajeevan Express. Navajeevan means new life. I feel, I may enter in new life. I take sit and see several candidates are going for RRB exam. I ask four or five candidates. All answer that they should appear examination for the C&W post. I take decision I must be appear in JE 11 (Mech. /DSL).

On 17-01-05 I reach at Ahmadabad at 8.30 P.m. and when I come out from station, one auto Rickshaw Driver tell me, he takes five rupees and shows two hotels. First, I go to a hotel rate 100 rupees per day in case of single room. Then I say, have any room 80 rupees per day. The Rickshaw Driver gets me far away and shows a room Rs. 200 per day. Again, go to previous hotel but that become fill up, hence return to 200/- rupees per day hotel and say have any dormitory system. Then get a bunker sit 60/- rupees per day. The rickshaw driver demand 60 rupees and telling other. It is right that three times traveled by me and that rate become Rs.10/- but want 60 rupees. I say that only I can give 30 rupees and I have no money to give you. Then by request of hotel owner rickshaw driver get Rs. 30/-.

Next day morning by a bus I reach at the exam center. I leave the hotel so get suitcase with me. In the way two girls meet with me, they come from Raipur, the capital city of Chhattisgarh state. They go to their center. I take food in the morning and then feel that it become necessarily goes to toilet. I request to the gate keeper, "Please give me permission to enter inside. I shall go to toilet and then shall return."

I go to toilet and feel very happy then return outside of the main gate. At 9.30 we enter into exam hall. I copy write Hindi and English paragraph then from 10 A.m. start to answer. Mechanical & Electrical question come in this exam. I feel I may be passing. After examination I meet with two candidates, they come from west Bengal. I introduce with them then go together. At night stay at a Dharmshala @ Rs.30/-.

Nest day morning at 5 A.m. get up and take bath. Then go to station and start my journey in the way of Chennai.

Already find out one better room nearby market in the Villivakkam area. I inform to Laxman and Santosh that I shift in a new rental room and if any letter comes into the GKM colony's address than kindly hand over the letter to me. The house owner's son gives me the return speed post which I send to Shipra. Today I have on line. AGM move to E. Road. I get the letter and mind crake; I feel I should participate at Christine Missionaries. I reach at Chennai Central and from a Baptist Church I phone and talk with the father of the church the Infant Jesus shine. I go on line to E- Road by Yard Card exp. Next day morning I phone to RS batch SSE Fatima Doss. I tell him, "I want to go at Kolkata." In this day N. Suryanarayana and Basant Topo set up the room and shifted some material.

Next day morning I return I talk with Basant Topo. He tells me he is going to Kharagpur because his sister is admitted to a hospital. I meet with Basant top at Basin Bridge yard. He takes one thousand from my balance which say to given as advance rupees to house owner. The house owner of 14/1 GKM colony Nandagopal is not return my advance money. On the other hand, Basant Topo gets two thousand rupees within one month. Now get one thousand more. Two thousand he gives for room advance to house owner.

I return to 14/1 GKM colony and all material shifted to my new room. N. Suryanarayana also helps me. In this time, I get mobile phone 3000/- from N. Suryanarayana. So, we contract through phone. In the morning I apply for a pass from Chennai to Howrah and return.

At 3 P.m. everything set up and again I go to yard and get pass then take reservation ticket. I go to Gunidi and find out Infant Jesus Seine church and meat with a brother. Father becomes absent. I talk with the brother and say details of my problem and ask I meet with my parent and then take decision to participate in the missionaries. He tells me, he discusses with father and payer to god to blasé me and give peace. I return from Gunidi and meet with Laxman Ram. Now I leave the room as open the door and tell to house owner that he must return my advance money and if any call letter comes to this address 14/1 GKM colony that must be given to me.

I know that a register letter is care by a peon but ordinary letter they not care about that. In post office the peon may understand my word or not, I also cannot think that. Hence, I am not contract with the pion of Pariyer Nagar post office.

I believe God. Every religion tells that the god is everywhere. In my life I realize that if you become worry about some things and you cannot tell or express to anybody. But you stand near by an idol of god and in your mind freely express the matter. Again, and again explain and payer to god blesses me and gives strength to my mind. You feel peace in your mind and can get strength in your mind. Many problems may come in your life but if you become confuse than you see someone get advantage from you, someone laugh at you. So, any problem you may not express to your friend or your neighbor and if you express that than you can face some problem. So, it is better to meditate about god or goddess and you may get peace into your mind. At the time of problem in your life, god can help you to give peace into your mind. The philosophers and talented persons express human being not mortal. I read one book of Ramakrishna Mission, "How control your mind" which written by Gokula Nandaji who express that if you have tension in your mind, you go to braid ground and see so many people were coming in the world and they become died and braid. You also die in future and either your body burn on a chulli (i.e. Wooden temporary oven or electric furnace) or braid into ground.

I complete diploma mechanical engineering and then complete 25 papers in B. Sc course from IGNOU. Only one paper remains in B.Sc. course but till now work in Group-D post in Southern Railway. I feel pain in my mind. In my life nine times pass in preliminary examination in deferent post in government organization and minimum fifteen-time examination chancel by RRB which I was appear and ten times I reappear to reexamination also but in reexamination I might not success. So, I think it is better to participate in a missionary. I shall meet with my parent last time. But some time think about Shipra and write so many letters to her. I express that if I make such that she become pregnant and then break the relation forever. What be done by her, she will think that may not be good because if I denied my sin then she will be along if she became pregnant. But I only build up such a relation as friend and are not build up physical relation because I should think that is better relation as a friend. In the meantime, I think the time period that I last time visit with her. She come near by a temple where we first time meet for secretly visit with each other. Then start to walk side by side and talking about Durga Puja. That is the month of October, according Bengali culture five days arrange worship in a temporary temple which is called as pandal. We beautify the spot by lighting and set the idol of goddess Durga, Laxmi, Sarasvati, Ganesh, Kartika and set up water pot with coconut and mango lives and use word of Sanskrit to payer the goddess of power. We start Durga puja on shasty (the six day of new moon) and set up water pot near by a pandal then idol set into the pandal (Temporarily cloth and bamboo use to made temple. Every Bengali people enjoy in these periods and Astami (the eight day of new moon) are more enjoy full for us. Then Nabami (ninth day of new moon) also arrange single time payer of goddess like as Saptami. Last day we call Dashami. We payer goddess last time and submerge into water of a river or a pond. Then wait for next year to visit Durga puja. Dashami is the meaning to us last day to visit to us. When Shipra was walking with me she indication to me Shasta, Saptomi, Astami, Nabomi and Dashami traveling in the area and told me, "In the time

Durga Puja period we may not visit the city and cannot entertain in our life, hence it is the time that it is like as Durga puja." I could not understand the matter that it was the last time she visits with me and forever she might not visit with me and for that region she indicated to me love some time remain as it was. She tells me in Bengali, "Shabe Prame Mala Pay Na" which means every love may not lead up to marriage and in our culture garland exchange at the time of marriage, hence indicate 'Mala Pay Na'. That is the life that our life turns into deferent rout for ever.

But some time thought she might meet with me hence some time drawn her picture and colourfully letter write for her then one day packed and was send to her by a speed post. Within one month that may not return to me hence think she except that.

Next again made another packet by a paper and was input remaining drawing and once more thought she might understand my condition but my friend Suryanarayana told me that she forgets me forever.

She sides as before that she meets with me at last time but I cannot understand. I am really foolish person that in my life think to make relation as friend with a girl but my friend may tell right thing that if anybody have no physical relation with a girlfriend then they leave him forever but if remain physical relation then think for him. In my life it may be mistake that I make only friendship but have no target to build up physical relation with them. In my life first friendship was done with Parbati and Gori who become friends as they remained two sisters. They remained in rental house and when shifted than friendship ended. Then come several friends but Surjatapa remain best friend in my life. Rima, Soma remained closer where I was not able to say to them that I liked them and neither try to kiss them. Surjatapa sometime said that if someone love anybody then she may explain directly to her lover. Then Rima came to my life who some time travel at Durga puja or some time called for her personal works or some time went to her student house with me. But Rima stopped to talking and day by day's hat me which is very pain full. Ultimately when Shipra came in mind become cool and once more think to marriage with her. At the beginning I told that if I may not able to marriage with her then shall participate at a missionary. Actually, in my life have no peace due to health problem but try to lead life like other. No body understand my word and in the first time when they meet with me then thought that I am an all-rounder person and that would be better to lead life with me. I become true friend but they left me forever. I only make friendship with them but think that it was better to build up physical relation with them.

LIFE ENJOY FOR A WHILE

Suddenly AGM programmed set up and it became necessary to go on line. When I return to my rental house at GKM colony from yard, house owner's son gives the parcel of which I had send to Shipra at Kolkata. Shipra who told me that she like me too much and want to live together. Hence, I had offer to her to get marriage and believe her that she may love me to much but she returns me which I send to her. She may love me too much but mind break and I feel very shade and payer to Jesus and thinking to participate at Christine missionary. From three month I was filling loneliness. Several times I was on the bed due to sick and suddenly when I want to lead life with love that propose me and Cheat me. I verify my life's activity and see in every step it become difficulty. I become ready to go at saloon coach from Chennai to E-Road by yard card express. But mind become faltering condition to the matter of life and when I reach to Chennai central station, I get dinner at Bengali Hotel and enter into a Baptist missionaries Church and setting on the chair for a while. Suddenly remember the telephone number of Infant Jesus shine church; I ring up to that from my mobile phone. Father is talking with me. I tell him I feel loneliness and I worry about some matter. Father says that whether I steady along. I answer, that so. Then express that I want to meet with him and now I go on line duty to E-Road, when I return from E-Road than I shall meet with him. He says he shall payer Jesus for me. I want to lead life with peace and harmony. I start to go at saloon coach. I spray the room freshener into the Coach. AGM come and set on a sofa. I supply drinking water to him quickly. His personal Assistant Nasir and his peon Narra tell me some things that at E-Road they get breakfast and lunch at Kaveri Rest house and I should get breakfast and lunch at VRR (Vegetarian Railway Restaurant). When they sleep, I go to berth. I think all the

LIFE TURN IN NEW WAY

It is my life that so many new matters came but, in my hand, only paper and pen remain. So, I try to write the matter to development which may be in real life. I am like as a child to travel into a desert to find out a jewel within a send but I may be success in my life or not, it only knows by god.

I join at Railway as a Junior Engineer and start training; my mind starts to do work but I feel very sorry to the matter that India is a large populated country and by land it is also a large in size. But all technology launch from foreign country like German, France, Russia, United Kingdom and America. When I think that we are technologically dependent and Indian people have no interests to done new invention than my mind crake into by part. Hence start to say to my new friend to do some things new. All friend laughs at me. In the mean time I observed a little boy kill a bird unnecessarily and I write a poem in Hindi. So many spelling mistakes are there but I read in proper and press to my friend. Someone say good and someone laugh at me that I write wrong spelling. In this period, I write some poem in Hindi, Bengali and English and read that, nearby my friend.

Girlfriend remain part of life and now I remain at Ratlam in a Rental House. The owner is two brother and both have four daughters and one son to each. When return to rental house then meeting with two families. Two family become too close. Their daughter Mina, china and their two sisters as well as Sona, Tina and their two-sister become friend as I am author so they like too much.

Remain along and writing some things,
Now come to a house sometime talking
At night sleeping on roof as load setting
Chin, Tina come on roof to talking.
Sing song together for some time,
Scientific works doing some time,
Sometime writing my biography,
They enter as new friend in my life.

One day I go to a temple called JVL temple at Ratlam and I tell to my friend that I also have done such type of sculpture which he has seen in these temples and I also know oil painting, water colour painting like these.

Chandrika and Lovely become friend of Diesel shed where taken training. After some month Our groups send to other shed training and we left Ratlam and visited Ahmadabad Sabarmati. My birthday celebrates by Chandrika to with as well as I offer Rasogolla Bengali sweet. One after another workshop visit Varanasi and Patiala. At Patiala some dunker making miss behave and that time protest. She became intimate friend who telling me she tries to transfer to Delhi and also try for me to transfer to Kolkata.

Two day pass out I suddenly go to a garden of the Ratlam diesel shed and discuss about culture which used to practice at Kolkata. Mr. Sanjib Kumar suddenly says to me, 'Leo Node De Vinci'. My favorite charter Leo Node De Vinci was a sculptor, an Artist, an engineer and a scientist. My name is Ishim Kumar which means Endless Young, my character as endless power and Sanjib Kumar use to realize my character to discuss with me than say non available non

Mr. Ishim Kumar stand on the Arun garden at Ratlam diesel shed. Shed staffs are make gathering to celebrate the republic day and Mr. Kuhara address to republican day and progress of Western Railway.

Barat Barsha as Geographical area: If we enter into history than we understand that Barat Barsha was a geographical area and its boundary indicated from Hindu Kush mountain to Burma where even to execute several countries. But in ancient time to Mughal period there execute several small countries in Barat Barsha. But in Europe the Barat Barsha was indicated as Indus which turn to India by speech slip to European.

Barat Barsha turn to Hindustan: Islamic rule enter to Parashah and Persian peoples enter to Barat Barsha because the also remain safe as to lead life as they believe Sun god, fire god as previous believer of natural power in Barat Barsha. Islamic peoples indicate the same land mark as Hindustan because the peoples of Hindukush mountain were indicated as Hindu and they shift from Hindu Kush to Indonesia but Bharat Barsha remain as Aryabarta (Land of Aryan) and Anaryabarta (Land of non- Aryan).

The word remains as Dave as superior people and Daveri as inferior peoples and Dave was means god where as Daveri means Danab(giant) Danab turn to Davir after long time and indicate the south Indian peoples. After long time the religious faith become submerge and as a whole called as

Hindu in the whole land mark of Barat Barsha where maximum time ruled by different king of Aryabhata (Land of Aryan) and Anaryabarta (Land of non- Aryan) separately. Islamic peoples indicate them as a same religious group as Hindu and the land mark indicate as Hindustan (Land of Hindu). As a heard that the land mark peoples used to habit to use milk to offer to god Shiva and the milk river flow from temple of god Shiva and temple had lump sum goal and money than greediness give to power to Islamic ruler of outer land. The outer ruler attracts to Barat Barsha and give the name as Hindustan (The land of Hindu)

Hindustan turn to India: weakness come after long time ruled by Islamic ruler in Barat Barsha and European start to come to sate commercial establishment in Hindustan and turn as ruler in different part. Pondicherry ruled by France community, Goa-Damon-Due ruled by Portugal's community and Bangla- Bihar-orisha ruled by British community (England-Wales and Scotland the independent three countries peoples). Bengal-Behar-orisha becomes the first spot of British ruled but after all maximum part of Barat Barsha ruled by British either direct or indirect ruled system. But the European indicate the land mark as India which one called as Hindustan by Islamic ruler. The European ruler indicate the land mark as France India, British India as per capture by the community.

Indian Independent Movement:

1. Agent Group of British wanted Semi Independent: MC Gandhi, Balavbhai Patel

2. Wanted to Full Independent as Birth Right: Mangal Panda, Bhagat Singh, Subhash Chandra Bose, Baghajatin, Khudiram, Praphula Chaki.

Independent India-Pakistan: British India divided to two countries due to decolonization and formed Bharat/ India Union and Pakistan

Independent Bangladesh:

Hindi Racism: Hindi Hai Hum Hindisha Hamada means we are Hindi peoples and Hindustan is ours. Hindustan means to Hindi peoples are as whole India where as in Non-Hindi peoples indicate Hindustani means only Hindi linguistic peoples

Now a days Hindi peoples indicating that they are superior than Non-Hindi peoples where as they are attended the competition examination in Hindi language which are there mother language and as well as they read write in Hindi.

Problem to Non-Hindi peoples: Learn one subject as English language and other subjects read in Regional language and hence remained weaken in English and Hindi not learn in life. Hence their form partiality and Hindi peoples getting continue advantage.

India-Barat: India required to implement Social Consulate Confederation System and nation required to form two autonomous zonal government As-

1. Hindustan to Hindi peoples
2. Liberal-Bharat for Non-Hindi peoples

Hindi the language of Hindustan: language of Hindu peoples indicated by Islamic ruler

Political system of Barat: Now remained federal system but BJP-RSS joint venture executing Hindi Racism and enforce Hindi culture to Non-Hindi peoples to abolish their identity.

Name required of country: United Republic of Bharat

as a single name

States name required to defend: West Bengal as Bangla Pradesh

Panjab as Gurumukhi Pradesh

Andhra Pradesh as Telegu Pradesh

Uttar Pradesh as Brojo Pradesh

Madhya Pradesh as Brinda chal Pradesh

Demand of us required as Non-Hindi:

Birth Right:

1. Mother language as Basic Educational System

2. Equality to every one as per qualification

3. Right to give speech in mother language or vernacular in parliament But

If vernacular not understand by other member than interpreter to require to give translated speech in bi- lingual system.

4.Compititive written and interview Examination should be given by vernacular recognize language in the state compulsorily.

5.Within India all peoples are not Hindi whereas the Hindi leaders defined as -

a. Sara Jahasa Acha Hindustan Hai Hamada (Everywhere are good mater that is our Land of Hindu)

b. Hindi Hai Hum Hindustan Hamada (We are Hindi Peoples and Land of Hindu is Only Our)

c. Buri Najar Na hamsa Dalo Sabsa Aga Hogi Hindustani (Ban view not to see to us Hindi Speaking peoples become in top most post)

d Jai Hind (Greeting Hindu Land)

In the above case it is clear that Hindi leaders are forcefully defined that the land Of Independent India Name as Land of Hindu and only Hindi speaking peoples have right to live in Independent India. Whereas as per constitution the Independent India have two Name as 1. India in English and, 2. Bharat In Indian Languages.

Within Enter Independent India the Written Competition Examination and Interview get in Either English or in Hindi but so many Peoples are in Non-Hindi areas are getting education in there vernacular and mother language which one are State official language and under continuation that are recognized language But if Non Hindi Peoples are become unable to attempt in their own language in their own state than what valuation remain the recognize and state official language. In Hindi State Hindi Officer input Hindi language and grammar question compulsory in competition Examination and get interview in Hindi. But in Non Hindi State there are education system implement in State language and English hence it required that to be given written examination and interview either in English or state language than the actual competition to give the proper result other wish the system favor to Hindi speaking peoples that they get like as mother milk in Mother language. Hence after the Hindi take in Examination field and interview than the Bihari's, UP's And other Hindi peoples come to the higher level in maximum number to ground level in governmental posts. After all Hindi Racism come by the system Hence Every Hindi Speaking Peoples explain that the name of country as Hindus then and they understand that the meaning of Hindustan as Hindi land and everywhere of Independent India required to implement forceful the Hindi Language or by greediness to give awards in case by Central Government and Akhil Bharati Hindi Parishad.

In my real life When I remain in Ratlam in Madhya Pradesh remain as Apprentices as Junior Engineer the Senior Section Engineer Mr. Harish Chanda Panda and others said that Why We live in Hindustan if we are unable to speak in Hindi and when I was in Ujjain in Madhya Pradesh in that time several period said by K. K. Mittal That why I live in Hindustan if I am unable properly speak and write Hindi Language and Said that I require to find out other county. Today such word said one after another and said all state required to implement Hindi language.

The above give alarm that Hindi peoples want to capture whole India as Oppose that to speak in State official language in parliament and in State Assembly Hindi speaking peoples or Muslim are given statement in Hindi and Urdu respectively. Afterall the Hindi speaking peoples support to Urdu speech because both have some things similar.

I Say to Non-Hindi Peoples that even today have time to wake up and alert to save us other wish we become bake and Hindi peoples said they are superior where as participate in Hindi by them.

We have required to demand by revolutionary mode as-

1. Give the right to give speech in vernacular state official language with interpreter in parliament.

2. In a State Either Cantal or State Governmental or public organization competitive examination and interview should to take in State official language and English.

3. In Local Assembly in State should be use the State official language in speech and written particular.

4. Want Birth right that our Mother language and state official language.

5. Want to demand compulsory State official linguistic question in competition examination at list 10 percent that if a candidate remain to do work, he should able to communicate easily in working field because maximum word use by common worker as vernacular language

6 In departmental examination there to be input State language as compeller because in Hindi State there are

remain compulsory Hindi Language in Departmental examination. Even in some case the question and answer remain and getting in Hindi.

6. Every letter and notice in State should remain in State official Language as Hindi States.

7. Hindi Racism to mention at international level and force to implement the system and required to help UN Department.

8. The Name of the country required to give as the United Bharat Republic because The India was given by European and Afterall the British ruler give the name British India where as previously Islamic invader called as Hindustan because that they enter land lived the religion of Hindu mainly and after lord Asoka ruled the land mark Buddhism start the flows in the religious under royal society but the Islamic ruler understand the land mark as Hindu land, hence the enter land mark called as Hindustan. But the real name of the land mark was Bharat Barsha and hence required the give name of nation as United Bharat Republic for create better integration of nation.

9. Name of the currency of our nation as Indiana by which reformation of economic system required and known by every citizen as Indiana whereas at present in different state call the currency name as Taka called by Bengali, Tanka called by Oria, Rupkani called by Marathi, Tokay called by Assamese and so on. On the Other hand, in Nepal, Indonesian, Pakistan the currency called the same as Rupees

and hence identification of nation required a special as for the national integrity.

10 In the verbally Hindi speaking peoples call them as Hindustani but in Non-Hindi State the Hindustani means as Hindi speaking peoples. Hence confusion create as that defining the propels as Hindustani, and the upper-class peoples indicate them as Indian in English but the Non-Hindi peoples indicate them as Bharati and these indicate the dissatisfaction of the peoples. The Islamic state and Islamic community indicate the land mark as Hindustan but they indicate them as Muslim but not things as Hindustani because that Hindu are attaching with the word with Hindustani. After all dissatisfaction create and terrorism increase around that part where the Islamic community remain maximum in number, hence it required to indicate us as Bharotian which to be easy to specified us as singe identity and hence the national integrity to be increase.

11. There are required the restrict by law that the name of nation and nationality should be indicate as Hindustan and Hindustani as well as India and Indian in Films and newspaper, magazine, and Journal respectively. The proper name to require as United Bharat Republic and in short to indicate as UBR and nationality should be indicating as Bharotian as single unity.

12. AS per constitution the name of country given as Union India and Sanga Bharat because the British India was ruled either direct ruled or indirect agent ruling and after all the religion remain as Hindu, Muslim, Shaik, Isai(Christian),

Jain, etc. and Hindustan if give the name of country than may airs problem that to feel Hindu Land but time pass out above 64 years but national integrity cannot try to increase by the identity of nation. No Liberty of tower or Liberty of Nation are not create by the government and peoples celebrating independent day near India Gate and some where the India Gate make as model by the peoples but the India Gate was made by the British Ruler in Respect of visit India by the king of England Gorge-V and he entered the Indian land through Bombay hence There also made as Gate way of India. But we become Prouder that we celebrate Indian Independent day near the India Gate which indicate that we have no feelings of nationality. Hence required to make the liberty of tower and liberty of Nation in respect of independent nation.

13. The parliament House, Governor General House (President house) in New Delhi and Right Us House Governor House in Calcutta (Kolkata) remain as the Administrations purpose as Central and state of West Bengal but we do nothings after independent as Our own building for local and central administration.

Area of as per language:

1. Hindi language States: Hindi use as Official language.

Haryana, Himachal Pradesh, Uttaranchal, Uttar Pradesh, Bihar, Jharkhand, Chhattisgarh, Madhya Pradesh, Rajasthani's the list of State and only union territory Delhi includes in the list of Hindi Language part of India.

2. Non-Hindi language States: Indo-English use as official language.

Jammu & Kashmir, Punjab, Gujrat, Maharashtra, Andhra Pradesh, Goa, Karnataka, Tamil Nadu, Kerala, Orissa, West Bengal, Sikkim, Assam, Meghalaya, Tripura, Mizoram, Manipur, Nagaland, Arunachal Pradesh as the state and union territory Daman-Diu, Pondicherry, Lakshadweep, Chandigarh, and Andaman & Nicobar where English use as official language and the peoples of that area participate competition written examination and face interview in English and they have no other option they may participate in recognize language whereas the peoples of these area use the recognize language in study and only one language paper remain English and become weak in English and remain unknown the Hindi language which have option to attempt Competition examination and interview. By the system Hindi speaking peoples give more and more facility and enter to Non-Hindi area where as have same qualification and same marmite as the Hindi speaking peoples whereas Hindi speaking peoples also have habit to take education in Hindi and have only one regular or optional English Language paper and they are also maximum weak in English. But in departmental and other competition examination one 10% question get in Hindi and become success in the competition by the system, hence partiality created by the system and the Non-Hindi peoples become downward in competition by system.

Policy to increasing the number of Hindi States: Divide the Hindi States to increase the number as UP, Bihar, Madhya Pradesh Divide int two parts as new states form as Uttarakhand, Jharkhand, and Chhattisgarh and previously the Hindi state form by division of Panjab State as Haryana and Himachal Pradesh. The resent year when Telangana state demand and central government give willingness to form the Telangana state than the Up Government and other political party as majority of Hindi Peoples want to divide as Up into different parts as Harit Pradesh, Bundle Khand, etc. The policy is to increase as numbers of Hindi States.

British Ruling in India

Direct British Ruled:

Indirect British Ruled:

Western Education and Indian Social Revolution:

British started Western Education and hence British direct ruling locality started Social and science revolution.

British remained foreigner but Hindi racism executing by Gujrati people leading who making fool to Hindi peoples and economy drain by black hand to Gujrat by cheating policy.

British are correlated with Indian peoples as they also Germanic branch group of peoples and originally Hindu that Kashmiri, Kalash, Nuri, Balti and Aryan Valley peoples are actually European. Hind are surnames of Irish and Saxion peoples. Hindas, Hindon City or village remain in UK and Sweden. Hinder peoples called as Hindu a Branch tribal Baltic European group. Arabian are Ashir / Assyrian branch group of European, Persian peoples are Prussian group of European. Aryan or Arian group of peoples are mixed group of Celtic and Assyrian. Sindi peoples are European who migrated to Indus through Russian locality Pamir plateau. All such above peoples migrated to Indian peninsula at primitive Himalayan period. Hence it is real fact that Old Anglo Saxion and Lithuanian languages matching with Sanskrit. Hence European should not called as Foreigner as actually they are our old generation relative but Dravidian are Mediterranean that West African peoples that Saharan And Sub Saharan peoples mixed with Australasians peoples. But All family's groups of World peoples migrated to India and Worldly community formed.

Britisher migrated and establish colonial ruled in India but remained so developer that they establish Railways and Development industrial technological development, Economic development done in colonial ruled and world connected with us. Britisher given well Administration, Judicial system Educational system and so much things and Afterall Education give to right to all and through Archeological, Botanical, Zoological, Mining researches works and serves and given scientific History on narcological evidence and through Western education revolution hold on to demanding independent also.

Thought about United Liberal Bharat:

He fell so much troublesome in life and now more trouble face that maximum works and study required to done in Hindi. When India became independent that time Bengali and Non-Hindi peoples remained first ranking in Administration Examination as there remained English and had not any personality. But Hinda make official language where Administrative post interview done mainly Hindi and some Hindi question remain compulsory in departmental exam also. In competitive examination there also remained compulsory Hindi written works to copy from question paper. It making discrimination and partiality by policy. In parliament Non-Hindi peoples have not right to given Speech but Urdu allowed as have somethings similarity. Interpreter provision not making for us. Non-Hindi peoples have not right to equality and behave as we come from foreign country.

1. Flow of life in Struggle

Harry seen a dreamed at night David and Abraham two person come to his house. David is younger brother and Abraham is elder brother. Harry asked them how be able to get responsibility of us at older age? Abraham said, "I shall take your responsibility." Abraham entered to Hurry's house.

2. Later behind David enter to Hurry's house

Harry gets up and goes to job and thinking his life. Harry has one Daughter name "Pearl" and thinking that next may have to be two sons.

After two years his dream becomes reality and his son Born and given name" Abraham".

After three years his one daughter born given name" Ziva" but next one year a son born. Harry become happy and thinking he was seen real dream and son name given David. But as new born baby activity peoples started to call Tapon (Temperament Always personally operate normalization)

Harry was in village but come to City as his has three brother and one sister and depending on elder brother becoming unhappy. And in empty hand come to city and at night school was getting education, there after get a job. Harry has poor family lead life with happy life.

Migratory Life: A job is essential in life. But how lead life as basic need required to full feel to survived life. Shelter and cloth as social need and food, life partner natural need that a root of life.

3. Life in Joy

Nanai (Neither Awarded Nor Achievement implement) and Santai (Simple Alive No Tension Always Inside)

At night seen a dream and write down the poem as I feel god come to my life in dream that somethings to be happened which should change my life. But life remain same but believed give inspiration to me and become positive in life.

Miracle dice

A bagger comes near the door
Want some things as bagging
Call again to give some things.
I heard the sound from inside,
Get some food and rice to give.
He wants milk from me to drink.
I get milk for him on a bawl,
Slowly drops the milk to his dice,
become empty again and again.
I became thought full for the event,
What I can do, I can't think again,

But little dice why can't fill by milk,
I drop total milk on the blacken dice.
Blacken dice suddenly become golden,
I fill miracle power create changed
The bagger gives me the golden dice
He tells me you give all remained
I give you the dice for your faith
He gone suddenly and surprised
The dice become full of milk
I drink the milk and fill the test
Test of milk become sweet and
Delicious milk flavored ever.
I feel a miracle dice get on hand
The dream breaks and feels better
-: Stop: -

I always love nature and love animals and want to save them from danger but it is reality that one animal eats to other animal and it became rule of nature to survival life. But unnecessarily when killed animal that hat me and such type even happen nearby me and hence write poem in life.

Night angle Bird

A night angle Bird set and song,
Remain happy and joy in life.
The night angle asked to his wife,
Feel nest to make to led life.
The night angle sings sweet song
A cruel little child heard the song.
Cruel little child shoot to him,

A small bust insert on his chest.
The night angle died by flopping wings
Little child kills him by cruelty of life.
Night angle body lay on the land,
Peoples pass nearby death night angle.
The little child left him forever,
Little boy should not remain hunger.
Little boy should not eat the flash'
Hunting becomes a hobby in life.
Unnecessary killed a bird become a fashion,
Sorrowful life styles make me unhappy.
I cried and weep several days in my life,
A beautiful bird left his life by cruel boy.

In our family it was hard condition that each and every brothers and sister thought negative. Father remained agree person and his self-decision given most priority in life. As early as possible gave marriage my elder sister but her husband remains Froude so one day my sister suicide. I tried to save her life but become unable to save her life.

Little heart breaks for ever

My young sister death body
Lie on the floor of hospital.
She Succeed as killed her life
The end sorrow is in life.
Her marriage holds six month ago.
What was sin of her life?
She was a girl and marriage

Remain statues in common family of life.
The India a male leading society
Female is depressed time to time.
Male gave flash statement and
His marriage is done with her.
It is not new matter in India that
Female depressed now a days but
From the long time the stories repeated
And end beautiful roses at any time.
My sister killed her that her husband cheated
And depress life where four sight dark in life.

I left house as love nature and it give experience that house is better than other and mother only love and wanted to her child. I remained youngest child in our family so mother mostly love me as remained quite all time.

Best on clapping hand of Mother

Little child wanted to travel mountain
And river sight at him remains at city life.
He wanted travel and travel to enjoy in life.
He left from house for sight of mountain,
North Bengal side had seen Himalaya all in his life.
Father fed up his child should not come
Again, he led life with his life.
He took him by force with him but
He weeps continuously and saw mountain
A beautiful seen as blue in color
After rain I feel happy in life.

Little child brought up and left
Calcutta is city of joy forever in life.
Door to door craving for a job as
Money is main things to lead life
Money provided food, shelter and cloth in social life.
For a job, for a shelter struggle and struggle
continuously but mind should not satisfy.
Little child brought up and came out from city
Where seen many mountain and river
Which give better slightness but
Mind craving continuously in life.
Young boy think it was better when
He was little child and remain on clapping
On his mother hand; Mother save him all the time.

I remain at Chennai and it relish that I should left Chennai. Dream come and given indication that somethings to be better in life. I see godliness dream which given pleasured in life as believed as secular that worldly and liberal that believe as Hindu by birth and as christen as rebirth in life. Worshiping to goddess of Hindu and payer to Jesus and Mary when to church. Jesus came several times in dream and guide in life. It is miracle that future matter seen in dream which come to reality in life.

Mahamya, the power of goddess

Mahamya saw at dream at night;
She walks on the surface of water.
Suddenly she comes nearby me;

She asked me what I want from her.
I answer to her whatever she
Want to give me to lead better life.
Then the goddess Mahamya enter
To a temple and set at sitting singashan.
She up her hand and from her third
Eye a light came to my body.
I feel hilling touch and feel powerful.
A series of lamp came from
Both side of the world Mahamya.
All the lamps came to my hand,
Then all lamps submerged to closed palms.
After all, promised that will be better to me,
And again, she meets at next night.
Next night remain as miracle matter;
In dream again Mahamya came nearby me;
She told me she should give me some things
A whorl pool come and tsunami formed.
Then again land mark seen nearby me;
She gave me a small snail scale than,
She tells me it would help me all the time.
They got up from slapping but nothing remains
Nearby me and thought the dream
Again, and again like as a good film.
Suddenly at Bay of Bengal a tsunami happened
And the Chennai See breeze covered with water.
The tsunami destructed all the shop of Marina Breeze
And disgusted harm to the poor peoples.
Polices cover the boundary of Marina breeze
And save to common peoples from natural digester.

After some month again several stalls set up;
I visit the Marina breeze again and
Saw a stall, a miracle power feel;
I find out same size and same type a snail scale.
I asked for that snail scale
But shop keeper denied taking any money.
I feel Mahamya gave me as a gift,
Value of gift came through human being
God and goddess are remained fever for us.
-: Stop: -

I got up and payer to god to somethings better and give me knowledge in life. It is life when you should not get any satisfaction in life and then only ways remained in life to payer to god. So, payer to god remain only ways to me.

* Oh God give me little bit of knowledge*

Oh God give me little bit of knowledge
We lead life with peace and joy.
I learn little bit and written little bit but
Other laugh at me what I get money from those.
I mentally satisfied that God help me to lead life;
They criticize again and again to insult other,
It becomes batter of second nature of them.
I believe that I know like as a sand particle in a Desert;
I believe that I know a droplet of water in an ocean.
But what I can do that they criticize again and again;
Galileo Galley got whole life imprisonment that
Have no answer that what he had done crim.
God help me and give power to lead life;

Give me little knowledge to pass out life with joy.

-: Stop: -

Later one dream come in life and feel better in life that spiritual power of life come which given satisfaction in life even problem come in life.

* Two stars meet together*

Joti means sources of light or stars,
In my dress sown go a goddess
Vishnu and Laxmi were standing on stage.
On their hearts two light resources create,
We called starts or joti in general view;
Two stars meet suddenly and only light seen.
A big star bon by two starts and idol fancied,
I should not understand any things but
Suddenly the big star moves toward me.
The stars meet with my harts and body,
And penetrated in my body and finish;
I feel freshness and powerful my mind.
A miracle power I feel which guide me,
Tell me what I have done right and wrong;
I become master of my own and guide me self.
My life run to new ways and guide to other,
So many people come to me for their help;
I help them and try to help them at any time.

-: Stop: -

I pass time to my life at different church and ultimately wanted to participated to Christian missionary as by rebirth story when came first time to India as David but rebirth again and again then only ways I should return to Christianity and prayer to Jesus in life to want last birth to be this life. All my girlfriends left and life fulfill with sorrow then what can I do that I see and wanted to meet to my parent last time but at train I have had seen dream and that become reality in life. It is miracle that god remaining with me and guide to me to walk along.

The dream of marriage

I want to meet with my parent in last time,
I want to participate at missioner forever in life.
Sorrow become integrated part old life,
I want to leave general life style to lead life.
So many friends make me sad in life all time,
They came and gone all time god by to me forever.
I like someone and want to love all time to live life,
She feels that I am stupid in my life without works.
I get service but unhappy all time in my life,
But I want to meet with them to left general life.
Oh God! I payer to you all time in my life in my mind,
I sleep at night where something seen as puzzle me.
I see three sisters remain at a hut and I enter to that,
The girl's name is same of goddess Laxmi's nick name.
I feel by heart goddess Laxmi become my wife as seen,
I remained unable to explain my friend for long time.
Faster than fieriest and which I want to go to my home,

I want to me with my mother and father at last time.
I catch an express train from Chennai to meet them,
When time will come that I return to Church.
Suddenly my maternal uncle offers to visit with a girl,
I visit to her with my mother and other.
I remain sure that I shall return with some language,
It makes me change forever to lead different style.
My father calls her brothers to meet at our house,
They come to visit with us as invite accept by them.
Father neither see to her face but marriage arrange,
Nothing asks to me as I remain unknown about that.
Ever things arrange suddenly in my life as miracle,
Marriage happens within one week at miracle sight.
I return to Chennai as other common man to lead life,
As a friend as a wife she become life partner in life.
Three years after I learn the meaning of Rama,
Her name remains the same as my dream.
I payer to God that he shown to me future,
The life will remain as per wish of god.
The name of goddess of wealth Laxmi,
AlterNet name Rama remain as life partner.
-: Stop: -

I was meet with parent and told to my mother that I should not return to our house again. Mother keeping but it was thought ever things to be normal after some time. My mother teaches me everything and told me you should adopted where you lead life. I learn philosophy and other knowledge from her as arts, sculpture making and many things as maternity gen is dominated to me and I remained most closer to my mother.

* My mother was one in all*

My mother a simple woman and simple life,
White cloth with red step was wearing in life.
Payer to lord Vishnu all her life for harmony of life,
She led life with knowledge of all and works.
All-rounder women are not seen in my life like to her'
She always said that spiritual truth of life to happy.
Her words as whichever discover and invent in world,
Somewhere those are use in same or modified form.
Philosophy of life is that mortality is ultimatum of life,
Birth is starting point but end may come at any time.
We are actor as parent and child as general matter,
Who is child to day next become parent as cycle?
Learning has not any end that knowledge is endless,
How long we live we learn up to ultimate time of life.
Lord Vishnu and Goddess Laxmi came to her dream,
She worships started and end to her life as death came.
She was teaching me first step of walking in life'
She was teaching household works, and other.
She was teaching worship, meditation and philosophy,
She was teaching useful material for our health.
She guides me all the field as learning and meditation,
She wanted to build me as all-rounder in my life.
I try and try but should not become like to her,
She was remaining to my mind and my heart in life.
Mammalian remain close to mother to primitive life,

The value of mother milk should impossible to return.
She remained as guide who tries to make happy life,
Her guide of step to first walk to higher in my life.
She was teaching craft works, and arts works,
She was teaching process of save life.
She remained artist, sculptor and household wife,
She guided me all the field to walk to lead life.
I love too much to mother to remain all time,
I came far away from her for service to earn money.
she remained at hospital at ending her life,
Her words as we should not bother to death in life.
I should alive long time without her all time,
Death came but she was leading as monk in her life.
-: Stop: -

After my marriage I return to Chennai and enjoying life and time came when I becoming as father and my son to be coming and before six months of delivery, I selected name of my son

I selected the name of my son

Before six month ago of birth,
I select the name of my son,
A miracle mater happens in my life.
Everyone selects son, or daughter name,
But there remain waiting for birth,
I select name without waiting time.
The life is like as river flow on land,
Life contain happy and sorrow on ways,

Sometime happy and some sorrow in life.
Thousands of peoples meet in our life,
Someone becomes friend in life,
Someone remains blood relation in any life.
Father become older and then died,
Son or daughter become young in life,
After all change relation time to time.
A Salween river flow from Tibet to Bay of Bengal,
It flows through china, Thailand and Myanmar,
An international river name selects for him.
Someone oppose as the name is like as Islamic,
Someone tell the name is like as Christian,
After all, ever one is human in life.
Suddenly I see a dream at night,
The next day written copy to fill a form,
Municipality certificate make by us.
We are swimming a river of heavy flow water,
Suddenly an invisible power pulls us upward,
We left river and remain at Atmosphere.
I select name on my son to remain which I select,
Any one may oppose but everything become normal,
God should wise him as he will be famous.
-: Stop: -

When took birth than seen Jesus that he told me as my some is replica of scientist and I thought if such matter happened then I am lucky person around world as I always wanted to scientific works but not done due to financial poor condition but if my some will become scientist then I should be satisfied.

He is replica of a Scientist

My son born I get news on mobile phone,
His name was selected before his birth,
I explain to my friend that Salween born,
I payer to god; kept good health in his life.
Health is wealth in our life than come money,
Money become valuable at civilized social life,
Health has value in any body life at anywhere.
At night to payer to god to kept happy to my son,
I sleep and on dream at night that a tall man come,
He indicated a child nearby us playing as he child.
The tall man explain he is replica of scientist you seen,
He will be a brought name in his life now as he child,
I awake and provide that I see such a dream at night.
I payer to God to wish at night to my dream,
I don't know that reality of future what will happen,
I believe god who wish to my child all the time.
-: Stop: -

* Last visit with my Father*

I remained at far away from my father,
I struggle in my life as lost so many times.
There remained mistake, misunderstanding,
And remain conflict in my mind to lass in life.
Frustration and fad up became a part of life,
Sorrow become as friend in my part of life.
Suddenly came to my house to meet with father,
But he arranged my marriage without willing to me.
He said that as a father had responsible to guide me,

I should understand when I should be a father in life.
The life started with new ways in marriage life,
I become a father of little son in my life.
I neither worry about my father property nor
I want anything other than love and affection in life.
Father oldest life as weakness became part of alive,
He became unable to talk clearly in that time.
He suffered so many problems in his real life,
So many years he was unable to sea clear vision.
He lost his father at early age of his life in 2 years,
He became sorrow as he should not see his father.
I feel sorrow his point of view and try to acting that,
But father always remain as father in any one life.
He was admitted at a Hospital in last time of his life,
I was meeting last time in his life and lost in life.
I was seen miracle matter of affection and love,
He last time told me that I should be happy in my life.
A clear speech came from his mouth as unexpected,
Which to God make me happy in my future life?

-: Stop: -

I rebirth again due to sin of that life

I remain land lord in several times
Life is rebirth again and again.
Rebirth is a believes but have not any proved,
In my dream I had seen rebirth story.
I devoted to lord Vishnu in my life,
I asked in my mind that why lead life bad.
In a land lord family I had born,
It was seen in dream at night.

As rich I was tortured too poor to poorer,
A young girl forcefully kept nearby me.
The Girl rebirth and make friendship
But she hats me again and again as return.
I left Calcutta and shift to Chennai,
I feel that I should remain only two years.
Then I left Chennai and shifted to Ratlam
I started to done scientific works also.
I remember the dream of my childhood,
I was coming from Scotland to India as young,
I was started to done scientific works in life.
I died to effect by Tuberculosis in that life,
In this life I also effected in such dieses.
My life safe as invention of medicine,
I followed British in my life to do something.
Mentality remain such as no factor as language,
Go to so far from my mother land in my life.
Today there are translations books, computer,
And other remains British discovery and invention.
I was love by heart to hear song of Indian in that life,
I rebirth again and again in India, I loved song.
I was rebirth in Islamic family called Badshah Khan,
Where I remain powerful in that life to rule an estate.
But after all I rebirth again as love dance and song,
Several girls become friends and they gone in my life.
They were a part in my previous old life and
Rebirth and meet again in this rebirth life.
When the sin of life apologies by god in life,
Then enter to rich to richer and end sorrow in life.
Christian remain as British, Islamic rebirth as Indian,
Again, rebirth as monk and had younger brother.

Goddess Kali as power of goddess worship in life,
Again, I was rebirth in a Hindu landlord family.
After all, in this life again Rebirth in Hindu family,
I believe the system of Christian, Hindu and Islamic.
Jesus Christ, Goddess of power came in my dream,
I Safe them as I believe as liberal faith in my mind.
-: Stop: -

There are five types of person

There are five type of person in life,
Someone gets advantage, someone tell lie.
Someone misses guide, someone tell only yes,
Only a few remain guide properly in life.
You may be understanding someone and
You may not understand someone.
If someone harm than you remain helpless,
You explain sorrow of life than fad up in life.
You only require believing God is great in life,
To whom only confide to cool mind to tell help.
A good friend can guide in your life for some time,
God remain all time with you as believe in our life.
Time should pass always and new period will come,
Mobility changes the allied peoples in new life.
New social life starts as friend and other changed.
We remain alive for sustain period of time,
Child becomes young and young become older.
Older become oldest and after all every one die,
New generation come and human remain in social life.
-: Stop: -

Mixed culture and worldly life

India is a name of country and
It was geographical of subcontinent,
Negros migrated at primitive stage
Ida was as Deccan Island in the ocean.
Deccan Island remained at fresh water age
Tithes Sea remained in Meditation Ocean.
But drift of Deccan island and erosion,
Tithes Sea fills up by mud and scraps of land.
Salt of ocean dissolved in water and flows water,
Climate formed and changed again and again.
New age of ocean came and old one end,
Ocean comes under salty water age.
The Deccan Island drifts nearby African super Island
Brown people's shifter from Mediterranean Island.
Human evolutions step by step happening,
Black, yellow, brown peoples formed in earth.
White and radish peoples later came in the world,
The pigment should not produce by them.
The climate and migration of life changed,
The colour of skin and life of leading changed.
At primitive stage white peoples was affected
But they become strong due to stability developed.
Yellow called Mongolian where white called Aryan,
Mongolian and Aryan migrated India in ancient time.
Mongolian people came at primitive Himalayan,
But Aryan came in Himalayan Mountain formed.
Aryan story of Hindukush, Tibet, Indus land,
Later Indus become India and religious faith as Hindu.

Hindu a large folk culture and believer of real life,
Sun, moon, and planets believe as gods by human.
Afghanistan, Central Asia came under Islamic ruled,
Calipha rule made Islamic believer and sped culture.
Persian came when Islamic capture Persian land,
They entered to India that titles are Irani, Turzai, Saho.
Irani culture mixed due to Persian came in Indian,
Peoples mixed as Hindu; Persian become Indian style.
Afghan and Mogul invaded India time to time,
Indian came under Islamic believer in Islamic ruled.
Jews Crucified deforms to Jesus Christ as the name,
Isa Moshi real name hidden in social life in time.
Christianity started when European in our life,
British ruled sped up Christianity as influence life.
Greek culture came at ancient India Alake Gander time,
Christianity started by Saint Tom's in primitive stage.
We mixed time to time and adopted culture of other,
Persian, European, Arabian, Chinese mixed up in life.
All culture, all religious faith came in historical time,
We mixed and mixed culture and mixed faith of life.
-: Stop: -

Offering become part of worship

King base society form in civilization life,
Common people's believed king and queen,
They respect them as god and goddess in life.
King and queen want food and need in their life,
The food and need full fill by follower in their life.

Common peoples some time offer to their king,
Otherwise foods and need full fill by force in life.
King the power of society, queen remain assistant,
Each remains happy and lead in their life with other.
King idol start to set up at different place in life,
At home king idol kept as they should not meet.
The name of king and queen known by common man,
King or queen come to visit with high profile respect.
Offer to king and queen remain a part of general life,
Then worship come as king believe god in life.

-: Stop: -

Music and dance become part of worship

Human started to lead life in village life,
They learn to farming and settled their life.
Wild ferocious animal harm in any one life,
Peoples want to save them from danger in life.
They discover fire to create by friction in life,
Fire divested woods at forest and finished life.
Primitive society fired at night to save them,
Then sleep later at night but became unsaved in life.
Dangerous animal came when fire stopped at night,
Then night stay and kept alert become system of life.
Meal makes sound by some things and invent drum,
Female are dance around fire as believed fire as god.
Night pass out with safety and early morning sleep,
King base society started to kept females to dance.
Apsara system indicated in the purana literature,
Dave dashi became later system of society in India.

Apsara was beautiful dancer of lord in ancient time,
Dave dashi became dancer of land lord in temple.
Civilization started and deformities system in time,
Invention and discovery are done one after another.
Peoples innovated and upgraded music instrument,
Society developed system of dance in their life.
Life style change as per time pass and development,
Music and dance become a part of worship in life.
-: Stop: -

Last Visit with my Mother

In March of 2010 I last visit with my mother,
Mother devoted to Lord Vishnu in her life.
I thought that paper works of property to done,
My mother told me you had come at June month.
I should not believe at June that I should came again,
The last visit to mother remains in my life at March.
I left Calcutta and join to Job again after leave avail,
I became sick and operations date given at May end.
I told to Mother the matter of operation of Hernia,
Mother became sick and admitted to a Hospital.
I asked her to went at Calcutta in that time to visit,
Mother told me with together not required to die.
I stop my travel in that time June month started,
4 Days pass and mother again admitted to Hospital.
I asked her what she feels in her mind in that time,
Mother told me there had not any matter in life.
Next day might be to end in her life to indirect ways,

10 June a sad news came my mother died.
I went to Calcutta immediately in my life,
I solved property works as mother said in life.
-: Stop: -

Monalisa friend of my Wife become Friend in my life as telling about social system in different place when she came to meet with my wife. Monalisa is very sweet and lovely beautiful. But she is hard worker as working as business. I meet with her one time but like to much as hard worker and too beauty. Now a day Android mobile come so what app masses and talking to phone used but I feel sorrow as some conflict crated when my son born then maximum house worked done by me. One day I told story to her as my friend but remained friend as beauty attracted that look as Monalisa as Lendon De Vinci. My character is same as Leonardo de Vinci as Author, Engineer, Artist, Sculptor, as mentality as Scientist. Sometime though an all-rounder multi field vehicle to build and that be very much useful to war field but dream of vehicle remained in mind not make in real life. Monalisa the printing of Leonardo De Vinci remained and now My Monalisa come as friend in my life as feel as look like that.

My Monalisa you are sweet like honey,
You attracted to me as hardy to in working life.
I like you as hard worker as you most beauty,
Your melody voice makes me happy.
As a friend you come in my life,
But freely telling of my life story.
I am able to shar sorrow,
A good friend encourage life too.

Sorrow forget as I talking too
You are lovely too my friend.
Monalisa I love too as friend
I share life story as become happy too.
-: Stope: -

I should love her from far always

I should love her from far always all time,
Affair is not good to build to anyone.
Love to someone; lick convert to love,
Affection attracted to each other nearby us.
Lovely face, sweet face and dear eye view,
Beauty of nature always attracts every one.
When a pair of meal and female remains closer,
They talking and thought more to each other.
The nature they attract to each other to form like,
Everything like sometimes convert to love.
Affair is always better with wife in any life,
You love far always it is better all time in life.
Which you like that may change any time,
But you should maintain life as social life.
First your family gives most priority in life,
Then you like or love to other from far sight.
-: Stop: -

At the night I sleep and get up in early morning I was crossing Jharkhand state I feel happy and remember about my friend and sings song one after another -

*Effect of love *

When I thought about you
My mind wants you nearby me.
When I hair your sound to ear,
My mind under tension many more.
When I see you nearby me?
I become happy in my mind.
When you remain far always,
I always feel some things less.
When I want to meet with you,
The heart is betting increase in body.
When we meet and talk freely,
I enjoy and excite in my mind.
When your look attracts to me,
I become powerless to my body.
When I want to tell you some things,
I forget everything which I thought.
When I see you are happy in life?
I become happy too much in my life.
When you become sad in your life,
I become sad too much in my life.
Whichever feeling in my mind,
It called affection and love in my mind.
When I payer to God for you,
God should bless to you in life.
When you talk with me,
I feel melodious voice in my ear.
When you look toward me,
I feel dear eye view in you sight.

When you walk on road,
I feel fairy queen come nearby me.
-: Stop: -

Even today remember her in my mind

I want to forget you but unable to do so,
You were long time waiting for me.
I want to tell you my feeling to you,
You should not hear my word of love.
You look toward me in bright eye view,
I should not understand you love me.
When you came to me to tell you word,
I denied hearing what you need to me.
You came with holy food in a dice,
I should not accept from you due to ego.
When I went to nearby you for confuse,
You should not hear any things from me.
You make mistake and I make mistake,
Our love and like crash in our life all time.
I explained to you as I love you by heart too much,
But you remained unable to explain your word.
When I was meeting last time with you,
You told I was everything to you.
When thought your word always,
Those times I was not understand you.
You loved me and waiting for me to visit
And talking with me as you had best friend.
I apologies to god as I wanted to you,
God is seen me in dream previously.
Your marriage would happen with there,

But I want you to much as life partner.
Ultimately reality came nearby us,
Our relation of friendship is beak forever.
I want to forget you from my life,
I am unable to forget at past event in life.
You may be remembering me or not,
But I remember you in my mind.
-: Stop: -

Love by heart submerges in mind

I thought about you always;
I feel, you should happy in life.
I want to help you by heart,
I want to come nearby you.
I want to catch your hand,
I want to kiss on your chick.
I feel you also want to meet again,
I think you also kiss me on chick.
I excite when hear your sound,
I want to see you nearby me.
All of my heart wants to submerge,
I want to see and hear your sound.
All time feel, I miss something's in life;
You love me and I love you in mind.
Mind submerge in good feeling,
Heaven should come nearby me.
Love is other name of faith,
Love is another name of godliness.
I love by heart but should avoid affair,
Affair creates bad effect in any life.

Love is faithfulness of your life as godliness',
Affair is killed mind as make mistake in life.

Heavenly feeling of love

I love you an easy word in life
But real love is very difficult.
In real love, there is like, love, affection,
Love is sacrifice and realization.
All word shares by each other,
Love makes a good friend in life.
Affair make want of body in life,
Love makes submerge of two minds.
You able to love to any one in life,
But you should not make affair.
Love is good matter in your life,
Affair other than wife is bad.
You love to your friend in life,
You love to your mother and other.
You make relation as sister and brother,
You make relations of friendship in life.
You shear sorrow and happy in life,
You help to your friend in life and guide.
You should not do any things in life
Which harm to her in real life?
You make happy in her life,
You should be happy in your life.
Love is heavenly feeling in life,
Friendship is integrated part of life.
-: Stop: -

I remain far way but love all time

I love you from far away,
I payer to god for bless her.
I should not break the system,
Even social system is manmade.
I do such things to make happy,
I love you by heart and mind.
You remain far away from me,
I love and payer to god in life.
You to be happy in your life,
Talking to be is part of life.
I love you in my life too much,
I like smile and everything in life.
-: Stop: -

Life remain Annoying all time and become simple railway employee and several time sicknesses disturbing all time. Sometime thought it was better if I die in early life than parent should weep for some time but whole life should not suffer in my life. I love too much Angela Agnes and become happy to see that she is happy in life. Angela Agnes is friend rebirth to rebirth and remained best friend in life as she remained in mind but not remained in life. I am married and it is responsibility of family life. Today it required to life as my liability to fulfill as my child are little and I have responsibility all time.

THE END: -

9 789393 385291

Printed by Libri Plureos GmbH in Hamburg,
Germany